Making Wicked Problems Governable?

Making Wicked Problems Governable?

The Case of Managed Networks in Health Care

Ewan Ferlie
Louise FitzGerald
Gerry McGivern
Sue Dopson
Chris Bennett

OXFORD
UNIVERSITY PRESS

OXFORD

UNIVERSITY PRESS

Great Clarendon Street, Oxford, OX2 6DP,
United Kingdom

Oxford University Press is a department of the University of Oxford.
It furthers the University's objective of excellence in research, scholarship,
and education by publishing worldwide. Oxford is a registered trade mark of
Oxford University Press in the UK and in certain other countries

© Ewan Ferlie, Louise FitzGerald, Gerry McGivern, Sue Dopson, and Chris Bennett 2013

The moral rights of the authors have been asserted

First Edition published in 2013

Impression: 1

British Library Cataloguing in Publication Data
Data available

ISBN 978-0-19-960301-5

Printed in Great Britain by the
MPG Printgroup, UK

To all our parents; both those present and those no longer with us.

Contents

Contents

Acknowledgements

We would like to thank various people who contributed greatly to this study. Dr Pauline Allen at the London School of Hygiene and Tropical Medicine was a great supporter of the original idea of commissioning research on health care networks and of getting the National Institute of Health Research's then Service Delivery Organization programme to commission a significant research programme on the theme of networks in health care. She was ably assisted by the programme's administrative team, then also based at the School.

We would also like to thank members of the project advisory board for their valuable insight and advice: namely Professor Janet Askham, Dr Jim Elliott, Dr Mike Kelly, Professor Mark McCarthy, Professor Julienne Meyer, Professor Adrian Newland, Professor Alison Richardson, and Roger Wilson. We much benefited from advice from Professor Janet Askham from the Picker Institute, especially on the older people's cases. Janet tragically died in the course of the study and was much missed by us all.

We much enjoyed discussions with colleagues working on the other networks projects commissioned by the Service Delivery and Organization programme, notably at the one day conference held at the School of African and Oriental Studies which brought all four teams together. We thank all our respondents for giving up their time to be interviewed and hope they find this monograph both interesting and useful. We also acknowledge we have used and extended some work in this book which has been previously published in journal form, namely:

Ferlie, E., FitzGerald, L. McGivern, G., Dopson, S., and Bennett, C. (2011) 'Public Policy Networks and "Wicked Problems": A Nascent Solution?', *Public Administration*, 89(2): 307–24.
Ferlie, E., McGivern, G., and FitzGerald, L. (2012) 'A New Mode of Organizing in Health Care? Governmentality and Managed Networks in Cancer Services in England', *Social Science and Medicine*, 74: 340–47.

McGivern, G. and Dopson, S. (2010) 'Inter Epistemic Power and Transforming Knowledge Objects in a Biomedical Network', *Organisation Studies*, 31(12): 1667–86.

The authors acknowledge funding from the UK National Institute for Health Research Health Services and Delivery (NIHR HS&DR) programme (HS&DR project 08/1512/102). Visit the HS&DR website for more information. However, the views and opinions expressed therein are those of the authors and do not necessarily reflect those of the HS&DR programme, NIHR, NHS, or the Department of Health.

List of Acronyms

AIDS	Acquired Immune Deficiency Syndrome
BASHH	British Association for Sexual Health and HIV
BHIVA	British HIV Association
CEO	Chief Executive Officer
CIR	Critical Incident Reporting
CQC	Care Quality Commission
DoH	Department of Health
EBM	Evidence-Based Medicine
EU	European Union
GDP	Gross Domestic Product
GP	General Practitioner
GRADE	Grade of Recommendations, Assessment, Development, and Evaluation
GTN	Genetics Translation Network
GUM	Genito-Urinary Medicine
HIV	Human Immune Deficiency Virus
ICER	Incremental Cost Effectiveness Ratio
ICTs	Information and Communication Technologies
IOG	Improved Outcome Guidance
IT	Information Technology
MDT	Multidisciplinary Team
MedFASH	Medical Foundation for AIDS and Sexual Health
NGO	Non-Governmental Organization
NHS	National Health Service
NICE	National Institute of Health and Clinical Excellence
NIHR	National Institute of Health Research
NpFIT	National Programme for Information Technology
NPG	New Public Governance
NPM	New Public Management
NSF	National Service Framework
PCT	Primary Care Trust
QUALY	Quality Adjusted Life Year
RCT	Randomized Control Trial

SAP   Single Assessment Process
SHA   Strategic Health Authority
STI   Sexually Transmitted Infection
UK   United Kingdom

1

Introduction and overview

Over the last thirty years or so, scholars of health care organizations have been searching for concepts and images to illuminate their underlying—but also perhaps changing—modes of organizing. Nowhere has this controversy been more intense than in the United Kingdom (UK), given the long succession of top-down reorganizations within the National Health Service (NHS) in the same period.

The debate historically has been between an established professional dominance and professionalized bureaucracy model (Freidson, 1970; Mintzberg, 1983), which tends to see clinicians as dominant, and a challenging New Public Management (NPM) counter model (Hood, 1991; Ferlie et al, 1996; Moran, 2003) which highlights novel governance mechanisms such as a hierarchy/quasi markets mix. The UK in general and the NHS specifically have been seen as high-impact sites for NPM reforming. But is this debate now dated? Specifically, are post-NPM developments emerging which require novel conceptualization? Or has NPM displayed surprising resilience even in the face of sustained criticism?

We will analyse this question in relation to changing modes of organizing in the UK NHS, a large and emblematic public services organization. A long period of radical right, 'Thatcherite', government (1979–97) was associated with NPM-based reforming, but was later succeeded by a substantial period of New Labour political control (1997–2010). The time has come to take stock of the New Labour period after it ended with the election of a Liberal Democrat/ Conservative coalition in May 2010. So what was the overall impact of New Labour specifically on the organization and management of UK health care? Did it preside over a minor rebalancing towards 'NPM with a human face' or were more fundamental changes apparent towards a novel 'network governance' reform narrative (Rhodes, 1997a; Newman, 2001; Osborne, 2006) which stressed the rebuilding of lateral capacity rather than the strong vertical reporting lines of the NPM? We explore these wider themes through an empirically informed analysis of one important organizational reform introduced in health care after 1997: 'managed networks'. Network-based principles (rather than hierarchy or markets) were used to achieve major service changes, but in a 'managed way' in that the new networks were charged with meeting national policy frameworks and standards and were accountable upwards. We argue that such network based reforms are a major strand of New Labour's policies towards the organization of health care and should be assessed as such in accounts of the period.

In the first two substantive chapters, we review streams of academic literature which are used to frame the study theoretically. In Chapter 2, we consider the NPM/post-NPM debate apparent in the academic public policy and management literatures. We take a view of the New Labour period which stresses their reliance on networks as well as on markets and choice as policy instruments. Here we introduce the 'network governance' reform narrative in more detail. We consider the nature of so-called wicked problems (Rittel and Webber, 1973) which lie beyond the jurisdiction of any one agency (examples include health inequalities or obesity/type 2 diabetes) and their implications for network based governance. We discuss the move back to principles of choice and provider diversity, especially in the later period of New Labour governments. We also note the shift from direct to indirect technologies of steering (Rhodes, 1997a), with weaker use of direct hierarchy. There are new arenas of clinical governance, patient safety and the Evidence-Based Medicine (EBM) movement, together with distinctive governance modes.

Chapter 3 introduces the Foucauldian concept of 'governmentality' (Foucault, 2007; Miller and Rose, 2008) as a key theoretical framing, including a consideration of a growing stream of such literature on health care organizations. Chapter 2 had suggested that managed networks display a mode of organizing based on neither market logic nor traditional hierarchy. Nor are these networks of the traditional tacit form well known in professional groupings; rather they are tasked with delivering national policy objectives. They draw energized clinical professionals into hybrid clinical-managerial roles in their core, displacing NPM-style general managers. They operate with a mix of self-regulation and intervention in 'loose/tight' governance regimes: so-called higher performers are accorded earned autonomy; whilst lower performers face interventions, sanctions and intensive 'support'. We outline core Foucauldian concepts and consider their development by the so-called Anglo governmentality school (Miller and Rose, 2008). It appears that the governance of managed networks requires retheorization as it does not fit either the traditional professional dominance (Freidson, 1970) or NPM models.

We then move into a set of four more empirically orientated chapters (Chapters 4–7) which outline and discuss our set of eight case studies of health care managed networks in a broadly comparable manner: taking clinical genetics; cancer networks; sexual health networks and older people's networks in turn. Methodological and technical issues of research design are considered in Appendix 1 and the development of a performance assessment framework is outlined in Appendix 2 which enabled us to distinguish between groups of higher and lower performing networks in our study.

We then explore three mid-range themes which emerged as important in both the literature review and the empirical cases. The first examines the effect of new Information and Communication Technologies (ICTs) on information and knowledge flows within the networks (Chapter 8). This was found to be modest in nature and strongly mediated by existing organizational and professional forces. The second thematic chapter relates to the nature of leadership processes in the networks where there appears to have been a significant shift away from the previous NPM orthodox model of vertical general management to new configurations (Chapter 9). The third thematic chapter explores the extent of inter-organizational learning in the networks which is found to be rather more modest than some literature had suggested (Chapter 10).

The final two chapters draw out the more general contributions of the work. Theoretically, we draw out the explanatory usefulness of the Anglo governmentality perspective adopted in Chapter 11. We highlight a number of policy and organizational developments apparent across the cases which stand out in sharper relief through the adoption of this theoretical perspective: the power/knowledge nexus apparent around the EBM movement and its key texts which powerfully legitimates decision making in these networks; the subjectification of local governing agents at the core of these networks which becomes evident through adopting a 'technology of the self' perspective and the emergence of novel but pervasive 'grey sciences' of calculation across the networks which include clinically as well as resource related technologies of calculation. We conclude that an Anglo governmentality perspective is helpful in theorizing modes of governance in the managed networks studied.

In terms of the public policy literature, we argue in Chapter 12 that managed networks are a broad, major, and perhaps enduring New Labour reform to UK health care organizations and that therefore its legacy should not be seen purely in terms of NPM ideas of strong performance management, choice, and quasi markets which characterize much of the present literature. Managed networks represent a neglected area of health policy reforming under New Labour which requires more sustained analysis. While the records of our networks were decidedly mixed (at least in the short period studied), they included a subgroup of stronger performers which we explore further. In addition, the 'wicked problems' conditions reviewed in Chapter 2 and seen as compatible with network governance were found to be pervasive in practice and we therefore argue should be persuasive in policy design.

From the case study evidence presented, we conclude by offering a limited defence of managed networks. In particular, we argue they may well be the most suitable governance mode in those many and expanding policy arenas characterized by 'wicked problems' (as opposed to alternative governance modes of hierarchy or markets) and should therefore be given more time to develop and reach their potential.

2

'Reforming' UK health care organizations—from New Public Management to network governance?

In this first substantive chapter, we explore the following question: does the academic public policy and management literature suggest a possible shift from established New Public Management (NPM) to post-NPM-based organizational forms in UK health care? In the first section, we briefly rehearse the well known organizational transition in the National Health Service (NHS) from a historic professional bureaucratic form to an embedded NPM form in the 1980s and 1990s and consider serious criticisms of NPM reforming. We then review academic literatures (notably the network governance narrative, see Rhodes, 1997a; Newman, 2001, Osborne, 2006; Rhodes, 2007) which suggests post-NPM and more network-based forms have been emerging across UK government.

We consider key milestones in public services and health care policy during the New Labour period (1997–2010), finding nuanced developments. While there are moves to network governance including an (ambiguous) shift from quasi markets to managed networks, other elements of NPM (such as performance management) continued or even intensified. As New Labour matured, so there seemed to be a reversion to policy instruments of choice and provider diversity which might erode the network forms set up five or so years earlier. Recent work (Mays et al, 2011) which conceives of New Labour's health care reforms purely in market terms still seems unduly narrow; their network-based reforms should be considered more fully. The extent of a post-NPM transition in UK health care organizations during the New Labour period towards network forms, however, remains an open question and requires more analysis.

5

1979–1997: From professional dominance to New Public Management

We start by recapitulating the well known rise of NPM during the period of high Thatcherism. Up to the 1980s, analysis of health care organizations conventionally drew on the related concepts of professional dominance (Freidson, 1970) within clinical care and of the professional bureaucratic form (Mintzberg, 1983) at an organizational level. The NHS was seen as a Weberian bureaucracy with a standard administrative hierarchy moving down from the Department of Health to the Regional, then District Health Authorities, and finally the operating units. It was organized through a well defined administrative line, with a permanent administrative cadre and a neutral management style which valued probity, stability, and due process.

However, these Weberian bureaucratic elements were overlain by continuing professional dominance. Elite professionals—notably senior doctors—were informally dominant so that the style of health care management was more facilitative than directive. Health 'administrators' (as they were modestly termed up to that point) implemented the many rules and regulations, drawn up after consultation with influential clinical advisory machinery rather than engaging in conventional line management. Sheaff et al (2004) paint a historic picture of modest exception management in the UK primary care organizations they studied with little managerial scrutiny of clinical practice.

At an organizational level, clinicians within such a professionalized bureaucracy (Mintzberg, 1983) typically set micro-strategy in a bottom up and decentralized way by developing their own services in isolation from wider considerations or even neighbouring professional segments. There are disadvantages of such forms of strategy making, particularly in volatile or retrenching environments. The top level managerial core has here a weak capacity to set macro-level strategy (Mintzberg, 1983), to manage corporate or radical organizational change and especially retrenchment, and to combat the long-term pattern of professionally led incremental growth.

Financially, the professional bureaucratic configuration tended to produce continuing growth in public spending, given the basic professional dominance over a highly decentralized and growth-based form of strategy making. This led in time to increased taxation to finance systemic growth, assertive public sector trade unions, and a rising proportion of Gross Domestic Product (GDP) consumed by the public sector. There was a growing fear in the political domain—particularly from an assertive New Right—that an expanding public sector would 'crowd out' the private sector and was even ungovernable, dominated as it was by strong public sector professions and trade unions.

These shifts in the political economy were reinforced by developments in the world of ideas. Rising ideas from public choice theory and organizational economics (Niskanen, 1994) from the 1970s onwards provided a more critical interpretation of the behaviour of public professionals and bureaucrats than conventional Weberian accounts. These new interpretations suggested public bureaucrats typically and rationally sought to maximize the scope, size, and budgets of their agencies to build influence and careers. In the absence of countervailing market forces, public agencies would grow inexorably and over-produce public goods beyond the amount that any true market would bear.

Organizational economics provided a strong intellectual rationale for the NPM movement which was one response designed to combat this long-term pattern of public sector growth, professional and trade union dominance, and insulation from market logics. A rising NPM model (Hood, 1991; Ferlie et al, 1996; Moran, 2003) informed cycles of UK health reform from the mid-1980s onwards. Traditional professional bureaucracy was challenged by a new configuration based on what might be termed the basic principles of the 'three Ms', namely: management, markets (or quasi markets), and measurement. Thus the NHS of the late 1980s saw the introduction of general management (replacing the old administrators) to implement central policy, and of more assertive and non-elected Boards bringing in more Non-Executive Directors from the private sector (as in the 1990 reforms to NHS corporate governance) to form a stronger strategic core (Ferlie et al, 1996). A core NPM doctrine was that 'management must manage' in a more assertive way than in the past.

NPM ideas helped develop performance measurement and management systems which visibly exposed a tail of 'poor providers' in publicly available league tables. It also led to the construction of an early health care quasi market (1990–97) experiment, designed to mimic market forces within a public sector setting. Within this quasi market, the old vertically integrated NHS disaggregated into purchasers (District Health Authorities and GP Fund holders) and providers (NHS Trusts and independent providers) linked by contract rather than hierarchy. While general management had been strengthened *within* the NHS Trusts, these organizations also had to compete in a more market-like environment.

Criticisms of NPM reforms

By the late 1990s, NPM principles, reforms, and techniques were firmly embedded in the NHS. The sceptical idea that such reforms would be symbolic, superficial, or merely another organizational routine appeared ill judged: these reforms had depth, breadth, and pace, leading to substantial and interacting changes (Ferlie et al, 1996). Yet even as they consolidated themselves, they faced serious academic and then political challenges.

The first criticism was that the NPM movement represented an excessive swing away from the well judged policy making of the old Weberian civil service to an exaggerated focus on operational management and productivity (Dunleavy, 1995), in turn contributing to high profile 'policy disasters' of the 1990s (such as introducing a new system of local government taxation which was later abandoned). Here was a reminder that creative policy making was important. The downsizing of the Department of Health could go too far if it hollowed out policy capacity in specialized areas which could rise in importance over the long term (e.g. public health and its policy level response to reviving epidemics such as tuberculosis) (Trenholm and Ferlie, 2012).

Secondly, critics argued that top-down and managerialist NPM reforms led to an unhealthy disengagement of insulated public services agencies from civil society and the public services workforce, including clinicians. A growing 'democratic deficit' (Weir and Beetham, 1999) characterized the appointed and non-elected State characteristic of the NPM, as the scope of local government contracted and that of appointed agencies increased. There was now a need to rebuild political legitimacy by taking a more inclusive and partnership-based approach (Newman, 2001). For example, appointed (rather than elected) Health Authorities lacked the democratic legitimacy to make contested hospital closure decisions which then might simply be rerouted to political and electoral arenas.

Thirdly, NPM reforms were argued by critics to be excessively vertical and with important fragmenting effects (Sullivan and Skelcher, 2002) as their contract-based forms of governance typically linked one operational provider to a single commissioner. The new executive agencies with their strong CEOs and Key Performance Indicators might well be more operationally efficient in terms of a focused task orientation and their ability to process high volumes of client-level decisions (in the case of operational delivery agencies), but also be 'silo like' and produce negative spill-over effects across the wider system, especially in those politically charged agencies where it was not easy to separate out operations and policy. Pollitt et al's (2004) comparative study of executive agencies pinpoints social security and prisons agencies as examples where operational and wider policy considerations mix in such an ambiguous fashion. Hypothetically one might ask: how do the policies of a prisons agency reinforce or contradict the policy of health care agencies in respect of mentally ill or substance abusing prisoners? Does a social security agency consider the health needs as well as income levels of elderly clients fully in its assessment process or is this eroded by the need to hit its throughput targets?

Such fragmenting changes might well erode lateral working and make system-wide or 'wicked' problems even more difficult (as explored in more detail below). The paradox is that new networks began to emerge after NPM reforms to pull together these increasingly fragmented policy arenas (Rhodes, 2007). It is also important to look at how health care commissioners were approaching their novel tasks within the quasi market to complement the usual focus on health care providers, especially acute hospitals. By the mid-1990s, there was some early evidence (Ferlie and Pettigrew, 1996) that the new health care macro-commissioners (District Health Authorities) were developing a distinct preferred style, specifically by developing strong networks with other agencies in their local patches to manage through influence and on a whole systems basis.

These academic criticisms were picked up in New Labour's thoughtful initial review of the machinery of government, the *Modernising Government* White Paper published by the Cabinet Office (Cm 4310, 1999), as some of these arguments migrated from academic work into public policy texts. A counter criticism from a pro-NPM position was not that NPM went too far; rather it had never been tried. The early quasi market in health care was always a 'managed market': over time, it became ever more managed and less of a market. NHS Trusts appeared more motivated by quality than cost-led competition (Crilly and Le Grand, 2004). The Department of Health acted as a strong market regulator and stabilized existing NHS Trusts. There were weak arrangements for market exit both from poorly performing NHS providers (beyond merger with more successful units) or for market entry by for-profit providers. The change of political control to New Labour in 1997 represented a potentially important break point when NPM doctrines and reforms could have been repudiated (but with a more nuanced reaction in practice as we explore later).

Academic discussion of a possible post-NPM organizational transition

While change in political control is potentially important in the politically visible and value-driven field of health care reform, various academic literatures suggest longer term and secular trends to organizing in both private firms and in government which might promote a post-NPM transition which we now review.

From Fordism to post-Fordism?

We start with a broad perspective within organizational analysis: post-Fordism (Amin, 1994). The historically evident tendency for vertically integrated large firms to replace small firms appears to have gone into reverse: Small and Medium Enterprises are growing and many large firms are delayering and downsizing. Large firms are typically outsourcing non-core functions to subcontractors while keeping core capabilities in house. There is here a shift in production in advanced capitalist economies from mass production to flexible specialization with a premium on higher quality, shorter life, and customized goods (as in the fashion sector) (Priore and Sabel, 1984; Amin, 1994). On the demand side, consumers become more sophisticated, discerning, and value greater customization of products to their personal tastes. Far from deskilling, workers in these faster moving settings develop broad skills which promote flexibility and quality. The ability to acquire and process knowledge, to respond to changing markets quickly, and to learn and change rapidly are important core competencies for post-Fordist firms.

This shift to a post-Fordist (Amin, 1994) mode of production produces specialized industrial districts populated by a network of small knowledge-based firms: Silicon Valley in California is an exemplar case from the 1970s onwards. Such networks are supported by powerful new Information and Communication Technologies (ICTs) (as considered below) which enable information to move easily within the network and across organizational boundaries. These networks are coordinated by high internal trust levels and by long-term and relational subcontracts rather than vertical integration, strong line management, or spot contracting.

Does the post-Fordist paradigm have implications for the changing organization of government as well as private firms? Just as wealthier and better-educated consumers demand higher quality, fashionable, and customized private sector goods, so they may develop higher expectations of personalized consumption and choice in the public services, especially in core services such as health and education. Over the last two decades, UK health policy has emphasized themes of quality, innovation, choice, and personalization consistent with a post-Fordist perspective.

Jessop (1994) explicitly considers the nature of the post-Fordist State. He argues for a transition away from the Keynesian Welfare State as a governmental analogue of the Fordist firm, both of which went into fiscal crisis in the 1980s. The Keynesian Welfare State promised full employment and universal health and welfare services on a Fordist model as a social guarantee. Jessop (1994) discerns a transition to a 'Schumpeterian Welfare State' which seeks to resolve the Fordist fiscal crisis through radical innovation within open economies to improve national economic competitiveness. It subordinates social policy to labour market flexibility and international competition produced by globalized capitalism. The full employment guarantee is abandoned and redistributive welfare programmes give way to production-centric social policy ('From Welfare to Work' programmes are a good example). This is a 'hollowed out state' (Rhodes, 1997a; 2007) where national governments lose functions upwards to the supranational sphere which alone can regulate fierce globalized capitalism, and downwards to strong and dynamized regions and cities that provide local and timely responses to economic demands.

This interpretation of the emergent post-Fordist State is fundamentally driven by the dynamics of globalized capitalism. There is a presumed crisis of the old Fordist model of the Welfare State with its high social costs and consequent restructuring of the supply side on productivist lines. The presumption is one of reduced social expenditures and the scaling down of the Welfare State. It does not consider an activated demand side, notably pressure from wealthier, educated, and less deferential citizens/consumers for higher quality and more individualized public services.

The post-bureaucratic organization

There is a growing literature on the possible 'post-bureaucratic' organization, succeeding the Weberian bureaucracy. Here we review two important recent texts which address this broader debate. Boltanski and Chiapello's (2005, Chapter 3) is the first text to provide a comparative overview of the corpus of the two management literatures of the 1960s and then of the 1990s. They suggest that the 'spirit of capitalism has undergone a sea change over the last thirty years' (p. 96). They found a distinct ideological reconfiguration in the 1990s when compared to the earlier management literature of the 1960s which had stressed ideals of meritocratic progress and job security for cadres in strong and stable firms. By contrast, the later management literature promised personal fulfilment at work through a multitude of shifting projects. At the organizational level, this management literature now supported a model of the firm as a network rather than a hierarchy: 'a slim core surrounded by a conglomerate of suppliers, sub-contractors, service providers, temporary personnel' (p. 74). There are high internal levels of trust and communication within the network. There is an emphasis on personal development and broader multitasking. While stable employment may no longer be guaranteed, the development of high skills creates employability so the flexible worker hops from one interesting project to another (although poor job security for less-skilled workers may be an achilles heel).

This later literature moves away from strong line management to broader leadership, centred on the projection of vision and creating a mission and strong shared meaning (Boltanski and Chiapello, 2005, pp. 75–7). Managers move into a range of wider roles, becoming visionaries, team leaders, or coaches. While vertically integrated firms are in decline, the new network forms still have authority and influence, even if taking different configurations. We explore this potentially important shift from management to leadership in the networks studied later.

Inspired by Toyota-style ideas, the new 'lean' and delayered firm is within the 1990s literature made up of flexible project teams which constantly seek to delight customers, energized by visionary leadership (rather than coercive management). Pursuing portfolio careers, workers move from one project to another (Reed, 2011), rather than staying within one organization for a whole career. The lean firm is able to learn, change, and adapt. There are obvious implications for restructuring in the health care sector, most obviously through the direct importation of lean programmes (Radnor et al, 2011) but also more widely in a broad shift from hierarchy to network, a stronger customer orientation, and energized leadership. This account suggests that the worker becomes more personally engaged at work, bringing qualities of creativity and personal emotional involvement as well as formal technical skill. This interesting account of a possible shift between two ideal types is however based on a review of texts rather than organizational-level evidence, so it will be interesting to apply these broad arguments to our health care cases.

These post-bureaucratic themes have been recently explored by Clegg et al's (2011) edition. The introduction by Harris et al (2011) notes that some literature claims to detect a meta shift from modernist to late-modernist or even post-modernist forms of organizing, with the ending of large vertically integrated firms or stable public sector bureaucracies (our particular interest). However, such claims have not gone unchallenged, with other authors claiming enduring advantages of the bureaucratic form (such as probity and due process) or detecting hybrid forms with surviving bureaucratic elements. Nor was it correct to talk of a simple decline of State agencies in the face of a neoliberal reforming wave in the 1980s. While some aspects of the State contracted; in other senses it expanded, with an increased desire to intervene in social and cultural spheres (e.g. promoting healthy behaviours).

Three chapters in Clegg et al (2011) deal specifically with the UK NHS, suggesting sedimented or hybrid organizational change there rather than a direct transition to a post-bureaucratic form. While not engaging directly in the post-bureaucratic debate, Buchanan and FitzGerald (2011) explore the effects of continuing policy changes on the underlying organization of the NHS. These shifts include on the one hand NPM-related policies such as the separation of commissioner and provider, patient choice, and the roll-out of Foundation Trusts with enhanced operational freedoms. On the other hand, there are network governance (and possibly post-bureaucratic) related reforms such as greater clinical engagement in leadership, lean thinking, evidence-based service frameworks, and networks. They use organizational archetype theory (which examines periodic transformational shifts between integrated constellations of structures, processes, and above all the ideological base) to consider whether a radical transition in the NHS from an embedded professional bureaucratic archetype to a business-based archetype is likely. They conclude (p. 77): 'we can see, therefore, a more or less traditional archetype "accessorized" with the trappings (structures, processes, discourse) of modern commercial enterprises'. They see considerable survival of the old professional bureaucratic archetype with some addition of business-like/NPM forces. The implication is that post-bureaucratic reforming is unlikely to prove impactful, as it is aligned neither with a dominant professional bureaucratic archetype, nor a challenging NPM archetype.

Speed (2011) uses the concept of 'soft bureaucracy' (Courpasson, 2000) to explore the growing rhetorics of choice evident in UK health care policy since the 1980s. This discursive turn is consistent with post-modernist forms of analysis and with post-bureaucratic organizations. Two key and interrelated features of health policy were defined as (p. 81): 'one of these is the principle of *post-bureaucratic* [our emphasis] network governance with more health care decisions being taken at a local level, and with the empowered consumer/patient located at the centre of policy thinking. A second related feature is a focus on quality and choice as the key determinants of effective clinical treatment'. He argues that this rhetoric of choice has two important effects. First, passive patients are converted into active consumers responsible for the effects of their own unhealthy lifestyles on their health status. It thus extends the extent of self regulation. Secondly, these more subtle processes of regulation are difficult for professionals to resist: how can any right-thinking person be opposed to principles of quality and choice? Thus, policies which advocate patient choice may also limit traditional professional dominance in health service provision.

So has there been a radical devolution of power to the active and choosing consumer? In practice, this has not happened as new 'intermediary mechanisms' and public agencies have appeared to mediate any such redistribution: 'organisations such as NICE function *bureaucratically* [our emphasis] to give the appearance of distance between the decisions of government and the provision of services' (p. 100).

Harris' (2011) chapter examines the case of the NHS National Programme for Information Technology (NpFIT). Radical new ICTs have been heralded by some authors as leading to new network forms and a regime of 'centralized decentralization' (but our later discussion of their impact in our case study sites finds modest impact in practice). Harris examined the career of the massive pan-NHS NpFIT programme (launched in 2002) with its strong centralizing ambitions to standardize and record local clinical practices. However, there was also a countervailing devolution of responsibility to a dispersed and networked consortium of private sector providers charged with implementation in local sites.

Harris' (2011) case study of NpFIT implementation in a Primary Care Trust found severe problems of clinical 'buy in' and resistance, given tight project timescales and the business process re-engineering approach used (as explored in McNulty and Ferlie, 2002): the clinical focus on patient outcomes

13

and the effective handling of clinical risk was eclipsed by the system's concern with indicators of productivity, internal markets, and patient choice. The network of local service providers in practice displayed few of the characteristics of dialogue, learning, and co-production that the literature suggests should characterize networks. Clinicians used the discourse of clinical risk to temper and reshape implementation, and to accord greater priority to local work practices. So the transformational ambitions of the NpFIT programme were blunted by clinical resistance and power to defend local work practices (McNulty and Ferlie, 2002). In summary, these three empirically orientated chapters on the NHS all suggest organizational hybridization and some survival of existing professional and/or bureaucratic elements.

Finally, Reed's (2011, p. 239) chapter directly explores the implications of the growing literature on the 'post-bureaucratic organisation' for changing control modes. He contrasts two ideal types of the rational bureaucratic organization (the Weberian bureaucracy) and the emergent post-bureaucratic organization: 'so the ideal type Post Bureaucratic Organisation is based on collaboration (rather than specialisation); flexibility (rather than standardisation) and negotiation (rather than formalisation)'. There is greater blurring between discrete decision-making 'jurisdictions' and an erosion of reliance on rules in favour of local bargaining and interpretation within the post-bureaucratic organization form. Strong collectivist values give way to values of individualism, personalization, and careerism, within a flexible but also mobile and more project-based workforce.

Characteristic rational bureaucratic organization and post-bureaucratic organization control regimes differ radically (Reed, 2011, pp. 238–9). Instead of Weberian externalized and rule-bound conformity, post-bureaucratic organizations stress the high internalized commitment of Foucauldian 'disciplined selves' (a theme explored later), but also leveraged creativity (rather than conformity) and high worker flexibility. There are expected shifts from explicit to tacit forms of knowledge (this is of course the reverse of the Evidence-Based Medicine (EBM) wave in health care) and from internal to external labour markets with a growth of project teams. There is a broadening of semi-autonomous and innovative teams as opposed to reporting to strong hierarchies. In the end, Reed (2011) is sceptical of the prospects for a radical paradigm transition but suggests a 'neo bureaucratic' hybrid may be emerging which combines elements of both ideal types.

Public policy literature: From NPM to network governance?

We now consider recent public policy literature, picking out specific implications for health care organizations. Closer to the discipline of political science (rather than organization studies), this literature explores the effect of political regimes and associated public policy reform doctrines on the public services. After a long period of Conservative political control (1979–97), New Labour won the 1997 UK election and remained in government with substantial majorities until 2010. New Labour criticized the failure of the Conservative governments to invest in the public realm and advocated extra spending, but linked to modernization and reform (DoH, 2000). The time is now ripe to take stock of the legacy of New Labour. With the benefit of hindsight, did it simply recreate NPM 'with a human face'? Or did it succeed in building an ideological, political, and organizational counter model (or archetype) which secured major changes in health care organizing?

Early New Labour thought reflected an overall strategy of 'triangulation', that is equidistance between presumed errors both of the Old Left and New Right. This positioning led to a nuanced assessment of NPM rather than simple rejection (Ferlie and FitzGerald, 2002). Giddens (1997) developed an influential early theoretical positioning of New Labour in *The Third Way: The Renewal of Social Democracy*. Within his overview, Giddens (1997) touches briefly on the specific question of the organization of the public services. A number of the New Right's criticisms of the public sector are accepted and there is certainly no desire to return to the Old Left status quo of the 1970s. Yet he develops two distinct and perhaps contradictory arguments.

On the one hand, Giddens (1997, Chapter 3 on 'State and Civil Society') argues that in a post-NPM period, democracy needs to be broadened and deepened to address the democratic deficit produced by NPM. This implies government should act in greater partnership with civil society to rebuild the public realm. The retention of high levels of autonomy and self organizing capacity by Non-Governmental Organizations is important if civil society is not to be swamped by over-mighty and distorting State power. This 'Democratic State' should be based on the principle of subsidiarity, supporting community renewal. This model stresses a non-NPM set of values of democracy, participation, and localization.

However, a second and more orthodox NPM model (Giddens, 1997, pp. 74–5) centred on the pursuit of administrative efficiency to rebuild public services' legitimacy. The Old Left collapsed in part because of a middle-class electoral revolt against the increasing taxation required to finance an ever-expanding public sector that provided poor value for money. Public services organizations should be redesigned to check constant bureaucratic growth. So government needs to consider how to get 'more from less' and deliver good value for the taxpayer. While government should not have recourse to quasi markets at every opportunity, it should use generic management controls (such as target controls, effective auditing, flexible decision structures, and increased employee participation) to increase performance. Performance improvement remains an important objective. Giddens calls for public–private partnership models to ensure greater private sector involvement in delivering functions previously contained within the public sector, while ensuring the public interest remains paramount. An implication was that some elements of NPM might well continue or even intensify. So this influential early New Labour text was ambiguous and difficult to decode.

A broader set of network-based ideas reflected other important academic work in public policy and political science literatures. As early as the 1990s, political scientists (Rhodes, 1997a) pointed to the 'hollowing out' of the traditional unitary nation state as functions moved upwards from central ministries (to the European Union) or downwards (to strong regions) or sideways (to executive agencies or public–private hybrids). Narrow 'government' was giving way to broader 'governance', where networks replaced the NPM markets/hierarchy mix as the preferred vehicle of coordination. The traditional Westminster- and Whitehall-based model of the UK State which privileged central political institutions was now outdated. Within more polycentric public networks, implementation was negotiated with many social actors, including the private and third sectors. So NPM regimes raised new governance problems (Klijn, 2005) in their turn. Their silos and high fragmentation paradoxically led to new inter-organizational networks (Rhodes, 2007) to restore coordination within the 'hollowed out' State. The State now steered through more indirect instruments such as contract, alliance building, partnerships, and persuasion as it had given up direct hierarchy or public ownership rights. Yet such contracts could be weak, poorly specified, or difficult to enforce (as in the UK transport sector with the opaque division of responsibilities between owners of infrastructure and transport providers).

Within this governance perspective (Rhodes, 2007), limits to direct state command become apparent and lead to a more diverse view of state authority (as in the Foucauldian governmentality perspective explored in the next chapter). Some authors (Stoker, 2004) see the state (here the local state) as playing a coordinating and network-steering role (similar to managed networks in the NHS) and as a still privileged actor. Rhodes (2007, p. 1256) challenges this view from a so-called decentred perspective, arguing: 'the instrumental or steering view of networks sees them both as a structure to be managed and a tool of central control'. Indeed, most networks in our study were constructed as 'managed networks' and as local delivery mechanisms for national policies. Rhodes argues that excessive central direction of networks will threaten their autonomy, distinctiveness, and effectiveness, and that a more bottom-up approach is needed.

Osborne (2006, 2010) positions what he terms the 'New Public Governance' (NPG) narrative as a potential successor to the NPM paradigm. The NPM period is seen in one account as 'relatively brief and transitory' (Osborne, 2006) rather than as enduring, although his later work (Osborne, 2010) raises the prospects of some enduring influence. The rise of NPG is predicated upon both a plural and pluralist state, with multiple independent actors and many legitimate policymaking processes. It assumes that the State does not wish to steer where it does not own. This perspective is theoretically aligned with network theory, unlike the organizational economics and principal agent ideas at the back of NPM, and also draws on ideas of social capital and relational markets. Trust, social capital, and relational contracts emerge as a 'soft' governance mode replacing the 'hard' spot contracts of NPM.

Newman's (2001) important overview explores the 'network governance' reform narrative influential in the early New Labour period. How does 'governance' differ from 'government' in her account? 'Governance' addresses a more complex polity in which government is no longer the only actor and negotiates with many social actors. It is a looser and broader term associated (Newman, 2001, p. 23) with such trends as: shifts from markets/hierarchies as policy instruments to networks; from a view of state power based on formal authority to one based on coordinating, steering, and influencing; from a state-centric analysis to a more pluralistic perspective on both the shaping of policy (through policy networks) and service delivery (through partnerships). The overall trend is towards more indirect steering and policy shaping within complex, multi-level, and multi-sectoral governance. Newman (2001, p. 24) suggests key propositions, some of which we pick out here as relevant to post-NPM modes of organization.

First, one would expect a move away from hierarchy and competition towards more networks and partnerships in policymaking and service delivery. Such partnerships would be inter-sectoral, involving public, private, and not for profit organizations. This marks a shift away from both the reliance of the Old Left on public sector agencies and the preference of the New Right for market-led solutions. The approach was now to be systemic and holistic, trying to move beyond the vertical silos of NPM to a 'joined up response' particularly in relation to 'wicked problems' (see later discussion) which could only be tackled systematically. There was an increased interest in whole systems working, as seen within the example of inter-agency Health Action Zones designed to promote the overall health of local populations within defined territories. Another example was promoting greater collaboration between health and social care—where there was a long legacy of flawed policy initiatives—through the 1999 Health Act which allowed for integrated organizations.

Second, there was recognition of blurred boundaries and responsibilities for tackling social and economic issues which went beyond State-centric models. Broader policy networks would bring in a wider range of non-State actors into policymaking. The new 'politics of inclusion' stressed the need for the State to combat top-down NPM-style managerialism by re-engaging with civil society, NGOs, and the public sector workforce. On the demand side, the new consumer-citizen was now less deferential and likely to demand higher quality public services. In health care, one would therefore expect to see greater user involvement in forms of care and a greater involvement by clinicians in management.

Thirdly, we would see the replacement of traditional modes of command and control by more indirect 'governing at a distance'. The centre would gather more information about the performance of local public agencies through expanded performance measurement and management regimes in relation to key national targets (e.g. waiting times in health care). Organizations are explicitly ranked in publicly visible league tables. 'High performing' organizations were given 'earned autonomy' and extra operational freedoms, such as the example of NHS Foundation Trusts. Low performing organizations were by contrast subjected to increased monitoring, directive 'support' from central agencies (such as the NHS Modernization Agency) and the replacement of senior management and NHS Boards within turnaround interventions to address their poor performance. We later bring in Foucauldian governmentality theory (Foucault, 2007; Miller and Rose, 2008) to help conceptualize these new modes of indirect steering.

Fourthly, developing more reflexive and responsive policy tools was an important aspect of a 'modernized' policy process. New Labour's initial and thoughtful reflections on the machinery of government (Cm 4310, 1999) argued that an excessive switch under NPM to operational managerialism was evident and more thought should be given to the redesign of government itself. There should be more creative policymaking and greater organizational learning with a focus on overall policy outcomes rather than narrow departmental outcomes. There should be more pilots, evaluation, and evidence in decision making rather than reliance on political ideology. Policymaking should be longer term, more outwards looking, and better at anticipating future shocks (Cm 4310, 1999). So policy formulation was to reflect 'what works', within the spirit of evidence-based policy which can be seen as an important spillover from the earlier EBM movement (discussed later). Budgets for research and development—including policy evaluation—increased substantially across the period. Health care was a leading example where the new National Institute for Health Research (NIHR) consolidated and expanded previous research programmes.

Overall, the role of government in this account shifts from direct control to providing leadership, building partnerships, steering and coordinating, and providing system-wide integration and regulation. The development of public services managers as broader 'leaders'—drawing in those from professional backgrounds as well as line managers—with the capabilities to act as local transformational change agents, supports the micro-politics of public service modernization (Newman, 2005).

However, it is too easy to see the network governance paradigm as a simple successor to NPM. Post-1997 policies (Newman, 2001) retained and even intensified some systems and policy instruments inherited from the NPM period, notably the use of 'targets and terror' (Bevan and Hood, 2006a, 2006b) as in the rapid replacement of NHS management teams who performed poorly against key targets. Poorly performing health care providers were also highly visible in publicly accessible league tables and rankings. The use of the Private Finance Initiative as an 'off balance sheet' mechanism to fund a renewed estate for the public services accelerated sharply after 1997. Proliferating NPM-style contracts continued as a mode of coordination replacing direct ownership and hierarchy which had now been hollowed out. Private partners were brought in within large-scale consortia, but some of them imploded (as in transport).

There is a debate within the governance literature about to what extent the role of the State declines or whether it more subtly takes new forms. Jessop (2000) (cited in Bevir and Rhodes, 2010, p. 86) suggests that the State has recourse to resources within network management which still give it a 'meta-governance' role. It can set the 'rules of the game', operating in the shadow of hierarchy (for example, making regulatory or ownership changes when it needs to or suddenly taking back control in a crisis, for example, by nationalizing failing banks). It can still steer by allocating money, authority, or political attention. It can steer other actors by providing a rhetorical narrative, telling persuasive stories, and building new identities, for example, as 'entrepreneurial' public managers.

Or back from network governance to choice and quasi markets?

This presumed turn to network governance has been contested by some scholars close to the New Labour project who advocated quasi market-based approaches more consistent with NPM ideas. Le Grand (2003) has argued that available evidence suggested the GP Fundholding aspect of the health care quasi market (1990–97) had been broadly successful—including the development of better-quality services—and that the incentive structure behind Fundholding had started to reshape GP behaviour but was too weak and overmanaged to exert major effects: here was a plea for less management and more markets.

A first argument for returning to quasi markets relates to the supply side, specifically assumptions about the motivation of public sector professionals and bureaucrats. While social democratic theorists traditionally assumed public services professionals were motivated by altruistic considerations and a desire to ascertain and meet social needs, the neoliberal and public choice orientated critics of the 1980s suggested public services professionals were instead motivated by different concepts of self-interest, bureau maximization, retention of monopoly of provision, and the marginalization of user voice. Le Grand (2003, p. 15) points to currents in centre-left thought (such as market socialist ideas) which moved away from traditional collectivist mechanisms to incentives and quasi markets as policy instruments. Market socialists seek to promote policy outcomes which go beyond a narrow pursuit of efficiency (although greater efficiency is still a desired policy outcome) but include broader objectives such as equity and responsiveness.

A second argument explores the demand side, especially the changing role of the user who moves to (or more normatively, should move to) being an active and choosing consumer, just as in privately provided services. This demand-side focus supports a move back to principles of choice, contestability, and quasi markets to empower the consumer (Le Grand, 2003) against public sector monopolies and over-dominant professionals. Fotaki et al's (2005) review of the concept of choice in health care literature suggests New Labour policy thinking recast passive recipients of public services as more active choosers, influenced by sociological thought (Giddens,1997; Beck,1994) about reflexive modernization. Reflecting the rise of the citizen/consumer, the delivery of public health care shifted from a rationed to a consumer-driven culture (Clarke et al, 2007).

These pro-quasi market arguments were influential in New Labour health policy circles. By the mid-2000s, pro-choice policies were re-emerging across the English NHS (see the review of policy developments below), rebuilding quasi markets but possibly also eroding the collaborative networks set up five or so years earlier. We can explore any such tensions between markets and networks as governance modes in our cases empirically.

Major developments in UK health policy and management, 1997–2010

We now move from reviewing academic literatures to consider different— and perhaps even competing—developments in UK health policy in the 1997–2010 period.

The content of public services reform: Networks or markets? NPM or post-NPM?

At the macro level, the tensions between different narratives of public service reforming replicated themselves in texts on public services reform coming from different UK Ministries (Ferlie and FitzGerald, 2002). Unsurprisingly, the powerful Treasury continued to espouse many NPM prescriptions as doctrines and practical policy tools used to control the behaviour of the spending depart-ments and ensure departmental performance in return for extra resources (Cm 4011, 1998). Each spending department (such as the Department of Health) signed up to a public services agreement in exchange for resources. The strong political desire to ensure policy 'delivery' was manifested in close central mon-itoring of departmental achievements against targets.

The Cabinet Office's analysis (Cm 4310, 1999) was different in tone, plac-ing more emphasis on institution building. This text contained critical reflections on the fragmenting effects of NPM. 'Joined up' or more lateral government was a key objective in a reformed policy process, along with an outcome orientation (which was more NPM-orthodox), a shift towards evidence-based policymaking, a learning organization approach, and a more future- and outwards-looking orientation. Given these internal tensions, New Labour reformative ideology might well be thought too incoherent to effect major change away from an embedded NPM paradigm (Ferlie and FitzGerald, 2002).

Novel policy arenas: Clinical governance, service improvement, patient safety and Evidence-Based Medicine

A set of major novel health policy arenas emerged within UK health care in the New Labour period, distinctively different from the NPM's focus on vertical line management and silo-like agencies. They typically take a lat-eral and whole systems approach, seeking to move beyond narrow agency boundaries and segmented professional jurisdictions, as in the influential service improvement and service redesign movements (Buchanan et al, 2007a) which consider the whole care pathway. Japanese inspired 'soft' ideas of continuous quality improvement and organizational learning had increas-ing influence, picked up by the later lean organizational change programmes. Clinical reaction to these ideas remained of prime importance (McNulty and Ferlie, 2002; Waring and Bishop, 2010), and included some resistance. These shifts invoked principles of 'soft autonomy' (Levay and Waks, 2009), whereby professionals absorb audit-like ideas which originally came from outside the profession but then use them in professionally influenced but more explicit forms of self-regulation.

The 1990s were marked by various scandals in the UK business world which led to corporate governance reforms (e.g. Cadbury, 1992), designed to strengthen the role of non-executives and Boards over senior management. Parallel highly publicized scandals in the health care domain (e.g. the death of patients at the Bristol Royal Infirmary and the Shipman case in primary care) suggested the need to strengthen traditional clinical self-regulation which had failed to deal with continuing problems, often caused by isolated, difficult, or on rare occasions criminal clinicians. The new term 'clinical governance' (Scally and Donaldson, 1998) proposed a mix of central policy frameworks and delegated self-regulation to assure professional competence and promote continuous quality improvement. It was more systemic and strategic than the previous fragmented stream of clinical audit work it built on.

Post-1997 statements of health policy (DoH, 1997; 1998) operationalized clinical governance ideas. The policy assumption was that if quality could be assured by such systems then consumers would not demand choice and quasi markets. Grey (2004) notes the first reference in the policy domain to 'clinical governance' in a Department of Health text (1997) which defined it as follows: 'to assure and improve clinical standards in local level throughout the NHS. That includes action to ensure risks are avoided, adverse events are rapidly detected, openly investigated and lessons learned, good practice is rapidly disseminated and systems are in place to ensure continuous improvement in health care'.

Here was an attempt to govern clinical practice with active participation of clinicians. Flynn (2004) explores this distinctive mix of regulation and self-regulation which recurs in other domains discussed later. He notes that a Department of Health text (1998b) states that while health care professionals should have the autonomy to set their own standards of professional practice and discipline, at the same time professionals 'must be openly accountable for the standards they set and the way these are enforced' (para. 3.43). It thereby combined devolution of responsibility with accountability for performance and transparency. Flynn (2004) notes that these systems reflect neither market, NPM nor traditional professional dominance models of government and require reconceptualization, suggesting an approach based on Foucauldian governmentality might be useful. We examine these ideas further in the next chapter.

The introduction of consultant appraisal in 2001 and of consultant job plans (McGivern and Ferlie, 2007) exemplifies clinical governance principles. Consultant appraisal combined defined assessment and developmental parameters, being: 'a formally structured opportunity for professionals to engage in dialogue and reflect on how their effectiveness might be improved rather than to catch those performing poorly' (DoH, 2000c).

Consultants were to provide evidence of 'good medical practice' in different domains and agree it with their appraiser to support revalidation. Consultants could be appraised only by other consultants and had the right to agree or object to the names of appraisers. Medical and clinical directors were the only managers with the right to view the content of the form; non-clinical managers were informed only of who had been appraised and the contents of job plans. These clinical governance reforms could not be reduced to simple managerialization but drew professionals into new processes of self-management. They structured local actions within central frameworks, mixing regulation, and self-regulation. McGivern and Ferlie (2007) found doctors defensively 'playing tick-box games' to provide the impression of compliance (specifically, within the new consultant appraisal process), while invisibly continuing as before. McGivern and Fischer (2012) noted unexpected and even perverse forms of 'reactivity' to such transparent professional regulation in the distinctive fields of psychotherapy and counselling, as it undermined aspects of professional practice within these fields characterized by histori-cally distinct modes of working.

Similar ideas underpinned developing electronic reporting systems for patient safety, given increased policy-level concern for reducing clinical errors. These systems were supposed to promote the organizational ability to learn lessons from service failure through systematic gathering of and reflec-tion on structured information about serious incidents and 'near misses'. At the national level, the National Patient Safety Agency was set up as an 'arm's length' body of the Department of Health to promote systematic data collec-tion and service wide learning. The National Reporting and Learning System (Currie et al, 2008) is a knowledge management system which gathers infor-mation about threats to patient safety. It sets up a dedicated incident report-ing system requiring front-line clinicians to record key information which is communicated to local 'risk officers' and then the centre, so increasing surveillance of clinical practice. Local risk managers were required to score and stratify incidents and conduct a 'root cause analysis' of serious incidents. The system was supposed to promote an open culture and avoid the public blaming and scapegoating of clinicians.

In a case study of a UK hospital, Currie et al (2008) explored tensions between the explicit forms of knowledge in the formal reporting system (with its tick-box forms) and tacit and local forms of knowledge held by clinicians. They noted low trust levels between risk officers and clinicians, with the latter still fearing a 'blame culture'. They commented on the partial reappropria-tion of the system by clinicians who excluded non-clinical elements by such tactics as: selectively recording information; shifting of blame to organiza-tional and managerial factors (e.g. lack of resources); and establishing inter-nally controlled counter systems which operated on higher trust, but also mimicked features of corporate-wide systems (Waring, 2007).

NHS plan: Investment and reform

The NHS Plan (DoH, 2000a) set out a long-term strategy for 'investment and reform', given a political commitment to move UK health care spend up to the European Union (EU) average as a percentage of GDP. The vision behind the Plan was one of an easy to access and consistently high-quality service designed around the patient, but which also remotivated public services workers, supposedly alienated by the managerialist excesses of the NPM. The text of the vision now appears somewhat producer-centric: 'our vision is of an NHS where staff are not rushed off their feet and constantly exhausted; where careers are developed and not stagnant; where staff are paid properly for good performance; and where child care is provided in every hospital. Ours is a vision of a renewed public service ethos; a system that values the dedication of staff and believes that trust is still the glue that binds the NHS together' (DoH, 2000a, para 1.2).

Our particular interest lies in chapter 6 'Changing Systems for the NHS', the tone of which now appears surprising given received opinion relating to New Labour's top-down and target-led approach to health policy: 'This plan operates a new delivery system for the NHS. It is a system based round the NHS as a "high trust" organisation. It offers standards and clinical frameworks set nationally. A leaner and more focussed centre with the Secretary of State devolving powers. And the chance for health professionals to innovate locally earning greater autonomy the better they perform. With support to spread best practice and pressure to raise consistently poor standards' (DoH, 2000a, para 6.1).

A market-led reform strategy was rejected in this text as the earlier experiment with quasi markets had led to fragmentation, a 'postcode lottery' of locally variable provision, and an erosion of teamwork. The centre would now retain strategic control, performance manage the localities, but progressively devolve operational responsibility. The strategy was to raise the quality consistently across the NHS by setting core national frameworks and standards. The localities were held responsible for meeting these targets, supported by monitoring from the centre (Ketley and Bevan, 2007).

Local actions would fall within four national policy frameworks. Firstly, the Department of Health would, with leading clinicians, managers, and staff, set national standards in clinical priority areas. Evidence-based National Service Frameworks (NSFs) were to be developed in mental health, coronary heart disease, cancer, older people's services, and diabetes, covering around half of NHS spending. The new National Institute of Health and Clinical Excellence (NICE, created in 1999) would undertake appraisals of best available evidence and produce evidence-based guidelines for the field. There would be a limited number of national targets such as shorter waiting times which were important to the public. We will explore the impact of evidence-based guidelines in our cases later, as they emerged as a major indirect steering mechanism.

Secondly, there would be nationally supported initiatives to redesign care across the patient pathway to improve coordination, remove unnecessary steps in the care process, and speed it up (Buchanan et al, 2007b). We note that this lateral perspective implied the easier crossing of conventional professional and organizational boundaries. There were examples cited and claims made in the NHS Plan of radically reduced waiting times as a result of early initiatives. Such service improvement and process redesign exercises would be championed at national level by the newly created NHS Modernization Agency as a specialist source of knowledge and support.

Thirdly, a new national Performance Assessment Framework would be developed across the NHS, in conjunction with advisory agencies such as NICE. New efficiency targets would be based on the achievements of the highest performing NHS Trusts. Depending on their performance assessment, NHS organizations would be rated as 'green', 'yellow', or 'red'. 'Red' organizations would face intensified corrective action from the centre, while 'green' organizations would be rewarded with greater autonomy and national recognition.

Finally, there would be a graduated national inspection regime undertaken by central regulators and inspectors. The new Commission for Health Improvement would inspect every NHS organization every four years, except for those rated as 'red' under the 'earned autonomy' framework which would be inspected more frequently. The NHS Plan quickly led to 'spin off' plans in major sectors such as cancer services (DoH, 2000b) which advocated similar ideas of evidence-based guidelines, service improvement, and care process redesign.

Mid-2000s: Back to choice, contestability, and quasi markets

After this early phase (1997–2002) orientated towards networks and lateral working, UK health policy moved back towards principles of choice and diversity in the middle New Labour period (2002–2006). Fotaki (2007) describes this shift as 'from quasi market and back to market'. Cooper et al (2010) note the confluence of three pro-market policies which, by 2006, were having substantial effects. The first was the introduction of a more sophisticated fixed-price prospective reimbursement system for commissioners (payment by results) to pay for hospital care. This enabled them to pay for each unit of care rather than crude volumes. The second policy was increased diversity on the supply side, with more private sector Independent Treatment Centres for elective conditions and the roll out of Foundation Trust status with more operational freedoms for those NHS Trusts that could demonstrate financial and managerial stability. The third policy was the introduction of patient choice policies nationally, after some regional pilots (such as the London Choice Project). From January 2006, every patient in England was to be offered a choice of four providers (including one from the private sector) when referred for elective care. Cooper et al (2010, p. 3) conclude: 'broadly the reforms were supposed to create significant incentives for quality and efficiency in the NHS. Policy makers hoped the new reimbursement system would increase activity rates, increase efficiency as well as encourage providers to compete on quality'.

These pro-market policies were more evident in the English NHS than in the newly devolved jurisdictions of Scotland, Wales, or Northern Ireland, which now had substantial control over health policy and were more resistant to market-based reforming (our case study sites are all drawn from England). Secondly, these pro-market policies applied particularly strongly to acute sector hospitals and to elective care. We do not have any elective surgical networks in the study—precisely because they are not there! Market forces were more difficult to apply in remaining sectors which were multi-agency in nature—including major clinical fields covered by the National Service Frameworks—where our networks are concentrated. Fotaki (2007) sees the policy shift as representing a 're-evocation of old archetypes', with a failure to unlearn from the flawed past of the old quasi market.

'Targets and terror' in the English NHS

Propper et al (2007) note a move in health policy in England to a more aggressive managerial stance after about 2000: the newly devolved jurisdictions in Scotland and Wales took a softer approach here too. The national policy focus was strongly on reduced waiting times for elective surgery within acute sector hospitals. After 2001, top-down pressure increased with the neo-Stalinist use of 'targets and terror' (in the graphic description of Bevan and Hood, 2006a; 2006b) whereby information on the comparative performance of hospitals was made public and boards and senior managers were sanctioned for poor performance, up to and including dismissal. Propper et al's (2007) comparison of falls in English and Scottish waiting times suggests that the 'targets and terror' approach was effective, at least in the narrow terms of reducing waiting times. We comment it may have also led to an increased internal focus by acute hospitals and a disengagement from cross-agency working. Increased top management turnover may have destabilized the composition of networks and eroded interpersonal trust. This policy stream represents a revival of NPM in the managerial domain.

These different health policy streams moved into tension with each other by the mid-2000s: an early New Labour reform narrative stressing collaboration, service redesign, and continuity of care with managed networks as the preferred organizational form conflicted with a middle period reform narrative stressing incentives, choice, and diversity; revived quasi market forces and a more aggressive managerial style. The latter account was better suited to acute hospitals and elective conditions; the former to complex health policy arenas, 'wicked problems', and enduring conditions.

Service improvement activity

New Labour public services reforms were also strongly influenced by 'service improvement' ideas. Such improvement has been defined by Boyle (2003, p. 223) as 'a closer correspondence between perceptions and desired standards of public services', taking a multiple stakeholder perspective. Such standards should include higher quality as well as greater cost effectiveness and also achieving sustainable service change (Hartley and Skelcher, 2008). 'Improvement evaporation' was a major problem encountered in the field as some services quickly regressed to the *status quo* once organizational development resources were removed (Buchanan et al, 2007b). Service improvement activity reflected ideas of continuous improvement, redesigning the whole service process as experienced by the user to remove bottlenecks (Ketley and Bevan, 2007, p. 13).

The 2000 NHS Plan contained many service improvement targets (e.g. reduced waiting times) and an ambition for more patient-centric care. Buchanan et al (2007b) explore specific implications for the modernization of health services, where the newly created NHS Modernisation Agency (created in 2001) diffused standardized techniques and interventions in an attempt to accelerate service improvement. These methods included the collaborative methodology developed by the US-based Institute of Healthcare Improvement (Kilo, 1998) which used repeated cycles of incremental learning and change. Key foci included cancer services (Ketley and Bevan, 2007) within the so-called Cancer Collaboratives. They are of interest here as we have two cancer networks in the study.

The various theoretical prisms through which improvement activity can be viewed (Ashworth et al, 2010) include the collaborative perspective (Entwistle, 2010, pp. 164–5). The theory of improvement through collaboration highlights reduced transaction costs when compared to alternative governance modes of markets or hierarchies. It suggests the need for active trust building and maintenance of supportive behaviours, such as high communication, reciprocity, and trustworthy conduct. Networks are seen as offering richer settings for the circulation of knowledge and for inter-organizational learning. The effects of a service improvement focus on the NPM/post-NPM debate are ambiguous. If narrowly defined in terms of performance measurement and management, then it may reinforce an NPM orientation. If defined more broadly in terms of continuous improvement, service redesign, and organizational learning (as in the original models), then it may support post-NPM forms.

The institutionalization of Evidence-Based Medicine

Timmermans and Berg (2003) see the growth of standardized evidence-based guidelines across the health care field as a key development in health policy internationally. An important UK development has been the institutionalization (literally so, with the creation of NICE as a national advisory agency) of EBM. NICE's advice supported the writing of National Service Framework documents including the NHS Cancer Plan (NHS, 2001). Senior clinicians and academics have been enrolled within well-developed scientific advisory committees so that the NSF reflect leading professional opinion as well as explicit evidence. NICE developed sophisticated stakeholder consultation arenas such as its Citizens' Council (Davies et al, 2006) to feed into decision making, so its consultation strategy is broader than sometimes assumed. Nevertheless, we will argue later that a clinical/academic nexus lies at the heart of its advisory apparatus in relation to evidence production.

These arenas produce an indirect steering technology—the standardized and evidence-based guideline—often seen as clinically and scientifically legitimate in the field, as it incorporates both expert clinical/academic advice and patient opinion. Such a development may well be consistent with post-NPM organizing as it supersedes general managers, local NHS Boards, or indeed quasi markets as governance mechanisms. We explore the impact of such evidence-based guidelines in our cases.

The managed network as an important network governance reform

The empirical focus of our study is a set of managed networks in health care, all set up around 2000. So there appeared to be a broad shift towards these forms in a number of health policy arenas simultaneously. Managed networks are therefore an important Network Governance reform (as highlighted in Newman, 2001; Sullivan and Skelcher, 2002; Bevir and Rhodes, 2010) which exemplify the arguments about post-NPM forms made earlier. They were often set up in complex cross-cutting policy arenas where it was difficult to apply market principles or to internalize line managerial control within one vertically integrated organization. They often related to well-known 'wicked problems', such as the health and social care interface. They were often set up to implement the new evidence-based NSF and their associated targets within local systems. Such managed networks were associated with demarketization, specifically rolling back the NHS quasi market, and a return to principles of collaboration rather than competition.

Cancer services policy in particular challenged the quasi market mode of organizing as unhelpful early on (DoH, 1995), even before the change of government in 1997. The new managed cancer networks built on and formalized existing patterns of professional working in cancer services, whereby specialist expertise was supposed to radiate out of teaching hospitals to associated district hospitals and primary care providers across a large geographical patch. In practice, there seemed to be sharp variation in patient outcomes by area or even hospital. The Department of Health (1995) sought to intensify this existing model of diffusion of knowledge and best practice by commending and formalizing a 'hub and spoke' model of networking. Local managed cancer networks started to emerge informally in the late 1990s and were formally mandated in the NHS Cancer Plan and follow-up policy documents (DoH, 2000b; NHSE, 2001). They were charged with effecting strategic service change, namely reconfiguring cancer services in the light of Improved Outcome Guidance (IOG) produced by NICE, to improve outcomes and reduce health inequalities. As managed cancer networks are an emblematic example of the wider form, we were keen to include them in our study. Similar logics were replicated in other major fields, such as sexual health and older people's services (both of which we studied), but also cardiovascular/stroke, children's services, and mental health (not included in the present study).

We explore in later chapters the extent to which we found a radical shift—or not—from NPM-style to post-NPM organizing in these networks. To do this, we explore three supporting domains and suggest that if there is little change in these three domains that new network forms will not consolidate fully (Ferlie et al, 2011a). Firstly, we argue that well-developed networks depend on effective cross-organizational ICTs and databases to share information meaningfully across agency boundaries: that is, they need a joint knowledge management strategy and capacity (Currie and Suhomlinova, 2006). New ICTs such as desktop computers, e-mail, the web, electronic data storage, databases, and electronic templates are now available to support network forms of organization informationally. We explore the impact of such ICTs empirically in our sites in Chapter 8.

Secondly, we argue in Chapter 9 that public services networks will remain weak without a well-developed capacity for inter-organizational learning and joint problem solving: there is an important cognitive basis to network working. The Network Governance reform narrative (Newman, 2001) argues that public policymaking should become more forward- and outwards-looking, adopting a continuous learning style. This requires the design of organizational forms—such as inter-organizational networks—better able to learn and change. We explore the nature and extent of inter-organizational learning in our case study sites in Chapter 9.

Thirdly, we explore in Chapter 10 the extent which managerialist NPM doctrines associated with empowered general management and non-executives on Boards have given way to a broader, softer, and more lateral idea of 'leadership' (Newman, 2005) exercised as an instrument of state modernization, provided by clinicians who have been drawn into the core of these networks as clinical/managerial hybrids as well as by NHS general managers.

Performance assessment and managed networks: A qualitative assessment

In our original research protocol and final project report (Ferlie et al, 2009b), we posed the question: which of the networks were doing 'well' and why? We were interested in assessing the 'performance' of the networks, although we recognized this was a complex task. We therefore needed to develop a framework for performance assessment, using qualitative and proxy indicators as we did not have data on final clinical outcomes. Details of the framework and how we developed it are contained in Appendix 2, along with problems encountered (we describe our methods in Appendix 1). This exercise is not an exact science but provides a useful heuristic device which enables us to comment on our case studies. We assessed the two cancer networks and one sexual health network as the 'fastest movers', using this method, and were particularly interested in exploring the correlates of faster progress in those examples.

Networks and the 'wicked problems problem'

We have already suggested that network-based forms may be effective as a mode of governance in tackling so-called wicked problems (see Ferlie et al, 2011a). But what is a wicked problem and what are its defining conditions? Rittel and Webber (1973) originally developed this concept within the social planning literature to refer to problematic social situations where: (i) there is no obvious policy solution, (ii) many individuals and organizations are necessarily involved, (iii) there is disagreement between such stakeholders, (iv) where desired behaviour changes are part of the solution, and (v) there may be a call for co-production with citizens. There may well be a legacy of chronic policy failure in such arenas (e.g. crossing the health and social care interface in services for older people). 'Wicked problems' (Clarke and Stewart, 1997) or the similar concept of 'cross cutting issues' (Sullivan and Skelcher, 2002) go beyond the scope of any one agency, and unaligned interventions by any one agency can have perverse knock-on effects. Examples of 'wicked problems' in health care include the growth of obesity/type 2 diabetes or HIV infection, where there are major social and behavioural dimensions to be considered alongside conventional clinical considerations, and also the case of elderly services with a myriad of agencies drawn from different sectors.

Sullivan and Skelcher (2002) emphasize important 'cross cutting themes' in public policy which go beyond any one agency. They point to high organizational fragmentation in UK public services following earlier NPM-style 'hollowing out of the state' reforms which now require the rebuilding of lateral links and systemic capacity. One question concerns the extent to which public policy arenas are indeed populated by 'wicked problems'. Are such arenas pervasive and hence persuasive in policy design or do they represent rare special cases? We explore later the extent to which the eight networks studied indeed addressed 'wicked problems'.

Concluding discussion: New Labour and health care organizations—an NPM and post-NPM hybrid?

We here reviewed the debate about a possible transition from NPM to post-NPM forms of health care organization during the New Labour era (1997–2010). We outlined three possible interpretations of what a post-NPM order might look like: post-Fordism; the post-bureaucratic organization and finally an influential Network Governance reform narrative. We outlined serious criticisms of earlier NPM reforms which had produced dysfunctional effects which strengthened the case for counter reforms. Some writers argued that the case for using network-based approaches was strengthened by the presence of 'wicked problems' and cross cutting themes (Sullivan and Skelcher, 2002) in various public policy arenas.

Examining developments in UK health policy, we found a wide spread of approaches adopted in practice during the New Labour period, ranging from an important strand of network governance reforms, through a reversion to choice/quasi markets, and even the retention of NPM-style 'targets and terror' (Bevan and Hood, 2006b). Quasi markets were used more in elective conditions (such as minor surgery), while networks were more apparent in complex and enduring conditions (such as older people's services). We argue managed networks are an important policy strand consistent with Network Governance principles which complement New Labour's more market-based reforms (Mays et al, 2011) and which should not be forgotten in the academic literature. In essence, we found an NPM/post-NPM hybrid at the national policy level, confirming Reed's (2011) analysis of more general trends. We will revisit this theme in the analysis of our empirical cases at the local level.

Our review of New Labour health policy also found a cluster of strands (clinical governance; patient safety; EBM and policy; managed networks in arenas covered by evidence-based NSF) which displayed novel and distinctive conditions of 'decentralized centralization' and of surveillance, self surveillance, and high levels of managerial commitment. This is an important observation. As already noted, both Flynn (2004) (in respect of clinical governance systems) and Waring (2007) (in relation to patient safety reporting systems) suggest Foucauldian governmentality is a helpful theoretical framing for the study of such arenas. We will therefore review this theoretical literature further in the next chapter.

3

A governmentality-based perspective on UK health care organizations

Introduction

This chapter seeks to conceptualize the novel developments found in UK health policy and organization in the 2000s outlined previously (such as clinical governance systems, Evidence-Based Medicine (EBM) policy arenas, patient safety systems, and our key example of managed networks). These settings mix regulation and self-regulation, 'earned autonomy' with central surveillance and intervention in failing sites, and also use legitimated evidence-based guidelines to underpin service reconfigurations. There is some local discretion accorded but only within policy parameters compatible with central policy. Managed networks typically bring professionals in hybrid managerial roles into their core so that middle-level general management roles become less evident. Such features fit neither the conventional professional dominance, choice, and markets nor New Public Management (NPM) paradigms and require novel theorization.

We argue that Foucauldian concepts of 'governmentality' help us make sense of such settings. The chapter starts by outlining core Foucauldian ideas, then considers literature on the changing governance of the advanced neoliberal State, and finally more specifically applications of these ideas to health care organizations, where a significant stream of Foucauldian work has recently developed. After this review, we draw out several broad themes used in our later case study chapters.

The Foucauldian perspective (Foucault, 1973, 1974, 1977, 2007; Burchell et al, 1991; Dean, 1999) is an influential one in many social sciences, notably including the disciplines of organizational studies and critical accounting (Burchell et al, 1991; McKinlay and Starkey, 1998; Dean, 1999; Reed, 1999; Miller and Rose, 2008; Townley, 2008). It has a broad scope but one branch has proved fruitful in the analysis of indirect steering mechanisms in the advanced neoliberal state which move beyond simple command (Miller and Rose, 2008) to more indirect steering. This literature also highlights the operation of a power/knowledge complex in knowledge-based sectors linked to the state, including in health care (Hasselbladh and Bejerot, 2007; Ferlie et al, 2011b).

Foucault's theory of power and rule is radically distinct from conventional pluralist, Weberian or Marxist/labour process approaches. Power here resides in mundane day-to-day practices, dominant languages, obedient and reformed subjects, taken for granted rationalities, and modes of thought. It is diffuse power rather than rooted in a single power centre (Clegg, 1998, p. 32), such as the sovereign, the State, or the ruling class. While many scholars (Knights and Willmott, 1989; Barker, 1993; Grey 1994; Alvesson and Deetz, 2006; Karreman and Alvesson, 2009) use Foucauldian notions of power critically, Foucauldian power may produce positive (power to) as well as negative effects (power over) (Townley, 2008). Foucauldian institutions (such as the reformatory and asylum) can contribute to a long-run civilizing process whereby spectacles of cruelty (such as public executions), once commonplace, were abandoned.

Foucault writes about the evolution of the French State and society in the 1750–1830 period, during which time major social and 'reforming' institutions, underpinning knowledges and proto professions, all simultaneously emerged. To understand his prolific yet complex work, we start with his most famous book (*Discipline and Punish*) with its startling image of the Panopticon in a reforming Benthamite prison (Foucault, 1977). In this site, the architecture enables an all-seeing but unseen jailor to keep all prisoners under observation from a central observation point. The Panopticon aims: 'to induce in the inmate a state of conscious and permanent visibility that assures the automatic functioning of power. So to arrange things so that the surveillance is permanent in its effects, even if it is discontinuous in its action; that the perfection of power should tend to render its actual exercise unnecessary...' (Foucault, 1977, p. 201).

So Foucauldian power seeks to make deviant social behaviours visible, transparent, and thus potentially reformable. There is a radical centre/periphery split so that: 'in the peripheric ring, one is totally seen, without ever seeing; in the central tower, one sees everything without being seen' (Foucault, 1977, p. 202). His focus on the prison—only one example of various reforming institutions, including the asylum (Foucault, 1973) and the clinic (Foucault, 1974)—exemplifies his recurrent concern with the management of socially deviant groups, including struggles for physical control over their bodies. Developing technologies of control do not just punish but also seek to reform such groups and create capacity for self-discipline. Some of the new institutions examined were founded by social or religious reformers (such as Bentham in the case of the prison or Tuke in the Retreat at York for the mentally ill) who sought to dispense with the cruelty and neglect they saw in earlier institutional sites (such as dungeons and leper houses). So the inmate may acquire a reformed identity through exposure to the day-to-day disciplinary practices of these total institutions. The authority of these institutional sites is bolstered by developing proto scientific knowledge such as criminology in the prison or early psychiatry in the asylum.

Townley (2008, p. 13) argues there are three principal axes in Foucault's work: the axis of knowledge (savoir), the axis of power, and the axis of ethics (the subject). Essentially, this knowledge, power, and identity triad organizes the Foucauldian thought system. She reminds us (2008, p. 16) that Foucault starts his analysis with the 'how' rather than 'who' or 'why' of power, mapping particular practices and technologies. Disciplinary power may be used by different actors in different ways in different societies and time periods, requiring a concrete analysis of how power is used in particular settings.

Complementing Townley's broad characterization, Dean (1999, p. 23) suggests four interrelated core dimensions to Foucauldian 'governmentality'. First, he highlights *visibility* and associated ways of seeing and perceiving. Second, there is *episteme*—ways of thinking and questioning, and associated vocabularies and procedures for the production of truth. Third, there is *techne*—ways of acting, intervening, and directing practical rationalities ('expertise' or 'know how'), which involve mechanisms, techniques, and technologies. Finally, one needs to be mindful of the process of *identification*—ways of forming subjects and identities.

While Foucauldian analyses often focus on internalized surveillance by docile subjects, his later ideas explore distinctive themes of desire as well as discipline (Starkey and McKinlay, 1998). In a process of so-called *subjectification*, individuals lose themselves in regimes of power but are also recreated by them. Starkey and McKinlay (1998) argue that the earlier focus on docile bodies moves in his later work to the ways in which individuals create their own selves and realize themselves through self-discipline and self-knowledge. Such processes may have a strong ethical dimension. So workers can use surveillance and discipline for self-development but within a set of social and discursive practices (Starkey and McKinlay, 1988, p. 232).

Governmentality

Foucault's work analyses the developing capacity of early modern states to govern populations in a more sophisticated manner than through crude physical force or direct rule by the sovereign. There is a growing range of social actors involved and a shift from direct to indirect control mechanisms. Foucault is interested both in macro shifts in the overall regime of government and the micro level of particular practices and techniques seen as the technical element of government (Dean, 1999, pp. 30–1; Miller and Rose, 2008, p. 15). Foucault's core concept of 'governmentality' (Foucault, 2007, p. 108) incorporates two key processes in the construction of the early modern state. First it refers to: 'the ensemble formed by institutions, procedures analyses and reflections, calculations and tactics that allow the use of this very specific, albeit very complex, power that has the population as its target, political economy as its major form of knowledge and apparatuses of security as its essential technical element'.

This definition focuses on a melange of various apparatuses, institutions, modes of thinking, and associated classifications and practices which enable the early modern state to generate a greater capacity to govern populations subtly. Note the stress on technical apparatuses as an important element. This is a melange rather than a single power centre so internal relations may be fluid and shift (unlike, say, the more centred Marxist analysis of the ruling class). Importantly, resistance to a governmentality project is possible and may lead to 'counter conducts' which sabotage governmentality regimes (Foucault, 2007, p. 356), for example, prisoners may (and sometimes do) reject discipline and self-reform, riot, and even burn the governor's office! We explore issues of clinical resistance to or indeed enrolment in governmentality later in the chapter.

The power/knowledge nexus

Secondly, Foucault (2007, p. 108) refers to: 'the development of a series of specific governmental apparatuses on the one hand and on the other a development of a series of knowledges'. Within the power/knowledge nexus in health care, political/medical knowledges and associated professions bolster this capacity to govern more broadly: thus psychiatry governs mental illness and public health governs epidemics. The State and learned professions are jointly involved in the construction of governmentality: the State licences professions such as medicine to undertake measures to protect the health of the population given expert knowledge. Townley (1998, pp. 193–4) suggests that for a domain to be governed, it must first be made knowable. 'Disciplines' (particular knowledge bases) provide micro technologies which enable a 'political anatomy of detail' to be stored and transmitted to the centre, surveying and classifying problematic domains and turning them into knowable arenas. We suggest the EBM movement promises to makes the health care field classifiable and 'knowable'.

Trajectory of the self and high commitment leadership

A third major Foucauldian concept is the 'trajectory of the self' and changed identity (Starkey and McKinlay, 1998; Townley, 2008) produced through governmentality: so the discipline of the penitentiary (Foucault, 1977) brings the offender to repentance, a reformed life, and a new identity. Foucauldian analysis explores the identities of those that govern and are governed (Dean, 1999, p. 32). His libertarian later work suggests subjects recreate themselves actively though 'practices of freedom' (Starkey and McKinlay, 1998): the self is developed and transformed by the self, with disciplinary practices playing an enabling rather than a punitive role. Social actors can discipline themselves to become ethical beings. This perspective suggests roles and identities may evolve over time. The 'technology of the self' (Foucault, 1986, pp. 10–11) represents: 'those intentional and voluntary actions by which men not only set themselves rules of conduct, but also seem to transform themselves in their singular being, to make their life as a collective *oeuvre* that carries certain aesthetic values and meets certain stylistic criteria'. While Foucauldian analysis has often traced changing identities of the governed (such as the transition to an active and choosing consumer of public services, Miller and Rose, 2008), here we use this perspective to explore the changing identities of local governors, specifically those clinical managerial hybrids who took on network leadership roles. We suggest that their network leadership represents 'identity work' (Alvesson and Willmott, 2002; Sveningsson and Alvesson, 2003), where they construct their own identities and the identities of their professional colleagues in relation to governmentality-related forms of knowledge/power.

This theme relates to a wider literature on high commitment levels supposedly found in 'post-bureaucratic' and network-based organizations. As suggested earlier, Boltanski and Chiapello's (2005) review of the 1990s management literature found a rising model of the network-based firm advocating an anti-authoritarian 'neo management' doctrine with distinctive self-control mechanisms. Coercive management gave way to leaders' attempts to achieve a visionary inspiration of the workforce, creating shared meaning and joint commitment to a project of the firm. Widespread coaching helped develop individual and organizational capacity, as the workforce developed broader skills in an 'upskilling' process. These internalized control regimes were supported by strong societal values of autonomy, including the achievement of self-discovery and personal fulfilment at work through creative projects.

Panopticon control

Fourthly, Foucauldian analysis vividly suggests 'Panopticon' control where the potential for surveillance by the centre is constant and inescapable. The image is taken from a Benthamite reforming prison where the central jailor can see everything without being seen. The prisoners do not know at any one time whether they are under observation but may assume that they are and so adopt reformed conduct.

Reed (1999) suggested that four sets of surveillance practices within the Panopticon are of interest. The first is spatial segregation and enclosure where institutional architecture enables physical surveillance by an all-seeing centre, as in prison. Clearly this does not apply to virtual or network-based organizations which are not physically defined or enclosed. The other three sets of surveillance practices identified by Reed (1999) have more relevance. The first implies continuous, remote observation and monitoring which historically took place through such instruments as timetables, scanning towers, and observational platforms. These micro practices enable the centre to keep the field under constant supervision, at least potentially. They may now take the form of audit routines or performance indicators. The second set takes the form of hierarchical ranking (as in visible league tables), public judgements by others and public examinations which may lead to reflection and self-criticism. Finally, there is pedagogic internalization and normalization. A therapeutic control apparatus within the educational sphere replaces the use of crude physical coercion. Educational and development programmes supporting professionals moving into management roles, but in a way desired by the centre, are a good example. Reed suggests the centre does not simply disappear; rather it steers through pervasive but mundane technologies of power. The extent to which the State still seeks to steer, even if indirectly, is an important question to which Foucauldians give different answers.

The Foucauldian analyses of organizations

The Foucauldian perspective has influenced the study of contemporary organizations (McKinlay and Starkey, 1998), alongside other academic fields. It has made a strong and creative contribution to critical accounting (e.g. Hopper and McKintosh, 1998) where dominant accounting logic can be seen as a pervasive day-to-day technology of control. The question of why accounting practices have recently expanded in public sector organizations is an intriguing one (Power, 1997). The concept of a power/knowledge nexus has been used to study behaviours in professionalized or knowledge-based organizations, including in health care (Ceci, 2004).

The original concept of the physical Benthamite Panopticon developed into that of the electronic Panopticon, fuelled by new Information and Communication Technologies (ICTs) and the informating organization. This produces a new electronic surveillance capacity for the centre as: 'Information systems that translate, record and display human behaviour can provide the computer age version of universal transparency that would have exceeded even Bentham's most outlandish fantasies' (Zuboff, 1984, p. 322).

Zuboff argues that the contemporary counterpart of the central tower is now the video screen. This Panopticon does not require physical enclosure or even human observers but can flexibly operate across time and space and through machines programmed to collect information in a certain way. The electronic Panopticon changes conventional superordinate/subordinate relations, providing routine information about subordinate behaviour to the centre, absorbing middle management, and lessening face-to-face engagement. The organizational requirements of informating organizations (Zuboff, 1984, p. 413) involve work improvement programmes, emphasizing high commitment levels, self-managed teamwork, and decentralization (under electronic surveillance from the centre). Middle management is delayered as the informating organization moves in a 'post-bureaucratic' direction.

Such a Foucauldian perspective helps reconceptualize 'post-bureaucratic' organizations (Ferlie et al, 2011a). Standard bureaucratic or neo-Weberian forms (e.g. line management, detailed supervision, many rules and regulations) are hollowed out as more flexible and mobile governance emerges. Reed (1999) asks whether there is a generic transition in contemporary organizations from a Weberian control mode ('the cage') to a Foucauldian one ('the gaze')? Such a shift in private firms may be driven by globalized capitalist production and consumption requiring more flexible and mobile control (Reed does not focus on the changing shape of government). Such restructured firms may be governed through Foucauldian modes: 'this model of a form of continuous, unobtrusive and pervasive surveillance combined with internalized cultural self management and discipline has provided the theoretical benchmark against which the emergence of a new organizational control regime that radically breaks with its bureaucratic predecessor has been analysed in recent years' (Reed, 1999, p. 31).

Importantly, this control mode reduces crude Weberian controls such as externally imposed intervention and direct supervision (Reed, 1999, p. 31). The implications of this perspective for the changing shape of government need further investigation, and may be problematic given high levels of risk management from the centre.

Within the academic field of organizational studies, Foucauldian ideas are increasingly influential. A preliminary review of papers on knowledge management in knowledge-intensive organizations (Ferlie, 2012) suggests Foucauldian analysis is widely used as a theoretical framing in that field. We consider specific examples from health care arenas (such as patient safety, Waring, 2007) later. This framing has also been used in recent studies of other professionalized and knowledge-based settings. Thus Brivot and Gendron (2011) take the Panopticon metaphor and explore its significance for an electonically based knowledge management system introduced in a case study of a French law firm. They find various responses by the professionals concerned, including lateral (as well as vertical) networks of surveillance, exhibitionism (showing off one's work to colleagues in electronic reports), and secrecy (hiding one's work from the knowledge management system).

Within the interesting field of academic work on management consultancy, Karreman and Alvesson (2009) explore themes of resistance, counter resistance, electronic surveillance, high work commitment, and identity formation in their examination of consent and obedience apparent amongst young management consultants in a case study of a leading consulting firm. Why did they work such long hours and do so willingly? Their research problem was to explain: 'a case where knowledge workers appear subject not only to a managerial division of labour, but also what they experience as extreme work conditions, in particular long working hours, and yet they subject themselves willingly'. Much conventional literature on Knowledge Intensive Firms sees them as highly decentralized, yet Karreman and Alvesson (2009) found subtle corporate control mechanisms which created the 'right sort' of motivated workforce. These controls included: (i) standardized and selective recruitment of able, ambitious, and similar young graduates, (ii) an extensive programme of training and development, (iii) formalized systems for evaluation and appraisal, and (iv) an elaborate internal knowledge management system. These corporate systems helped the firm to resist possible workforce resistance.

Strong identification from the young consultants with what was seen as an elite firm happened quickly, given strong socialization mechanisms. There were strong norms of cooperation found within task-focussed teams and high conformity. The authors concluded that this combination created a context in which 'compliance is not only desirable; it is almost irresistible'. These two examples from law and consulting illustrate the way in which Foucauldian analysis helps analyse subtle and indirect control systems in knowledge-based and professionalized private firms.

The anglo governmentality school and UK neoliberal government

We now review important British work on governmentality which examines the changing shape and strategies of advanced neoliberal *government* as a theme of particular interest in the UK policy context. This school takes the same public policy developments apparent within an NPM perspective, but analyses them in a distinctive way. While clearly based on Foucault, Armstrong (1994) argues this is a distinctive 'second wave' concerned with the ability of the neoliberal State to steer society, operating at a distance and through indirect technologies of power. The steering centre does not disappear but rather operates through new and more indirect modes.

For the last thirty or so years, this school argues that a neoliberal UK State has been shedding direct ownership and control over functions previously provided directly through privatization and outsourcing (Miller and Rose, 2008, chapter 8). While a greater range of actors becomes involved in government, the State still acts as a steering centre: Rose et al (2006, p. 89) refer to 'governing at a distance' where the State acts as a remote 'centre of calculation', seeking to act on the desires and activities of others who are spatially or organizationally distinct. This strategy goes beyond NPM's empowered internal line management combined with strong contracts and incentives as typical implementation strategies to include indirect steering technologies and incorporation of more social actors within State-influenced arenas.

Miller and Rose (2008, p. 212) ask: what is it to govern in a neoliberal way? While the direct economic domain of government shrinks with privatization, it still has overall responsibility—as reflected in blame strategies in the mass media which highlight government failings—for problematic social domains such as crime or health. Irrespective of party political affiliation, governments developed new policy instruments which typically: 'created a distance between the decisions of formal political institutions and other social actors; conceived of these actors in new ways as subjects of responsibility, autonomy and choice and hoped to act upon them by shaping and utilising their freedom' (Miller and Rose, 2008, p. 212).

There are three characteristic shifts in the governance of the advanced neo-liberal State. The first is termed *a new relation between expertise and politics*. Miller and Rose argue that the old autonomy and dominance of public services professions has been breached through new calculative technologies. New indirect technologies include the 'accountization' of public services through budgeting, accountancy, and audit activities which enable the behaviour of public services professionals to be recorded and challenged. An example is the ever growing remit since the 1980s of the Audit Commission (before its abolition in 2010 by the new UK coalition government because it paradoxically felt it offered poor value for money) as it expanded its 'value for money' studies. Miller and Rose (2008) see these 'grey sciences' as both modest and pervasive, applicable to almost every public services domain. Their analysis is accounting led and they do not consider the 'grey science' of the EBM movement in the health domain which retains a role for clinically orientated knowledges and techniques of calculation, and indeed professional representatives (we explore EBM-related knowledges in our cases).

The second shift is *the pluralization of social technologies* with the 'destatisation' of government, that is detaching the State centre from the old

40

apparatuses previously built up (such as National Health Service (NHS) vertical line management which was strengthened by policy changes up to the late 1980s but which then retreated). Government fragments into a looser collection of quasi autonomous non-governmental organizations (quangos), agencies (such as the National Institute of Health and Clinical Excellence (NICE), created in 1999), regulators, purchasers, and providers. The old divide between private and public sectors blurs, with new hybrid forms, more partnerships and consortia, and a broader range of stakeholders in public policy arenas. Direct political and democratic control erodes as key functions (e.g. the post-1992 'new' universities) become self-governing corporations. While these 'hands off' agencies have a certain operational autonomy, a Foucauldian prism highlights the new managerial technologies that indirectly govern these looser arenas without line management: contracts between the centre and the agency, key performance indicators, audit, monitoring, and evaluation. The centre governs at a distance but through a novel and regulated form of autonomy.

The third and final shift is a *new specification of the subject of government*, consistent with Foucauldian subjectification and the technology of the self. The active and 'responsible' customer/citizen values high quality, personalization, and a choice between public services. Miller and Rose (2008) draw attention to social technologies that support such subjectification and transmit information about consumer behaviour back to the centre: mass media, opinion polls and market research, health and lifestyle experts. The problem for the centre is how to encourage 'responsible' lifestyle choices by service users, using indirect technologies and knowledge about patterns of consumer behaviour (e.g. sexual behaviour, smoking cessation, diet, and exercise). Miller and Rose's (2008) analysis concentrates on the behaviour of the governed as opposed to the reconstruction of local governors. We will consider the subjectification of public sector producers (such as clinical managerial hybrids) as active governing agents in our cases, linked to post-bureaucratic discourse about high commitment and leadership (Reed, 2011).

Townley (2008, p. 16) uses a Foucauldian framework to analyse the operation of performance measures in another UK public service: the criminal justice system. Her interesting book is not primarily about the substantive setting of criminal justice services, although it draws examples from them. Rather, it is about how novel practices and technologies play out in this organizational context. She sees performance assessment systems as a disciplinary technology, that is a power/knowledge nexus which produces both positive and negative effects. Such performance measures are intended to 'cascade' through the organization, linking the front line with the observing centre to give a 'snapshot' picture. Townley's (2008) analysis represents a Foucauldian perspective applied to a public service other than health care.

Foucauldian perspectives on current health care organizations

Health care institutions have been strategic sites for Foucauldian analysis, given the power of medicine, its ability to control the body, its advisory role to government, its influential underpinning science and research base, and its diagnostic systems of patient classification. Foucauldian framing has provided a new theoretical purchase on patterns of health care reforming and health policymaking. Johnson (1995) used a governmentality perspective to get beyond a conventional state (vs) professions binary in analysing health care organizations, looking instead at the institutionalization of clinical expertise. Various writers internationally used a Foucauldian perspective to study contemporary health care organizations, typically examining three themes.

The first theme explores the surveillance effects of new ICTs within the electronic Panopticon (Zuboff, 1984), together with clinical resistance or enrolment. Clinical enrolment or absorption is as possible as counter conduct and resistance: we need concrete analysis of how behavioural dynamics play out in informating clinical settings. Doolin's (2004) New Zealand study of the implementation of a new case mix system in a hospital highlighted the potential capacity of the new technology to increase remote surveillance of clinicians and establish transparent norms of performance and calculability. ICTs could make clinical practices visible to the organizational centre, reported upwards and stored in comparative data. However, implementation depended on the enrolment of senior clinicians, which was weak. Doctors engaged in resistance and 'counter conduct', circumventing systems seen as too finance-led so that the case mix system was not widely used in clinical practice. Timmons (2003) similarly found non-compliance by nurses in their interaction with new computer-based case management systems. On the other hand, an Australian study (Iedema and Rhodes, 2010) involving video recording of a spinal team to focus on an infection control problem questioned the assumption that surveillance was always negative. It could trigger adaptive or creative responses by a reflexive clinical subject, engaging in clinical learning and using it to develop the professional self.

A second Foucauldian theme explores the dynamics of new clinical governance and patient safety systems. Flynn (2004) analyses emerging UK regimes of clinical governance from the late 1990s from a governmentality perspective. He argues clinical governance is based on quality improvement ideas, with a mix of professional self-regulation but also open accountability. They reflect 'devolution of responsibility combined with accountability for performance...and dispersed and devolved systems of policy implementation'. Flynn (2004, p. 20) argues: 'clinical governance is a form of governmentality, where audit is linking in with regulation and accomplished through new forms of self surveillance'.

Medical expertise is co-opted into managing health risks, requiring both surveillance and self-surveillance. The normative style emphasizes commitment, entrepreneurship, and flexibility rather than neutral affect and rule-bound behaviour. Sheaff et al (2004) examined new clinical governance systems in UK primary care, as a shift away from the old professional dominance. Using Foucauldian concepts, they saw the clinical governance discourse (with associated categories, concepts, and techniques) and its links to explicit national policy frameworks as a power resource which legitimately presented itself as 'soundly evidence based'. Non-compliance to such a legitimated discourse would be both clinically and scientifically impossible. Clinical governance was operationalized through semi-formal and clinically related networks, rather than the contracts/hierarchy mix typical of NPM. At the heart of these networks lay a clinical/managerial core extending its surveillance over the primary care field. The old pattern of professional dominance and exception management gave way to a continual and mainstream scrutiny of primary care doctors, using routine, comparative, and directive 'technologies of power', such as explicit practice-level performance indicators.

Empirical studies suggest varying clinical reactions to these new systems. Waring (2007) sees developing UK patient safety systems as a contest between two alternative power/knowledge discourses. The first is a managerialist discourse of 'safety science', enabling managers to develop and use novel techniques such as: root cause analysis, incident reporting systems, and electronically based risk management systems which gather information across the clinical field and route it to a specialized central unit so 'a managerial gaze is therefore turned upon medical practice'. Initially clinicians failed to complete key forms, seeing the new system as an illegitimate form of non-medical control. Yet most medical departments in the hospital went on: 'to enhance their techniques of quality improvement by applying what could be described as more "managerial" forms of risk management. Significantly, these initiatives had been justified by the recent hospital wide developments in patient safety'. In obstetrics, for example, reports on risky incidents were collected by an experienced midwife and analysed by a lead clinician in a popular local system of self-surveillance. Waring (2007) sees this 'adaptive regulation' as going beyond superficial compliance by professionals, so disciplinary discourse is internalized within self-surveillance. Such arenas reshape forms of knowledge as they move round the system. Waring's (2009) later ethnographic study of hospital risk management systems found tacit forms of clinical knowledge about safety-related incidents were decontextualized and codified as they moved up from clinicians to the new central grouping of risk managers.

Levay and Waks' (2009) Swedish study of how clinicians are actively involved in 'transparency projects' (e.g. accreditations, quality registries) does not explicitly draw on Foucauldian concepts but produces comparable findings about mixed surveillance and self-surveillance. Clinical professionals became involved in transparency projects, finding them meaningful and even internalizing some aspects. At the same time, they remained in control of evaluative criteria and procedures: 'the professionals submitted themselves to the gaze and judgement of others, but in the end they retained considerable control over the judgement criteria'. McGivern and Fischer's (2012) study of the impact of new transparency and regulatory regimes in UK psychotherapy and counselling found strong reactivity effects, as doctors learned to manage the 'blame game' and engaged in defensive practices.

Iedema et al's (2006) Australian study of Critical Incident Reporting (CIR) found a move from bureaucratic to narrative or interpersonal modes of control, whereby doctors were engaged in constructing narratives about their practice: 'what I did'. The intent behind CIR was not to blame but rather to learn and shape work practices, by combining systemic rationality and personalizing morality, obligation, and inspiration. It constructed an arena of 'governmentality' where intimate aspects of clinical work became available for scrutiny and intervention by the self or by others, having the effect of increasing participation from front-line clinical staff. This post-bureaucratic 'hot' control mode brings in elements of personalizing morality, obligation, and inspiration rather than the neutral affect and 'due process' of public bureaucrats. It focuses analytic attention on the roles, style and perhaps high enthusiasm, and the value base of clinicians drawn into the new systems of regulation/self-regulation.

The third theme relates to the power/knowledge nexus which might well be thought to be highly developed in health care. Ceci's (2004) Canadian study of a legal enquiry into why nurses were not believed when they correctly tried to draw attention to a major loss of safety in a Health Sciences Centre argued that this was because nurses lacked access to a societally authoritative discourse that the clinicians and the judiciary that later publicly examined and judged them both possessed. Shaw and Greenhalgh's (2008) discourse analysis of how 'official' research agendas are formed in UK primary care research uses the power/knowledge nexus concept. They argue research policy is currently redesigning primary care settings as population labs for large clinical trials conducted by networks of dominant biomedical researchers who marginalize qualitative or experiential clinical knowledge. Behind this shift lies a set ('ensemble') of powerful economic, political, and academic interests, institutions and disciplines that together have the power to define 'high quality' clinical knowledge.

Pickard explains the development of medical specialisms, such as General Practitioners (GPs) with special interests (Pickard, 2009, 2010) and geriatric medicine in a Foucauldian governmentality framework. Pickard argues that the backing of government (a strategic actor in this account), with policy concerns about an aging population, was crucial to the development of geriatric medicine, enabling it to overcome resistance from other medical professional sub-disciplines to its formation. She suggests that this 'imprinted the profession with the stamp of governmentality' (2010, p. 1072). Pickard (2009, 2010) suggests that particular medical specialisms are internalizing the rationalities of government and constructing their professional identities accordingly.

However, there is room to develop national policy level analysis further, looking at the *what* of EBM. Bearing in mind Townley's advice (2008) that a Foucauldian analysis should start with the *how* of power, rather than the *why* or *who*, we examine in our cases the nature and impact of texts, technologies, and techniques which populate the EBM field. These include clinical guidelines produced by NICE, incorporated in National Service Frameworks (e.g. *NHS Cancer Plan*, DoH, 2000b). This technology of guidelines provides the possibility of a form of indirect steering persuasive to health care professionals, although we should still be open to processes of local sense-making or even resistance (Dopson and FitzGerald, 2005). One argument is that the clinical guideline may prove effective as legitimated sapiential authority in polycentric networks with weak hierarchical or market power.

Governmentality in managed health care networks—some broad themes

Drawing on our earlier literature review, we now define some broad governmentality-related themes to explore in our empirical study of NHS managed networks.

Theme 1: A power/knowledge nexus—the ensemble of Evidence-Based Medicine

A power/knowledge nexus is a core part of governmentality, referring to an ensemble of institutions and associated knowledge bases, techniques, and practices. Foucault has a major interest in analysing the effects of different rationalities (Townley, 2008, pp. 10–11) on social relations. The government of the modern state is linked to policy arenas which draw on well-developed knowledge bases and associated learned professions, notably medicine in the case of health policy. Clinical medicine has developed a biomedical research infrastructure of vast scope and scale over the last sixty years (the first Randomized Control Trial (RCT) did not take place until about 1950 but has since grown exponentially and acquired great authority).

A sustained development in health policy (including the UK NHS) has been the growth of EBM as a mode of medicine based on explicit analysis of clinical research ranked in a formal hierarchy of evidence. Such 'high quality' knowledge tends to be produced by an elite group of academic clinical researchers who publish within peer reviewed journals using a restricted range of methods. Such knowledge is then synthesized by health services researchers who are developing novel knowledge bases. Such synthesis supports production of formal evidence-based guidelines and protocols for implementation by the clinical field. As a mode of knowledge production, such EBM steers the field away from clinical experience, intuition, tacit knowledge, or group consensus building.

Taking a social science perspective on EBM, Timmermans and Berg (2003) ask: what is being ordered, who is involved in the ordering, and how do explicit EBM standards remake the practice of medicine? They point to a melange of influential authors, new academic journals, government agencies (including the US Agency for Health Care Research and Quality), and major research funders which populate this emergent arena. They trace the emergence of new disciplines (such as Health Services Research) and research themes (such as outcomes research and standardized disability assessment) within such knowledge production.

Taking their steer, how might we characterize the ordering of UK EBM arenas? Up to the late 1990s, the UK EBM arena lacked national policy frameworks and agencies so implementation processes were locally enacted by the clinical group (Dopson and FitzGerald, 2005). This pattern changed as new national policy frameworks in relation to clinical governance and EBM (see Chapter 2) were elaborated. The EBM policy arena now includes major central agencies such as the National Institute of Health Research (NIHR) and NICE, as well as the international Cochrane Collaboration, which all act as institutional sites of knowledge production. NIHR produces a growing volume of scientific evidence which feeds into NICE's synthetic work. Often held up as a role model internationally, NICE is a high volume producer of evidence-based clinical guidelines which now cover much of the UK health care field.

NICE, its advisory machinery, and its core 'product' of the clinical guideline represent important sites for Foucauldian analysis (Ferlie and McGivern, 2011). NICE's 'Manual of Guidelines' is a key text available on its website (NICE, 2009) which outlines a standardized process for producing clinical guidelines, specifying core tasks and who should be involved. For example, the manual refers to the Grade of Recommendations, Assessment, Development, and Evaluation (GRADE) international working group and its approach to the assessment of the quality of evidence, indicating that NICE is migrating to the GRADE model.

Curiously, the composition and operation of the EBM power/knowledge nexus has not been fully explored in recent Foucauldian studies of health care, except for Shaw and Greenhalgh (2008). They analysed texts produced within national policy and did not examine the advisory apparatus, analytical techniques, and knowledge classification systems apparent within clinical guidelines. Our initial scan of NICE's core methodological text (NICE, 2009) suggests bounded pluralism, with strong elements of patient involvement (Davies et al, 2006) but where it appears the methodological core resides in advisory groupings of expert clinicians, clinical academics, and health services researchers (Ferlie and McGivern, 2011).

Theme 2: Subjectification, the technology of the self and clinical managerial hybrids

Our earlier review of the governmentality literature suggested it addressed characteristic ways of forming the selves, identities, and orientations of those who govern (Dean, 1999; Townley, 2008) as well as the governed, through subjectification and the technology of the self (Starkey and McKinlay, 1998, p. 230). Our focus here is on the changing self of clinicians drawn into managed networks as governing agents but now under the surveillance of the centre in terms of implementation of visible national targets. The high legitimacy of evidence-based clinical guidelines as an indirect mode of steering and of associated managerial tasks (such as service improvement activity) may enrol such hybrids in an EBM-based governmentality project.

Clinical managerial hybrids are originally from clinical backgrounds but have been progressively drawn into management roles (for example, as a Network Clinical Director). They are not just the clinicians they were originally, but nor are they general managers with line management power, so how can they be characterized? Using a concept of 'identity work' (Alvesson and Willmott, 2002; Sveningsson and Alvesson, 2003), McGivern et al (2012) distinguish between two groups of clinical managerial hybrids: *incidental hybrids* who undertake managerial roles for only a short period, and a smaller but significant group of *strategic hybrids*. This second group still see themselves as 'good doctors' but are now permanently interested in organizing clinical care and improving service quality as well as treating individual patients. Rather than being 'forced' to become managers and enact roles framed by governmentality-based knowledge/power (such as evidence-based guidelines and associated performance targets), this transition may be one of self-development and the realization of a desired new identity: individuals become what they desire. Changing how patient care is provided within health care networks to align with evidence-based guidelines could fit with what a 'good' clinical managerial hybrid does.

This perspective highlights the strong normative commitment likely within transformed selves (Boltanski and Chiapello, 2005; Reed, 2011). So we might prima facie expect to see a 'post-bureaucratic' management and leadership style based on self-belief, dedication, high energy levels, inspirational qualities, and ethical commitment rather than the neutral affect and due organizational process typical of bureaucratic settings. We would expect such hybrids to be successfully enrolled in an EBM-led governmentality project rather than demonstrate counter conduct and resistance. So the trajectory and style of these strategic hybrids is an interesting theme to study in our networks.

Theme 3: Transparency: The grey sciences, risk management, normalization, and external examination

Governmentality seeks to make problematic social domains knowable and manageable. One approach to achieving such governmentality is through the collection of transparent data which can readily be moved from the localities to a surveying centre, electronically as well as physically. Such data produce classifications, identify and manage sources of risk, and promise to contain potential social danger (Foucault, 2007). For example, elaborate risk-management systems in UK mental health services (Castel, 1991) seek to make an unpredictable and potentially dangerous field 'knowable' by surveying and classifying individuals and subpopulations (e.g. through forensic psychiatry) and formally assigning levels of clinical risk through structured assessment tools (Fischer and Ferlie, 2012). Collecting clinical audit data is another method for making clinical practice more transparent.

Miller and Rose (2008) highlight the role of mundane yet pervasive 'grey sciences' in promoting governmentality in the advanced neoliberal state. They see such grey sciences as emanating from the world of accounting and colonizing previously professionally dominated public services organizations. Examples include audit (Power, 1997), costs data, and clinical risk management systems (Castel, 1991). This perspective provides a fruitful avenue for examining the operation of financially or indeed clinically orientated 'grey sciences' in health care arenas.

The Foucauldian perspective implies the use of 'normalising sanctions' (Hopper and Mackintosh, 1998) to eradicate non-conformity and to move behaviours of those observed back to the desired and visible norm. These sanctions can be positive as well as negative, mixing reward and punishment. Systems of personal accounting emerge in Foucauldian control systems whereby individuals are ranked according to observed behaviours: 'punishing, ranking, sanctioning, promoting, demoting, were integrated into a cycle of complete knowledge about the individual. Each teacher, officer, master, overseer or reformer was required to perform the essential surveillance, ranking and punishment functions and to keep a written record of subordinates' progress and comportment' (Hopper and Mackintosh, 1998, p. 137).

The public examination is a major Foucauldian control technology (Hopper and Mackintosh, 1998, p. 137). It transparently but also ceremonially establishes the 'truth' about each individual who is classified and ranked according to his or her attributes. The need for examinations produces an examining apparatus, most obviously examiners in educational settings but also doctors in clinical settings. Hospitals are in Foucauldian terms enclosed organizational vehicles for the continual examination of patients by clinicians. These examination processes leave behind detailed records used to construct tables, averages, norms, and subgroups.

Can we move this analysis up to the organizational level? It suggests transparent examination of health care organizations and clinicians by the centre, as in patient safety reporting systems (Waring, 2007; Currie et al, 2008). So one would expect elaboration of surveying and examining technologies along with visible assessments of performance. Poor performers can be 'named and shamed' in publicly visible league tables, putting on pressure to improve performance and to conform to field norms. Periodic accreditations (e.g. designation of Academic Health Sciences Centres) undertaken by expert external panels against specific and stated criteria are another indirect control technology. Accreditation reduces the need for direct hierarchical control and provides a public examination of sites' competence.

Theme 4: Panopticon surveillance and electronic reporting

As previously discussed, Zuboff (1984) suggests the informating organization provides opportunities for Panopticon-style control through electronic reporting to the corporate centre, cutting out conventional line management. Here the centre develops electronically based performance management regimes and also knowledge management systems to convey key information in a timely fashion upwards. The development of electronic knowledge management systems is apparent across professionalized service organizations, notably law and consultancy firms, as well as health care.

Authors have explored the various and sometimes unexpected behavioural effects of such surveillance and knowledge management systems on health care professionals. One question is whether the logics inscribed in the reporting systems are internalized by clinicians, or whether they retain power to reject or adapt such systems (linking back to professional dominance). Currie et al's (2008) analysis of knowledge management in the NHS's National Reporting and Learning System explored the tension between contextualized tacit clinical knowledge at ward level and the way in which it became more explicit and decontexualized as it moved through the risk management system. However, doctors remained the most powerful group and resisted the new risk management logic and reasserted some control by, for example, selectively participating in recording information or shifting blame for incidents from clinicians to managers in discussion.

As discussed previously, previous studies have found various clinical reactions to electronic surveillance systems, ranging from resistance (Timmons 2003; Doolin, 2004; Currie et al, 2008), through defensive reactivity (McGivern and Fischer, 2012), adaptation and self-surveillance (Waring, 2007; also Currie et al, 2008) to internalization and a creative clinical response (to video-based surveillance) (Iedema and Rhodes, 2010). Patient safety, clinical governance, risk management arenas, and also recent work on infection control arenas (Murray, 2012) all represent important empirical sites for such analysis, with some evidence of reassertion of clinical control over originally managerially orientated reporting systems (Currie et al, 2008; Harris, 2011).

Important questions emerge for empirical analysis (as in Genetics Knowledge Parks cases): how frequently do local clinicians and managers fill in electronic reporting templates? Who fills them in and how? What information is concealed and what revealed (Waring, 2007; Currie et al, 2008; McGivern and Fischer 2010, 2012) or changed as it moves around the system? Are the performance indicators embedded in the templates internalized by clinicians or scientists, adapted, or simply rejected? Does the centre take action where such reports signal potential concerns or it is overwhelmed by a flood of data so that they are not used in practice but act merely as a 'ritual of verification' (Power, 1997)?

Concluding discussion: Governmentality as a theoretical prism for analysing managed health care networks

So we suggest that a governmentality perspective—as developed in these four broad themes—is a useful theoretical framework to explore in reconceptualizing empirically evident 'post-bureaucratic' developments in UK health care. As Rose et al (2006) argue, scholars in more practice-connected academic fields (and we might well include health care management here) are drawn to a governmentality perspective because it may make theoretical sense of important and novel organizational changes in the field.

Foucault's work is dense, complex, and sustains multiple interpretations, including those that take a more post-modernist and post-structuralist view than adopted here (Bevir and Rhodes, 2003, pp. 22–4). We here operate within a more conservative 'Anglo Foucauldian' school (Bevir and Rhodes, 2010, p. 49), using such foundational texts as Miller and Rose (1990, 2008), Rose et al (2006), and Starkey and McKinlay's (1998) work on the technologies of the self.

There are two implications of this more conservative theoretical position. The first is a strong interest in examining concrete and substantive technologies of calculation and steering (such as NICE's evidence-based guidelines) which are not just another form of linguistic discourse but powerful techniques of inscription. The second implication is a notion of the State (still with a capitalized S) operating as a distinct centre of calculation and steering. Other interpretations of Foucault's work see the role of the State as much diminished and as 'hollowed' out by underlying Foucauldian processes. Some authors even see it as an effect more than a cause: 'the state should be addressed as an effect of the detailed processes of spatial organisation, temporal arrangement, functional specification and supervision and surveillance' (Mitchell, 1991).

We do not take this radical position: we suggest that the State still seeks to steer even in post-bureaucratic settings. The paradox is that as the direct role of the UK State contracts; so its indirect role expands. At one level, the old nationalized industries have been privatized; at another level, direct ownership has been replaced by new forms of regulation. There is an activist style of governmental reforming, sustained over a considerable period (Moran, 2003). Expanding public–private hybrids (such as Public Private Partnerships) have double-edged effects. On the one hand, they import private money and business logic into previously publicly funded services. However, such partnership logic also extends governmental influence into new sites: 'with Foucault's work in mind, we can perhaps theorize this not as a decline but an expansion of governmental power: the power to constitute individuals, households, communities, social entrepreneurs, NGOs, public organisations, businesses, voluntary organisation as active partners' (Newman and Clarke, 2009, pp. 14–15).

In professionalized organizations in the UK public sector, long-term growth of indirect surveillance and control mechanisms in both the universities (research assessment exercise, quality assurance) and health care (clinical audit, clinical appraisal, EBM guidelines) (Power, 1997) is evident, justified through goals of transparency and high performance. Within health policy, central government appears still to undertake a shaping, brokering, and surveying role, operating in broad concert with various social constituencies and on the basis of influential technical advice (e.g. the strong example of NICE).

How does the governmentality perspective differ from other theoretical prisms? Foucault does not specifically analyse the rise of capitalism or the capitalist firm. Unlike neo-Marxist analysis, a Foucauldian perspective does not highlight macro drivers from the economic sphere, such as the search for shareholder value in health care enterprises, privatization, or financialization. There is little concern for work intensification and the ramping up of control and productivity seen in labour process work (see Smith et al, 2008 on controls over nurses in NHS call centres): indeed jobs may become broader, team-based, and more inspirational (Reed, 2011). Power is linked to accredited knowledge rather than owning the means of production. It is most suitable for the analysis of sectors not experiencing privatization or financialization and with a well-developed advisory apparatus.

We suggest that this pattern broadly fits much of the UK health care system in the 1997–2010 period. There was no substantial move to a market-driven health care system in the UK NHS (at least within our networks) and little growth of a private sector (e.g. in cancer services). There was surprisingly little supply-side change. Instead, there were buoyant increases in public funding so health care remained a publicly funded system with a strong governmental/professionalized/scientized core, as our cases suggest.

Unlike Weberian or New Public Management perspectives, a governmentality prism does not highlight the line management hierarchy or succession of 'offices' as a control mode. It suggests limits to direct managerial control and detailed supervision, envisaging more flexible 'smart' and non-Weberian control modes (Reed, 1999). This Foucauldian perspective also suggests a delayering of traditional middle management and their replacement by ICT-led surveillance.

Finally, a governmentality perspective sees the State and the health care professions—notably academic and quasi managerial subgroups—as part of the same power knowledge nexus rather than as engaged in zero sum conflict (Johnson, 1995). This is radically different from the professional dominance and NPM models. It accords attention to subgroups of clinical professionals who link the two domains. At the individual level, the subjectivization perspective suggests hybrids may develop and realize themselves at work as they move into managerial or advisory roles and pursue their long-term agendas in an energized manner.

We conclude that the Anglo Foucauldian governmentality perspective provides a potentially creative theoretical prism with which to examine patterns of organization and governance in managed networks in UK health care.

4

Genetics Translation Networks: The continuing autonomy of academic science

We now move from two early chapters which reviewed key literatures and set initial theoretical direction to a set of empirical chapters where we report our case study material. We start with Genetics Translation Networks (GTNs) (a pseudonym designed to protect the identity of our sites). These were selected as science-oriented networks which sought to bring together the National Health Service (NHS), universities, and other stakeholders in a new form of 'translational science'. The attempt to link clinical practice and basic science is a distinctive feature. It is important to note that the fieldwork for one case (GTN1) started three years before the fieldwork for the other cases, as one of the team was involved in the earlier study of its creation (2002).

The chapter is organized as follows. Firstly we present the common national policy history, which shaped the career of the two cases discussed. This is followed by the story of 'tracer issues' in the two cases (GTN1 and GTN2). Finally, we present initial reflections on the case material in relation to the overarching themes of the book namely, governmentality, the 'wicked problems' problem, the management and leadership of networks, Information and Communication Technologies (ICTs), and shared learning. The continuing autonomy of academic genetics science and its ability to evade a governmentality project is a common feature of both cases.

Policy history of the two Genetics Translation Networks

The creation and funding of a set of GTNs across the UK was fuelled by hype about a nascent 'biotechnology revolution' in the early 2000s. New academic science in the field of biotechnology in general, and in genetics in particular, was seen as having the potential to radically improve medical practice in developing new personalized treatments, diagnostics, and service delivery mechanisms (Pisano, 2006). Some authors are sceptical of such a rosy pro-spectus. Pisano (2006) suggests that the prospect of rapid translation of the new science into routine practice may have been oversold, given high uncer-tainty, difficulty in codifying tacit scientific knowledge, and the need for col-laboration amongst the many stakeholders involved (where network-based approaches were often used). Wainwright et al's (2006) ethnographic analysis of the translational pathway for stem cell research for diabetes found it had to negotiate a fraught transition from the world of basic research to the different world of routine clinical practice.

In 2001, the UK government's Department of Health (DoH) and the Department of Trade and Industry came together to provide £15 million funding over a five-year period for a UK 'Genetics Fund' to establish six regionally based GTNs with the aim of improving the health and wealth of the nation. The idea was to bring together academic scientists (includ-ing social scientists with an interest in genetics), clinicians and health care providers, private companies, patient groups, and ethical/legal experts to encourage more effective collaboration and to foster practical improvements in health care from breakthroughs in genetics and genom-ics research. In early 2002 six GTNs were launched, commonly located in elite research-intensive universities around the UK, with some very senior scientists involved.

The GTN initiative formed a major strand of the government's strategy for realizing the potential of genetics science, reflected in the DoH's (2003) White Paper *Our Inheritance, Our Future: Realising the Potential of Genetics in Health*. It was expressly set up to promote genetic science and its commercial applica-tion, whilst simultaneously promoting public dialogue regarding the social, ethical, and practical issues arising from developments in human genetics.

Two major problems immediately arose following the launch of the GTN programme. Firstly, it was problematic developing a tender that adequately encompassed all the demands being placed on the GTNs. A member of a Genetics Research Advisory Group, a national body monitoring the perform-ance of the GTNs, commented:

> It appeared very late in the drafting of the NHS plan, virtually just a sentence, just a throw away sentence that took everyone by surprise and when [the then Minister for Health] was questioned what it meant—he said: 'You tell me'. We then had to develop some themes. We felt GTNs were about focusing on an aspect of genet-ics knowledge and really becoming a centre of excellence, a world leader...the objective of the GTNs was to prepare the NHS for the genetics revolution...it rolls off the tongue very easily, but what does it actually mean?

The tender highlighted the need for GTNs to demonstrate regional activity a number of key areas: developing genetics services in healthcare, society (i.e. public engagement), education (public and clinical professionals), translation of science into practice, and commercialization of genetics science. Aside from this broad specification, the tender was open to considerable interpretation and so provided the opportunity for those involved in submitting GTN bids to develop their own ideas unencumbered by central guidance around any 'GTN Model' with differing emphases on each of the four major areas.

A second issue related to the competitive nature of the commissioning process. The bidding process fuelled competition between specialists across regions. Prior to this 'a harmonious genetics community in the UK' (GTN member) had existed (Swan et al, 2007). Whilst competitive bidding is a fact of life for all UK clinical genetics centres, the scale of this initiative, together with the commonly shared view that there would probably be subsequent funding following the initial five-year period, meant that much of the informal collaboration occurring across regions effectively ceased at this time. Initially, at least, the old genetics community was severely disrupted by the bidding process and the implementation of this initiative.

We examined two GTNs, which we label as GTN1 and GTN2. The tracer issue examined in GTN1 was the development of a genetic test for an inherited cardiac condition (which we describe as a cardio-genetics test). This was an activity where multidisciplinary work was required and many different actors were necessarily involved, each with their own distinct interests and epistemic orientations towards their common task. The tracer issue in GTN2 was the application of genetics knowledge to a broader public health agenda, again spanning the boundaries of a number of diverse disciplines.

Genetics Translation Network 1

Description of the site and its structure

Genetics Translation Network 1 (GTN1) was situated close to a leading British university. The university's scientists involved with GTN1 included some elite international experts in the field who had been at the forefront of research in basic human molecular genetics research for many years. GTN1 was also connected to a local hospital providing NHS clinical genetic services, including a testing laboratory and genetics department.

It was reported that there were significant communication issues and tensions between those whose work in genetics was considered 'academic' and those who contributed to NHS genetics work. The differing cultural and employment practices of the university and the NHS were seen as important in explaining how GTN1 developed.

Formation of the Network locally

The policy interest in genetics, and in particular the interest in securing the funds associated with the GTN initiative, initially pushed university and NHS practice more closely together. It is illuminating to examine how the bid for the Network was put together locally, as this initial process crucially shaped the nature and characteristics of the Network (see McGivern and Dopson, 2010).

A senior medical professor from the university first heard about the GTN programme and its potential funding from a contact in the DoH. Then:

> It was a question of pulling a team together. But from our point of view it was just using additional funds from government to add to the broad area of information about genetics out there. (Medical Professor)

Two other senior medical academics wrote the initial application for funding, with others becoming involved for a variety of reasons such as to ensure representation for their function:

> When I learned about the bid I got involved early on to make sure clinical genetics was represented. (Genetics Professor)

Other academics were approached because the tender asked for a specific contribution that they were able to make; for example, a social science professor commented:

> The original call for bids did say something about ethics, X knew me and said 'well I know someone who might be able to do that', and presumably that's how it worked. (Social Sciences Professor)

Other medical professors were approached to participate to lend their reputation and credibility to the proposal, as the DoH: 'wanted prominent geneticists on the bid' (DoH Official). So the bid was dominated by the 'great and good' in the university medical school.

Some senior academic clinicians were keen to get involved as they saw the GTN bid as an opportunity for channeling this new money into existing research or practice. A cardiology professor commented:

> It became fairly clear that we might be able to fund an area of work that I was having difficulty in covering... in very pragmatic terms... [GTNs] are very attractive as a resource. (Cardiology Professor)

Another medical professor noted:

> It provided additional terribly useful funds to do the work we wanted to do but it was maintaining the momentum we were building elsewhere. (Pathology Professor)

So for these medical academics originally involved in the GTN1 bid the espoused purpose of the GTN, that is translating genetics science into practice, appeared less important than simply getting new money into pre-existing clinical practice and academic research. As a genetics professor put it:

> The GTN means nothing; it is a way of getting money into clinical practice. (Genetics Professor)

The window from the tender document becoming available to the final deadline for submission was two months, and the speed of the application process for funds was a source of irritation to the managers in the NHS hospital involved. One commented:

> The bid got rushed through, it didn't really have the opportunity to go through the correct channels and so the trust was concerned about implications like space, was there enough money for consumables, did we get our fair share to enable us to deliver. There was a concern it was a cavalier process at a time when the trust was in financial trouble. (NHS Lab Manager)

Another NHS manager was concerned, even at this early stage, about the different orientations of NHS and academic stakeholders, noting: 'I had little expectation, partly because the people who are active in the GTN want to do their science, not influence services'. NHS doctors were too 'worried about the question of how it is going to impact on the patients we see' and reported 'a huge gap between academic and clinical genetics' (NHS Geneticist).

In theoretical terms, we highlight within the history key differences between the diverse range of 'epistemic communities' (Knorr-Cetina, 1999), each with distinct orientations towards developing knowledge and practice linked to wider structures of knowledge/power. At the same time there was at this stage no clear governmental episteme to frame and make the GTNs' activities visible, due to the nascent nature of genetics as a discipline. As Clegg et al (2002) note, the success of such interdisciplinary collaborations may rely on a shared form of governmentality, which did not emerge in this case, and this absence enabled academics to pursue their pre-existing agendas.

The GTN1 bid was successful and the Network was formally set up in 2002. The GTN1 tender was split into four projects, each largely based on the university's existing core competences. We here focus in particular on Project 1, which was the development of a clinical service for the identification and genetic management of a cardiac genetics test. Project 2 related to the viability of routine molecular testing for genes influencing susceptibility to cardiovascular disease and/or response to treatment (cardiovascular genetics). Project 3 focused on developing genetic microarray technology. Project 4 involved social science, relating to the ethical, economic, social, and legal factors in translation (which we also examine in Project 1).

Project 3 made some progress but became redundant as cheaper alternative microarray technology was developed commercially elsewhere. There appeared to be little interdisciplinary networking or translation in respect of Project 2, however, and yet a cardiology professor commented that it had produced:

> Very good science...we'll have good publications and will be internationally well regarded by peer reviews.

Similarly, another medical professor commented:

> We are generating results now that we wouldn't be able to do if it had not been for the GTN...academic type of stuff leading to more grants, more publications...I would say that the [GTN] was a success...[translational networking] is almost irrelevant.

The various stakeholder groups involved in GTN1's formation

At its conception, GTN1 was dominated by elite academic medical scientists who had worked together for some time, knew and trusted one another, and shared an epistemic orientation towards GTN1's projects. Their motivations for joining this Network were clear; the GTN represented an opportunity to win more money to push on with existing academic work and leverage other funding opportunities. This is not to say that they disregarded other possible benefits of the Network. For example, as one interviewee argued, 'it could provide an umbrella to bring people together'. So the GTN was collectively imprinted with the epistemology of the medical professors.

NHS managers who were tangentially engaged with the bid worried about cost implications, yet failed to get such concerns on the agenda early on. As a stakeholder group, they were marginal and engaged in a tokenistic way. Another stakeholder group included research scientists working in a research institute within the university. Their epistemology was similar to the medical researchers, although they appeared somewhat less powerful because they lacked the academic clinicians' understanding of patients.

Another important stakeholder group were the NHS scientists who worked in the NHS labs, and were enrolled in the Network to perform vital genetic tests. This community had a distinct epistemology from medical researchers and research scientists. The NHS labs saw the GTN as useful in providing new funds and equipment and raising their local and national profile.

The call for tenders emphasized the need to engage social science stakeholders. A professor with an interest in the ethics of genetics was identified as important. Patient representation took the form of a member of a patient interest group invited to attend the executive meetings. Later on (2005), NHS commissioners became another stakeholder group involved in the Network in a more influential manner. So a range of stakeholders with distinct episte-mological orientations towards the GTN's projects were involved in its forma-tion and development.

Management roles, relationships, and management style

A Network Director was appointed in late 2002, coming from a research sci-ence background. The Network Director was accountable to the Chairman of the GTN Board (a medical genetics professor) and the manager of the laboratory in a Directorate of an NHS hospital who, in practice, was virtually absent. The Network Director's style was personable and focused, liaising with the four projects' staff in a regular and systematic way to keep them up to date with developments. The Network Director personally dealt with and completed the quarterly reporting forms demanded from the DoH. The actions taken to deal with the bureaucratic reporting demands were univer-sally appreciated by other Network members. Consistently, interviewees com-mented on the Network Director's credibility, excellent interpersonal skill, intelligence, integrity, work ethic, and passion to make the GTN succeed.

Non-managers played crucial roles in the development of the Network, par-ticularly in its later stages. A consultant geneticist working in the hospital and university proved able to move across the boundaries described. He had previ-ous experience of and understood laboratory working; he was therefore able to negotiate between the NHS labs, the university, and the NHS hospital. Like the Network Director, he had excellent interpersonal skills and was passionate about using genetics science to benefit patients, having had frequent contact with patients adversely affected by the cardiac condition linked to Project 1.

A third key negotiator and boundary-spanner was an economist working within the social science institute. Despite coming from a social science back-ground, the economist developed good relationships with clinical researchers and scientists who saw value in the work, which was more quantitative than some of the other social sciences. The fourth important boundary-spanning figure was the NHS commissioner, who had a background in nursing, expe-rience of managing specialist units, and a MBA. The commissioner too had experienced changing careers, which perhaps made it easier to transcend the boundaries between the different 'epistemic communities' which often dis-played different assumptions about the nature of preferred forms of knowl-edge (Knorr-Cetina, 1999; McGivern and Dopson, 2010).

Governance

The governance arrangements of the GTN changed over time. The shifting membership of the Executive Committee proved an important aspect of the story. The Executive was chaired by a professor of clinical genetics and its meetings were held quarterly. DoH and Department of Trade and Industry representation was expected but in practice the representatives appeared at the first few meetings only. The patient representative also attended for a few meetings at the start-up stage. In addition, the Principal Investigators of the four projects, the Director of the NHS genetics labs, the Directorate Manager and the Network Director were all on the Executive Committee. A GTN Board was set up as the overseeing body of the Executive Committee and consisted of senior members of the 'stakeholder' institutions. It met twice a year and had responsibility to review and contribute to the strategic direction of the GTN.

The story of the Network following its formation

While GTN1 assembled executive and supervisory boards, some senior medical academics who were originally and centrally involved in the GTN bid soon withdrew to more distant supervisory roles, playing little practical role in the GTN's activities.

The early period of the Network was characterized by the hiring of new people, start-up research activity, the introduction of governance arrangements, and getting to grips with the expectations of the DoH. By mid-2003, there had been several changes to the Network. Firstly, the Network in practice revolved around an even more limited number of key individuals, particularly medical academics, the NHS labs, the university clinical science research institute, and the social science professor. Representatives from primary care, patient groups, the hospital, and the university's innovation unit (which was meant to help commercialize science), had little practical involvement with the GTN, other than formally sitting on the Supervisory Board.

At this early stage the Department of Trade and Industry, despite having jointly funded the GTN, started to lose interest in the project. As it became apparent that commercial applications were unlikely it withdrew from its role in managing the GTNs. Acknowledging disappointing progress, the DoH now brought in a Genetics Research Advisory Group as a governance mechanism to help regulate GTNs (with the first meeting in early 2003). Members of the Group included genetics experts from various institutions (including the DoH, universities, and the pharmaceutical industry) and disciplines (including medicine, biology, and sociology).

The DoH now imposed standardized quarterly performance reviews on the GTNs to help them understand what GTNs were doing. A DoH official commented: 'The collective way of reporting across the six [GTNs] made the work of the advisory group quite easy'. A member of the Genetics Research Advisory Group similarly noted that GTNs were: 'reporting in a particular format so we could judge performance against criteria'. These criteria were expressed in terms of translation rather than academic outputs, but subsequent reports still showed little translational activity or networking between the six GTNs.

The DoH put pressure on the Network Director, who in turn put pressure on the four GTN1 Projects, to meet the espoused goals of 'translation' into the NHS. In theoretical terms, the DoH can be seen as attempting to re-establish jurisdiction over the Network by imposing a form of governmentality and steer it away from academic science towards the original objective of translation.

However, medical professors and scientists in GTN1 contested the legitimacy of introducing reporting, which they saw as 'changing the rules' halfway through 'the game'. They suggested that the Genetics Research Advisory Group was vague about what they wanted the GTNs to achieve and provided little guidance on objectives, targets, or methods of reporting. Interviewees commented on finding reporting time consuming and feedback limited, vague, and unconstructive. Typically feedback took the form of a half-page generalized commentary with little concrete advice or evaluation, leading to a perception that reporting was a 'box ticking' exercise (McGivern and Ferlie, 2007):

> Even though it is a quarterly report... it seems that you blink your eye and the next one is due... constantly doing something that is wasting your real time. You are ticking bureaucratic boxes. That is how it feels... All you end up doing is writing pretty much the same as last time and then you just change a few of the numbers. (Academic Scientist)

Performance reporting systems now surfaced as a major tension between the DoH's desire for faster translation and the professors' primary focus on academic publication and accessing further funding. This is not to say that professors had *no* interest in translation, rather that translation of academic science into practice was not a key objective within their epistemic community (knowledge/power regime) where publication and funding was seen as the currency of academic careers. An additional complexity arose when the Advisory Group put pressure on the GTNs to collaborate rather than compete. This attempt to change the interaction style between GTNs at short notice was problematic, leading to tokenistic efforts to collaborate such as joint seminars.

Clashing knowledge/power regimes in GTN1

Within GTN1, pressure points emerged in relation to turnaround times for the cardio-genetics tests. Scientists in the NHS labs were oriented towards a knowledge/power regime which prioritized the accuracy of test results over the speed of the testing process, whereas academic clinical and medical researchers were concerned with getting results quickly with reasonable but not necessarily complete accuracy. As one genetics professor put it, 'we are competing with the best in the world and frankly we are not funded to compete with them, so we need to use every intellectual trick in the book'. Tension over the turnaround times of cardio-genetics produced strained cooperation between these two groups. Academics felt that the service did not understand the nature of academic research, while lab scientists resented academic attitudes to practice. As one NHS lab scientist put it 'when [academic scientist] says the ROUTINE lab, I mean I could just shoot her!'

A second clash between university researchers and the NHS labs emerged in relation to Project 4 (social science). Increasing national competition for business between NHS labs began to undermine the local labs' willingness to disclose costs information to a health economist in Project 4 trying to calculate the health economics of cardio-genetics testing nationally. The NHS labs feared that this information might leak and undermine their competitive position. The health economist expressed concern about the labs' uncooperative behaviour, especially as other labs nationally were providing this information. As an academic scientist commented:

> Health economics...were trying to do costing but [the NHS labs] basically didn't want to give any prices...it a complete barrier...[and] embarrassing because you have got [NHS labs in other universities] collaborating.

The health economist was, however, able to engage effectively with medical professors and academic scientists as they shared a quantitative epistemology and could see the practical value of her work. This contrasted with perceptions of the contribution of the sociologists in Project 4, who were described as 'weird sort of sociology people' doing 'woolly' research (NHS Lab Scientist). An academic scientist noted:

> Our world is very black and white...[sociologists'] terminology, it does not mean anything to us...it was quite obvious that we were providing material...to write some interesting papers...it was not of mutual benefit...it was a one-way flow...a clash between people coming from a scientific point of view, or what you feel is scientific, and things that are not.

When it became clear that his position on Project 4 would not be refunded, the sociologist concentrated on producing academic sociological papers, valued within his own disciplinary community to secure a job in a sociology department. So we see fundamentally different orientations towards the translational work undertaken within GTN1, shaped by the wider epistemic (knowledge/power) regimes, which undermined the translation of science into NHS practice.

By mid-2006, the DoH decided not to refund the GTNs given the slow pace of translation activity. As a Genetics Research Advisory Group member stated:

> Academics don't seem to focus on the deliverables in the NHS and that has been my experience of the GTNs...A lot of academic work going on would have gone on naturally and it was not going to benefit the NHS...They need to focus on the end game...The lack of translational awareness was disappointing.

As far as our tracer (Project 1) is concerned, the development of a genetic test for the cardiac condition was seen as successfully completed by members of GTN1 in academic research terms by 2005. A health economist in Project 4 provided evidence that the test was economically viable in terms of its effect on the health of the population. At this point, local NHS commissioners, responsible for funding, emerged as important actors affecting the adoption of the test. They were concerned about possible costs as the new test moved into the NHS with implications for health benefits and fairness issues. Testing people with a family history of the particular cardiac condition would be expensive, not least because those at risk would need defibrillators. An NHS commissioner suggested that members of GTN1 had failed to conceive of the translation process as a whole, noting:

> They hadn't thought through the process to completion...the whole...It sort of comes back to the Network thing that we can't just think about genetics in isolation, you have to think of how does that fit in with the rest of the cardiac services...you just can't do your little bit. You have to think of the knock-on effects, the unintended consequences...You have to be more conscious of the bigger picture. (Commissioner)

A small group of scientists and doctors working on Project 1 met with the commissioner to try to persuade him to fund the adoption of the test. As we gathered our final data in late 2007, as GTN1 closed, the local commissioner had not yet been convinced of the cardio-genetic test's clinical and economic benefits, which he regarded as 'academic'. However, in 2008, and interestingly after GTN1 had shut down, we heard that the cardio-genetic test had been commissioned (without pressure from the DoH to produce translation). So Project 1 did eventually achieve its translational objective, but only after GTN1 had been judged to have failed and closed down.

Genetics Translation Network 2

Description of the site and structure

GTN2's bid proposal stated that GTN2 would be interdisciplinary and facilitate the transition from genetics research into public health and policy interventions.

One respondent described the Network as 'an interdisciplinary think tank, to engage and educate the public and make policy recommendations' (Research Fellow). The Network had four stated aims:

1. Participating in the development of national policy on genetics and genetics services and enhancing the transition from genetics research into public health and policy interventions.

2. To transform information from scientific studies on genetics into knowledge through its validation by critical appraisal, by seeking the perspective of patients and the public and by placing it in its ethical, legal, and social context.

3. To stimulate the transition from research into clinical practice through programmes that promote the dissemination and sharing of genetics knowledge.

4. To create and support a network of individuals and organizations in the local area with active interests in human genetics.

Formation of the Network locally

GTN2 was situated at the periphery of a city with another university and NHS hospital. Its aims and objectives mirrored the long-established interest of GTN2's Network Director, who was passionate about public health contributing to the field of genetics and had managed to secure a stream of funding for this work previously. He commented:

> My model is not at all an academic model, it's a corporate model, it's about change management, and we are about getting research into practice. We do not see ourselves as doing primary research, we do secondary research, we bring knowledge together.

Like those creating the bid for GTN1 and GTN2, the Network Director saw GTN funding as a way to continue existing work. In effect, the monies enabled this longer-term project to continue:

> When the [Genetics Translation Network] money came along we just set up the structure and we moved from having a 50 square metres of space to 250 square metres of space. Most of our expenditure is on people. (GTN2 member)

The Network Director similarly commented:

> When I was the [previous public health genetics initiative] I was working on a project with £10,000s a year. And then we got the Genetics Translation Network funding so we were about a million pound a year...It was extremely helpful.

Stakeholder groups involved

The Network's stakeholders consisted of over twenty people (some part-time) working in multidisciplinary teams (including public health medicine, human genetics and molecular biology, epidemiology and biostatics, policy development, industrial liaison, education, public involvement and communications, and information management). This core team was complemented by part-time lecturers, associates, and honorary consultants in law, ethics, social science, health economics, and primary care. Surprisingly 'obvious' stakeholders such as the NHS/academic genetics community and public health were not involved and this gap became an important part of the subsequent GTN2 story.

Management roles, relationships, and management style

The dominant management role was the Network Director. As a GTN2 member noted:

> There is no doubt that the concept and the driving force was [the Network Director] himself. But he is a very astute and politically aware individual.

An NHS manager agreed that the Network Director had played a powerful leadership role within GTN2. He also commented on the Network Director's political skills and ability to make things happen despite the resistance of clinical stakeholders:

Some people reported finding working for the Network Director's frustrating because, they argued, his ideas were not always thought through.

The managerial style of the Network Director is striking in this case. He was an entrepreneur, passionate about his own vision, strong minded, and a skilled resource investigator with a distain for top-down performance management and governmentality. He noted:

> I have this entrepreneurial view of life and I actually hate the environment of the UK at the moment with this emphasis on performance management and stuff.

Governance

The Network Director chaired an executive team of five people which met fortnightly. The four key members of the executive group had line management responsibility for different activities within GTN2 and reported progress at the Executive meetings.

There was also a supervisory board, chaired by a distinguished scientist, consisting of representatives of the DoH, Department of Trade and Industry, a research trust and the NHS hospital trust, and social care. This supervisory board considered budgetary issues as well as monitoring the work of GTN2 but was, in essence, a sounding board for the Network Director.

The story over time

GTN2's funding went down badly with some members of the local health genetics community, who acknowledged that they were caught 'napping' and had failed to capture these resources themselves, and relationships were described as 'not good' with the regional genetics centre. One respondent commented:

> The GTN had zero science in it when it started and that meant it had zero connection with the [genetics] Department. It was more public health stuff...very soft. (Clinician Geneticist)

Another respondent spoke of a loss of local goodwill following the award of GTN monies. So unlike GTN1, GTN2 was isolated from the wider local genetics network. The Network Director claimed they had approached the clinical genetics department at the university at the stage of bidding, but argued they weren't interested because it 'wasn't proper genetics'. This was confirmed by other GTN2 interviewees, suggesting a desire to retain autonomy for basic science:

> [X] approached the clinical genetics department but they weren't interested because it 'wasn't proper genetics'. When the GTN was funded, clinical genetics then resented them getting money that they should have had. (GTN member)

After a year of GTN funding, the Network Director again attempted to reach out to the genetics department by ring fencing some money for a research laboratory. However no substantive collaboration with the GTN Network flowed from this gesture. The Network Director commented:

> The main fault line is not between the different disciplines...the fault line was between the academics and the rest of us. (Network Director)

So there was little evidence of the Network extending to or influencing local health service delivery. There was no reported interaction with managers or commissioners. However, the events and publications arising from GTN2 were acknowledged as being used by NHS commissioners.

Several interviewees believed that GTN2 was particularly puzzling to the Genetics Research Advisory Group and other GTNs. An interviewee noted:

> The Department of Health sort of changed its stance. And the individuals changed and of course the focus of the R&D programme changed during the period of

the existence. And so that and I think to some extent they wondered about this cuckoo in the nest. (GTN Supervisory Board member)

Like GTN1, GTN2 was not refunded, and when it became apparent that future funding was unlikely to be forthcoming, members of GTN2 spent its last year trying to secure funds from private sources to get longer-term activity going. The outputs from the GTN included publications and web-based materials that targeted public health and social science communities. Like members of GTN1, however, despite a lack of demonstrable translation, members of GTN2 suggested their involvement in the GTN programme had been beneficial:

> We have decided to revert back to our core business public health genetics. Our profile has grown throughout the world...we are at the stage where we may possibly set up a charitable arm that would offer what we do to other parts of the world. (GTN2 Manager)

Like GTN1, GTN2 appears to have been captured by powerful academics who used GTN funding to pursue their own purposes, which, in retrospect, the DoH might not have supported.

Several interviewees suggested that the disappointing outcomes from GTN2 stemmed from, first, the nature of the way the GTN programme was established (in line with other initiatives beyond GTNs), and, second, the complex nature of the nascent genetics discipline.

A member of the GTN supervisory board suggested the complex nature of translating genetics science into practice was too complex to be governable:

> How are you going to measure success and I think that may have been part of the reason the Department of Health always struggled with the GTN because what is success? (Member of Supervisory Board)

Another interviewee commented that DoH's disappointment with GTN2's progress was a symptom of the way government sometimes commissioned research without a clear prior framework of what they wanted to achieve and how to evaluate its outcome:

> I have a funny feeling these guys [in GTN2] knew what they wanted to do...and the government didn't quite understand. And to be honest that is usually the case isn't it...Some minister or somebody would have an idea, civil servants would turn that idea into a much wonderful phrase, somebody who had a bit of knowledge would turn that to a hint of reality. It would then be sent out as an opportunity. Experts would fill in the forms and non-experts would read them. And the reality would become reality and then people who...had some expertise would review what was happening and suddenly realize it wasn't what the original concept was. (NHS Manager)

Discussion of themes arising from the two GTN cases

These science-orientated Networks involved multidisciplinary 'epistemic communities' (Knorr-Cetina, 1999) working (albeit imperfectly) to translate scientific and indeed social scientific knowledge into NHS settings. GTNs sought to align the NHS service field with the different world of academic research through developing new translational pathways. Both cases—in different ways—suggest the ability of academic genetics science in these research-intensive university settings to capture new funding while maintaining their old focus on producing academic publications and distancing themselves from more translational and governmental elements of this research initiative.

An unsuccessful governmentality project?

Governmentality can be defined within the Anglo governmentality school of analysis (Armstrong, 1994) as a process in which a wider group of actors internalize and identify the ways of recording, assessing, and behaving promoted by a surveying 'centre' (Miller and Rose, 2008). This implies the generalization of a way of 'seeing the world in the terms of those governing it'; here from a surveying centre of senior managers at the DoH and members of the Genetics Research Advisory Group. The centre set up a quarterly reporting system from the GTN sites through electronic templates but with little effective feedback. On this basis, we argue that the GTNs represent a broadly unsuccessful governmentality project.

Influential stakeholder groups (especially in the academic domain) continued to promote their own agendas, behaviours, and preferred outputs with considerable success in securing long-term refunding for academic research. This inability to construct a governmentality project was partly an effect of the nascent nature of the genetics field and knowledge base, not readily amenable to the short-term reporting of quarterly performance outcomes. It was also partly due to the rushed specification of the GTN initiative, and the late development of performance evaluation, which stakeholders had not signed up for when they originally agreed to be part of the programme and which they successfully resisted, and the change to a requirement to collaborate rather than compete half way through.

As discussed, the DoH eventually established the Genetics Research Advisory Group, containing genetics and other experts to help monitor the GTNs and evaluate performance. This new Group potentially strengthened the policy community in challenging medical researchers for jurisdiction over the GTNs; its formation heralded a possible transition. But trying to control the way performance was monitored did not in the end create an effective jurisdiction over GTNs. Rather than facilitating dialogue between the medical, scientific, and policy communities, reporting upwards took the form of superficial 'tick box' compliance (cf. McGivern and Ferlie, 2007; Waring and Currie, 2009), delegated to the Network Director in GTN1 and decoupled from core work practices of senior professional staff. These data were collected but did not appear to be used: at central level, key stakeholders (e.g. the Department of Trade and Industry) also withdrew from participation in the Genetics Research Advisory Group, perhaps sensing how developments were proceeding.

Some key stakeholders did not want their work to be governed by the centre and had the power to defend this position (notably, medical professors in GTN1 and the GTN2 Director) and resist top-down pressures for change to academic working practices. In Foucauldian terms, this is an example of successful resistance to a governmentality project using a strong pre-existing power base. Elite science was here decoupled (or decoupled itself) from a DoH-sponsored translational research initiative, socially constructing their knowledge as too complex to be subjected to a governmentality project, retaining professional autonomy to continue focusing on academic publications.

The wicked problems problem: A weak response given strong internal conflicts

These translational research Networks necessarily involved many different stakeholders (including both academic scientists and NHS practice), which needed to be aligned if genetics science were to flow readily into health care practice. The projects undertaken in GTN1 and GTN2 also sought to mobilize social science as well as science knowledge, given the complex sociological, legal, and ethical issues thrown up by the new genetics. So the arena showed characteristics of 'wicked problems'. However, the cases suggest that different groups within the Networks constructed their work in different and often incompatible ways so that an integrated and systemic translational research pathway did not emerge.

Thus the policy and government community needed to produce governable forms of knowledge (demonstrating translation within a reasonable timeframe), whereas academics needed to produce academic publications to maintain credibility within their own epistemic communities, more important to them than the espoused aim of GTNs to translate research into practice. GTN funding provided an opportunity for academics to 'do their science' and produce academic publications and credibility within their own epistemic community (McGivern and Dopson, 2010). Equally, in GTN2, public genomics academics captured the new jurisdiction, which enabled them to develop their reputation, but found it difficult to engage with their local genetic research community or NHS services.

Management and leadership of Networks: Notable individuals and boundary spanners

In GTN1, leadership centred on the Network Director (a former research scientist) who was well regarded and built up influence and credibility from an initial low base by taking on much of the unpleasant work (in particular Genetics Research Advisory Group reporting) and acting as local progress chaser. The Network Director developed expertise in the translation of meaning across epistemic and professional boundaries and had the credibility to negotiate cooperation between the different stakeholders. The Network Director's style was personable and focused, liaising with all the GTN1 Project leaders in a regular and positive way.

The Network Director was also supported by other individual 'boundary spanners' who emerged by chance. An important emergent boundary spanner was a consultant geneticist with previous experience of working in NHS laboratories who linked the scientific and translational worlds. He could negotiate between the labs and the university/NHS hospital. He had excellent interpersonal skills and a passion for using genetics to benefit patients. Another boundary spanner was a health economist working in the social science institute who established good relations with clinical researchers and scientists who were able to understand and value her work, although she was in conflict with the NHS scientists over the disclosure of information. A further boundary spanner was an NHS commissioner who had a varied career (moving from nursing into management and then commissioning), helping him to move between, understand, and engage with the different epistemic communities in GTN1. He explained to clinicians the financial practicalities of commissioning services and had the resource power and social credibility to convince them to reframe their cardio-genetics test in a way that could be commissioned.

These boundary spanners were not a purposefully constructed team but rather an opportunistic emergent collection of individuals motivated to develop a cardio-genetics service that would benefit patients. Other individuals in more formal leadership/boundary-spanning roles (such as the NHS lab scientists and the sociologist) found it difficult to cross boundaries. The case demonstrates the limits to boundary-crossing actions and the important constraining role of epistemic fields at a more macro level.

GTN2 presents a different leadership pattern from GTN1. It can be seen as an individualized fiefdom more than as a network, with a strong and enduring founder. It reveals the impact that a determined, visionary, and entrepreneurial elite actor, with high personal social capital, passion, and vision makes in developing a translational network. Influential actors from outside the site had been enrolled in the Network. The founder invested much of his personal energy into creating and protecting the Network, acting as an effective policy entrepreneur and as a maverick in the system.

The weakness of this leadership style was the limited impact in developing effective partnerships with the local genetics and public health communities; the Network remained an enclave. Field-level and epistemic forces again appeared to play an important constraining role. While the Network Director provided a powerful vision for the Network, this vision was also not balanced with operational management, meaning that new ideas were not seen through to completion, and indeed may not have been possible in practice. Moreover, the leadership style did not evolve over time and was difficult for junior members of GTN2 to challenge.

Limited shared learning

GTN1's track record in the domain of shared learning was limited. The quarterly meeting of the Network's Executive Committee and biannual meeting of the Board could have been fora for shared learning across the different stakeholders, but in practice this did not happen. They concentrated on ensuring the implementation of the grant plans but opportunities for reflection on the Network as an organizational and management entity were not seized. Considering alternative forms of shared learning would have enabled the Network to keep in touch with the progress of the projects and promote a deeper understanding of the different paradigms of research evident within the Network. Some clinicians and scientists were not always clear about the value of the social science component of the Network—or of the qualitative methods employed—reflecting the challenge of moving different forms of knowledge across professional and epistemic boundaries

GTN2's core purpose was to promote shared learning, yet impact here was limited too. There was some evidence of learning within the emergent academic domain of public health genomics. It proved difficult to construct the broader multidisciplinary alliances and spaces needed for shared learning. Those with an academic background tended to retreat into their base disciplines rather than spend time moving into a new space. Some were unsure about crossing boundaries into what was seen as a highly technical arena. Also, there were no joint intellectual forums, as opposed to managerial meetings. There were, as in GTN1, continuing epistemic barriers between the clinicians and the social scientists in the Network. So while promoting multidisciplinary learning and knowledge diffusion was one *raison d'être* of these Networks, evidence for success is highly limited. It is also unclear whether learning from the GTN experience occurred at a national policy level which could have informed the future commissioning processes in relation to further large-scale research investments.

There was little evidence of ICTs facilitating the work of either genetics Network, which spanned different organizations with different information technology systems. The most significant use was the introduction of electronic performance reporting in a standardized template, but as we have noted, while this was an attempt to refocus GTNs on translation, its impact was limited and produced frustration rather than changing activity.

Overall discussion

In summary, the GTN cases demonstrate important obstacles to establishing fully functioning managed networks within the domain of translational science: the core of academic genetics science remained ungovernable in both sites. The scientists were not enrolled in a governmentality project or a power/knowledge nexus in alliance with the centre (DoH/Genetics Research Advisory Group) but retained professional autonomy and distance, successfully finding new funding for their ongoing academic projects after GTN funding ended. They resisted a governmentality project by mobilizing current 'taken for granted' dominant assumptions. While the DoH set up quarterly reporting systems, based on an electronic template, it appeared such data were collected but not actively analysed and effectively used in ways that changed how members of these Networks thought about their activities.

Key central sponsors (e.g. the Department of Trade and Industry) withdrew from active participation rather than engage in effective monitoring, as scepticism about rapid translation emerged. We note the marginal involvement of venture capital or University Innovation Units in the process—there was little private sector involvement in practice and it was to the NHS that the Project 1 group turned to for funding. So these cases demonstrate that governmentality is far from a totalizing and inevitable influence. However, in the next case studies of cancer networks, we discuss ways in which governmentality can have a more powerful influence.

5

Managed Cancer Networks: Exemplars of evidence-based governmentality?

Introduction

This chapter discusses two case studies of Managed Cancer Networks, taking as its tracer issue their reconfiguration of urology services. We begin the chapter by briefly discussing the background of government policy and a major push to improve cancer services. This in turn triggered the creation of Managed Cancer Networks supposed to lead the evidence-based reconfiguration of cancer services. Managed Cancer Networks are often taken as exemplars of the experiment with network-based working, so we were keen to include two such sites in our study.

We then introduce the 'County' and 'Urban' Cancer Networks (which are pseudonyms) and present narratives of how they both reconfigured urology services to conform to national policy and standards. We conclude with a comparative discussion of both cases, linked to the book's two key themes of governmentality and wicked problems.

UK cancer policy and Managed Cancer Networks: Some organizational issues

UK cancer services are a major and highly visible subsystem of the health care system and exhibit a difficult inheritance. Survival rates for cancers have historically been worse in the UK than the rest of Europe. There is significant variation in access to treatment and care at the local level (DoH, 2000a), with deprived populations often facing poorer access and outcomes. Since the mid-1990s (Calman-Hine, 1995), there has been a sustained national policy push to improve cancer services, matched with substantial new investment.

Some important organizational issues arise in the delivery of cancer services. The patient pathway is often complex and long term, moving from primary care, through local hospitals and on to teaching hospitals, and then back again. The expertise contained within teaching hospitals has not always diffused outwards to other hospitals in their geographical patches, contributing to local variation in outcomes. Voluntary sector agencies (including hospices for end of life care) and health promotion units are also involved in service delivery.

Policy suggests care for a cancer patient should be provided by a Multidisciplinary Team (MDT) which can meet social and psychological needs as well as medical needs. So many agencies and professions are involved in the cancer patient pathway. In addition, there is a major research complex in the academic and scientific domains developing new drugs and treatments, which are then translated (perhaps too slowly) into clinical practice.

The Calman–Hine Report (1995) reviewed the overall organization of cancer services. It proposed that historically poor outcomes should be remedied through service improvements associated with partnership-based working and specifically through creating local Managed Cancer Networks. Calman–Hine was the first policy document across health care to call for a break with the then dominant quasi market model (1990–97) and for a move back to collaboration and networking. These principles fitted cancer services well, given its complex pathway and history of strong, informal, clinical networks. A 'hub and spoke' model was proposed where clinical expertise would radiate out from centres of excellence across large patches. Managed Cancer Networks were an opportunity to diffuse knowledge, clinical expertise, and evidence-based best practice across organizational and professional boundaries, leading to higher-quality care and reversing the negative effects of competition engendered by the internal market.

The *NHS Cancer Plan* (2000) and the subsequent, operational, *Manual of Cancer Services Standards* (NHS Executive, 2000: 9) outlined national standards for cancer care in England, based on Calman–Hine (1995). The 2000 *NHS Cancer Plan* promised substantial resource investment in improved services. Managed Cancer Networks were now mandated and required to deliver these standards and targets locally, and network management teams mandated to manage these networks. Thirty-four Cancer Networks were created across England, typically covering populations of between one and two million. Some Managed Cancer Networks had already developed in a bottom-up fashion locally following Calman–Hine (1995). Others were established after the National Health Service (NHS) *Manual* (2001) made them mandatory.

The National Institute for Clinical Excellence (NICE) developed a series of Improving Outcomes Guidance (IOG) (NHS Executive, 1999; NICE, 2002) notes which outline standards of best practice on an evidence-based and tumour-specific basis. NICE guidelines often recommend the centralization of specialist services, given evidence of better clinical outcomes in units with greater volume. The Urology IOG, for example, states that

> patients with cancers which are less common or require complex treatment should be managed by specialist multidisciplinary urological cancer teams...in large hospitals or Cancer Centres, and each team should carry out a cumulative total of at least 50 radical operations for prostate or bladder cancer per year. (NICE, 2002, p. 29)

This statement implied that hospitals operating below this threshold would no longer be allowed to conduct these major operations: NICE guidelines pushed network management teams into managing major service reconfigurations.

Local network management teams were charged with brokering such reconfigurations, aided by other indirect pressures placed on service providers by the wider NHS system (such as financial penalties if they failed to meet targets for cancer waiting times). Network management teams were not part of the vertically integrated management on the provider side, notably large acute hospitals that had the most to gain or lose from service reorganizations. Nor did they have the power of the purse which instead lay with the NHS commissioners, notably the Primary Care Trusts (PCTs) (at least within the period of fieldwork). Instead, managed networks operated on the basis of providing expert advice to both NHS providers and commissioners, recreating some systemic capacity and thinking across the purchaser/provider split which had been a core element of the internal market model. Managed Cancer Networks are therefore a major early experiment with the managed network form, operating in a visible health policy arena and with a demanding agenda of strategic reconfiguration.

'County' Cancer Network

'County' Cancer Network was established in a bottom-up way in 1996 as a formal clinical network, in a local response both to the Calman–Hine (1995) report and local cancer services focus groups funded by the local Health Authority. County Cancer Network covers a relatively small area (with a population of just over one million) which is relatively affluent but had below average cancer outcomes due, in part, to a high proportion of elderly people.

In 2001, when the NHS Cancer Plan mandated formal network management, the Network then appointed a Lead Manager who was a manager already working there (and who was the Network Director at the time of our research) alongside a lead clinician; an oncologist from a local teaching hospital. The current Medical and Nurse Directors came into their roles in 2003. The challenge was how to move from a local clinical network to a *managed* clinical network and to meet standards laid out in the NHS Cancer Plan. At the time of the research, County Cancer Network described itself as a set of collaborative partnership relationships and services, which underpin cancer services and cut across organizational and professional boundaries.

County Cancer Network relates to all the local organizations involved in cancer care, including: County Teaching Hospital (a pseudonym) which is a teaching hospital with a reputation for high-quality services and teaching but which suffered from recent financial problems and faces difficulties redeveloping its aged and cramped site; Eastern Hospital (a pseudonym) is smaller, operating on two modern and spacious sites in the east of County; Western Hospital (also a pseudonym) is based in the west of County, comprising two sites, one providing cancer services. Western Hospital is the smallest hospital and threatened with closure, so was particularly keen to retain cancer services to justify remaining open. There are also four PCTs (down from eight before mergers in 2006) and seven independent hospices within County Cancer Network.

Cancer networks operate in an evolving national policy environment. The *Shifting the Balance of Power* (DoH, 2002) document, and the later 'payment by results' and 'patient choice' regime (DoH, 2005) increased competition between the three hospitals to provide services. They created a tension within County Cancer Network over the reconfiguration of cancer services and between NHS commissioners and local provider hospitals. This was exacerbated by County Teaching Hospital's financial problems and Western Hospital's threat of closure. Although NHS organizations within the County must meet cancer standards and targets, County Cancer Network has no formal authority or budget to purchase services, but relies on influencing member NHS organizations through recommendations, which limited its impact:

> The biggest problem for the Network...[is that] the executive board is not statutory and it has to rely...on cooperation...[local NHS Organizations] come out of the woodwork [only] if there is a financial issue that might affect them. (Patient Representative)

> The Network would be far better off if they had money. As long as people don't have money in the NHS then they are not really interesting. (Urologist)

Network structure

The Network Executive Board supervizes the County Cancer Network. It meets on a bimonthly basis and contains representatives from local organizations, including NHS hospital and PCTs' Chief Executive Officers (CEOs) (and/or their senior staff); a CEO representing the seven hospices; two patient representatives; Network Management Team Directors, a service development manager and the Network cancer services lead. One interviewee described the Network Executive Board's role as:

> ratifying the work that has been initiated and...done at the committee group stage...bit of report monitoring...performance...horizon scanning. (Hospital Director)

Interviewees complained about being overloaded with reading before the meeting:

> The paperwork that is generated...you just physically don't have time to read through all those papers before one of those meetings. (Hospice Director)

So interviewees suggested that the Network Executive Board simply 'rubber stamped' or ratified decisions and disseminated information rather than make a decision:

> I just get a feeling that those decision-making processes happen outside...the Network Executive Board is more like a rubber stamping. (Hospice Director)

We focused on the 'Urological Tumour Group' and its reconfiguration of urology cancer services as a tracer of complex service change, exemplifying wider processes within County Cancer Network. The Network has eleven clinical tumour groups, meeting to discuss specific cancers and containing clinicians and managers from the organizations within County Cancer Network. The Network Management Team usually attend these meetings too. The Urology Tumour Group develops local guidelines for the treatment of urological cancers (prostate, bladder, and renal), based on national and international guidelines. It also functions as a professional advisory group, involved in 'horizon scanning' for new cancer drugs and treatments. Urologists dominated the Urology Tumour Group meetings, often using aggressive language and puerile humour. For example, in a meeting we observed, one rubbished a presentation on patient-level data on procedures collected by a nurse by commenting:

> If a patient can't even remember having a large probe stuck up their arse how can we trust this data?

County Cancer Network also has a 'clinical advisory group' containing a representative range of clinical professions, healthcare managers, and patient representatives, who scrutinize decisions made in tumour groups before they are taken to the Network Executive Board to be ratified, and 'generic working groups' focusing on professional groups to represent particular areas of work and provide a forum for sharing ideas and best practice.

The Network Management Team

Our previous research (Addicott et al, 2007) suggested that Network Management Teams can contribute significantly to the effectiveness of cancer networks. The Network Management Team that led the County Cancer Network contained a mix of clinical and administrative staff. County Cancer Network's Chairman was a PCT CEO busy running two organizations, so took a 'hands off' approach. In practice a trio, Network Director, Medical Director, and Nurse Director, led the County Cancer Network. These three key leaders were highly regarded locally:

> The three of them are on the whole very sympathetic and they have the interest of cancer patients at heart. (Patient Representative)

> It is a relatively good network and that must be credit to them. (Consultant Radiologist)

The Network Director joined the network in 1999, becoming Network Director in 2004. She had a nursing background. She emphasized her clinical rather than financial or operational background, although the Network Director post was an exclusively managerial role:

> My background is nursing and then audit and clinical risk and all that sort of element. It has not been through an operational route or a finance route. (Network Director)

She had a clear passion to improve cancer services, stemming from personal experience:

> My leadership style comes from the passion I feel, we can make a difference...for the sake of the patient...it is about...vision...trying to maintain...enthusiasm...the belief that working within a managed clinical network is the only way you can make a difference to deliver their pathways...The minute you have a relative go through that pathway you suddenly understand how complicated it is...I had quite a lot of relatives and people with cancer. (Network Director)

The Network Director had an excellent reputation, being described variously as:

> A huge driving force. (Network Management Team administrator)

> Very good...very focused...works phenomenally hard. (PCT Manager)

> We would be lost without her. (Oncologist)

> ...has her life and soul into it [the Network]...I think extremely highly of her. (Patient Representative)

Interviewees commented on the Network Director's skills:

> Fantastic...she is assertive without being aggressive. (Oncologist)

> Her knowledge base which is phenomenal...she has been around since the inception of the network. (Nurse Director)

Network Management Team members enjoyed working for her too:

> A very good role model...inspires you to work at high level...I wouldn't want to work anywhere else. (Network Management Team member)

The Medical Director was a consultant radiologist at Eastern Hospital who had been involved with County Cancer Network since 1997, having chaired tumour groups before being appointed Medical Director in 2003. Like the Network Director, he was seen to work hard and had an excellent reputation:

> [Medical Director] puts in a huge amount of personal time and effort. (Hospital Director)

He had responsibility for medical issues within County Cancer Network, crucially including managing consultants, which was 'a difficult balancing act' (Urological Surgeon). Doctors commented:

> [Medical Director] is in a very difficult position...he is very good at his network role but it is in huge conflict with his clinical role...clinicians like to know are dealing with a clinician or they are dealing with a manager? He is both...we don't know where he's...on our side or their side. (Oncologist)

> There are areas that were controversial and therefore [Medical Director] had to make decisions and sometimes he didn't have all the full support of all clinicians across the patch...I think he found that difficult at times, but he did a good job. (Urologist)

Interviewees commented on Medical Director's interpersonal skills and assertiveness:

> If there is someone who doesn't tow the line, he [Medical Director] is not adverse to going to see them and saying, look this is not a reasonable behaviour and you know we can sort this out. But I will have to put it in writing to your Medical Director and Chief Executive Officer...he [Network Medical Director] is pretty well respected by all his clinical colleagues and they do see him as being fair and reasonable and having to make some difficult decisions and generally he has got them right. (PCT Manager)

Another important role for the Medical Director was

> chatting behind the scene and getting clinicians to work together...if you don't have any discussions outside the meetings nothing would ever happen. (Network Director)

The Medical Director commented on his leadership style:

> You have got to have a bit of a vision...[and] emotional intelligence; you have got to understand yourself...[and] understand other people. (Medical Director)

The Nurse Director, a MacMillan nurse by training, had previously worked as a service improvement manager for a cancer collaborative. She was seen as:

Just fantastic. (Medical Director)

A work horse. (Network Administrator)

Very good...I should not really underestimate her role...the one who most often says to me, what about the patients. (PCT Manager)

The Nurse Director commented about her leadership style:

I suppose it is about enthusiasm, commitment...remaining quite grounded... being out and about...focusing on the key things I need to achieve...being passionate...assertive...supportive...accessible and...human. (Nurse Director)

The Network Management Team was 'very much a team' (Medical Director), which brought together collective expertise within a collaborative and distributed form of leadership:

We [the Network Management Team] are all essentially going in the same direction...[Medical Director] will be looking at it from you know the doctors point. I [Nurse Director] will be...looking at it from my perspective and [Network Director] looks at it from her perspective...the combination of all those collective expertise I suppose which brings it together as a kind of you know a unified sort of collaborative. (Nurse Director)

This team spirit developed organically and was based upon a shared collective belief in improving cancer services:

We share a belief that what we do makes a difference...we share pleasure in seeing change happen for the better. (Network Director)

Urology Improving Outcomes Guidance: Reconfiguring services

To explore County Cancer Network's operation in practice, we focussed on the reconfiguration of urology services following the publication of NICE's (2002) urology guidelines, which involved: (i) the centralization of urology services; (ii) the development of MDTs and team meetings; and (iii) standardization of work practices and the development of joint protocols. We particularly focused on the first aspect, which was the most challenging change.

CENTRALIZATION OF SERVICES
The Urology IOG recommended the centralization of urology services within a specialist cancer 'centre' treating rarer cancers, based on the evidence-based premise that specialization and more volume leads to better outcomes, with common cancers still being treated in local 'units'. Only surgeons who had done at least fifty specialist operations (radical

prostatectomies, the complete removal of the prostates and radical cys-tectomies, complete removal of the bladders) in the previous year should continue to do them. Surgeons in County Teaching Hospital, both Eastern Hospital Sites, and one site at Western Hospital had all been doing fewer than fifty specialist procedures per year and so a single specialist centre was needed to comply with guidance, but this involved major changes to urologists' clinical practice.

THE DEVELOPMENT OF MULTIDISCIPLINARY TEAMS AND BROADER DECISION-MAKING

The IOG proposed the development of MDT meetings to discuss patient care, on the premise that a range of people with diverse skills, experiences, and knowledge would improve the multifaceted care needed and diffuse good practice between professionals and groups. Urology was seen as a lag-ging service in this respect. The difficulty in developing MDTs was firstly getting such a diverse group together at a single time and place across a large county and secondly that urologists had traditionally dominated patient care so this represented significant broadening of multi-professional decision-making.

STANDARDIZATION AND DEVELOPMENT OF JOINT GUIDELINES

The Urology IOG also recommended the standardization and development of joint local protocols for urological cancer services, based on national guidelines (IOGs or National Service Frameworks) or indeed European guide-lines, to be developed in Urology Tumour Group meetings by local clinicians who had knowledge of local conditions and best practice. We note that local clinicians were given some discretion about which evidence base to adopt, as long as they adopted one.

THE SERVICE RECONFIGURATION PROCESS

The reconfiguration of urological cancer services took place during 2003–2007 and was ultimately successful, partly because it was relatively straightforward (at least when compared to the other case we discuss later) and partly because the Network Management Team had learned from an earlier problematic local reconfiguration of upper gastro-intestinal cancer services (Upper GI) where there was a 'clash of personalities between the two teams...people were literally having to hold people apart in groups...very unpleasant...it was about defending their patch and...clinical practice...We just try not to mention Upper GI' (PCT Manager).

The Network Management Team learned the importance of 'process' in the reconfiguration of cancer services; making sure everyone was signed up to the decision-making process, which provides an example of organizational learning. The Network Director noted:

> We realized through our lessons with the upper GI that if we were going to be rationalizing where the surgery was to take place, we needed a formally agreed process...for the bidding, we laid out all the criteria...We have been quite pedantic about process...decisions have to be made that can be quite hard...if they all agree the process by which that decision is...made then they can't argue with the outcome...process agreed through the tumour group...[so] they feel that they own that...if you don't, they will spend...years arguing about who said what and when. By having the processes there with the evidence if anybody challenges it. (Network Director)

Initially there was little progress towards deciding where the cancer centre should be, with urologists resisting the process, contesting the legitimacy of IOGs, and hoping the need to reconfigure services would 'go away'. Various interviewees commented:

> [Urologists] have been a sticking point...have taken a lot of persuading...they are probably the most senior participants...If they are not intending to be cooperative...you are banging your head against a brick wall. (Patient representative)

> The whole issue [reconfiguration] was kind of centred around the consultants not wanting to move. (Nurse)

> People have their own private interests...ambitions, their own careers...in urology you have got a lot of piddling little operations and then a big gap and a few big operations. So if you are sort of surgically inclined and like the cutting and became a surgeon to do that, then you don't want to give up big operations...if it is going to affect your interesting practice...your way of life, which hospital is going to get more resources. (Urologist)

> They are fighting for the politics of it and saving their own individual departments and hospitals...there will always be something about private practice thrown in. (Consultant Oncologist)

One argument against having a single specialist centre in the County was that travel within the region was problematic. After a period of deadlock, the Network Management Team then decided to apply to the national clinical director or 'Cancer Czar' (note this appeal to a top-level advisory figure, although formally he had no role in such processes which had been supposedly delegated down to the localities) for permission to have two centres, one in the east and one in west of the county. This was duly agreed and helped break the deadlock within the reconfiguration process.

The Network quickly agreed that Eastern Hospital, which had appropriate clinical expertise (five urologists) and facilities, should host the eastern centre, with Eastern Hospital Urologists amicably agreeing to operate on a single site. The western centre was more contested. County Teaching Hospital was keen to provide urology services which were profitable under the payment by results regime and could improve its financial difficulties, while Western Hospital feared losing urology services would further undermine the hospital's viability. The decision about the western centre was put out to external review, which finally reached no clear conclusion, so then it came back within the Network. Finally a commissioning meeting decided that because County Teaching Hospital had four urologists whereas Western Hospital had only two (one about to retire), linear accelerators (machines for radiation treatments), a renal unit, and radiotherapy centre that the second centre would be in County Teaching Hospital. A key factor was the Network Management Team's role in conducting audits which provided data about local services. The Network Director commented:

> We had to do all the number crunching to demonstrate to all the clinicians actually if you look at our numbers versus what this Guidance is recommending we can't sustain four teams doing all of that work.

The Medical Director added:

> ...in my experience if you ask a doctor how many of something they do a year, whatever the figure they give you if you half it you will be about right...at a urology tumour meeting we took them [urologists] the house data and it showed I think 106 major urological operations in a year in [the Network]...[Urologists] just went, ridiculous...I gave them fifteen minutes to ramble on, and I said, okay...take this data, go through it...you have two weeks to challenge the data and you get back to us. Otherwise this will be the basis of what we use. And I only had one response...The data was pretty good. The crucial thing early on in the phase was getting good valid data, because if you don't have data you [are] struggling. (Medical Director)

Consequently, the Medical Director concluded:

> we decided on County Teaching Hospital...[because] surgical activity data...showed a reduction in Western Hospital activity and increase in County Teaching Hospital activity.

A hospital director commented:

> Urology has gone quite well. The clinicians very much led the process...There was very good communication and engagement with all the clinical teams...extensive consultation with lots of people, patients, and everybody concerned. (Hospital Director)

A Western Hospital urologist who had been vocal in resisting the reconfiguration described the decision as fair, despite Western Hospital losing urology services:

> County Teaching Hospital had the linear accelerators and was the biggest hospital and with probably the best advanced bladder surgery...[the decision]

was perfectly fair...It was inevitable. The problem is there are no beds, room, or parking in County Teaching Hospital...but the cancer centre is very good. (Urologist)

Another urologist commented:

Now it has been going on for several years that the testosterone has gone out of the argument. It is not as aggressive as it was before...nowadays we swallow more than we did before...in the beginning it took ages about every single decision...now we accept...that certain things have to be done...as long as they are reasonably sensible. (Urologist)

MULTIDISCIPLINARY TEAM MEETINGS AND THE
DEVELOPMENT OF LOCAL STANDARDS
The Urology IOG also specified that patient cases should be discussed in MDT meetings, enabling different professions to discuss best treatments from different perspectives rather than urologists alone deciding as had historically taken place. Their meetings had a macho tone to them. The Medical Director commented that:

The urology tumour group are a rather fierce group for the uninitiated...the kind of mentality of some of the surgeons [is] almost a gentleman's club type of thing.

An urologist agreed that 'as a group sometimes we appear very oafish' (Urologist).

Initially urologists attempted to retain control over Urology Tumour Group meetings by agreeing decisions outside Urology Tumour Group meetings. The Medical Director commented:

[Urologists] all like to go for a beer afterwards [Urology Tumour Group meetings] and they go, oh well, let's discuss this one later in the pub...my view of that, of course, is we discuss it in the room [at the Urology Tumour Group meeting], it is not some kind of surgical carve up with your mates. (Medical Director)

Urologists were accused of 'waffling' and engaging in 'apathetic sabotage' of multidisciplinary discussions.

[Urologists] are talking about carrying on having their own local MDT meetings despite the fact that we agreed that we would have one local multi-disciplinary team meeting for both [hospitals]. So they still are paying complete lip service to it but don't want to do it. Completely resisting it for as long as they possibly can. (Consultant Oncologist)

As stated earlier, travel within the County Cancer Network site was difficult and presented significant problems for professionals attending an MDT meeting on a single site physically. Clinicians had to spend several hours travelling to these meetings. County Cancer Network invested over £300,000 in teleconferencing equipment for virtual MDT meetings. Here we see an example of how Information Communication Technology (ICT) can facilitate the functioning of networks. We did not hear any complaints that the quality of discussion in teleconference-based meetings was reduced. Having teleconferencing equipment in place helped overcome resistance among urologists to the idea of MDT meetings. The Network also has a good website which contains up-to-date information about its activities, as well as cancer and cancer care more generally. MDT meetings eventually facilitated conversations between different disciplines and led to changes in practice:

> Having the multi-disciplinary team meetings and that side of it has changed practice. (Urologist)

The development of local standards was relatively straightforward, although urologists insisted on keeping flexibility in local pathways to respond to local circumstances.

'Urban' Cancer Network

Urban Cancer Network's structure

'Urban Cancer Network' (a pseudonym) was formed in 2001 in a local response to the NHS Cancer Plan. It covers a large urban site containing 1.6 million people, encompassing six PCTs, various hospitals, four hospices, and some voluntary organizations. The Strategic Health Authority (SHA)—the intermediate or regional tier of NHS management—both hosts and performance manages the Network.

In organizational terms, Urban Cancer Network comprises four NHS foundation trusts and a number of specialist acute trusts, including three small specialist hospitals (Smaller Urban Hospitals 1, 2, and 3), and three teaching hospitals, including Urban Teaching Hospital 1 (a pseudonym) which is the leading teaching hospital in the region, with two main units. Urban Teaching Hospital 2 is another big teaching trust, which has undergone a series of mergers and now consists of three main units and two smaller ancillary units. Urban Teaching Hospital 3 is a smaller teaching hospital.

Urological cancer services were historically delivered at five different units within four trusts. Urban Teaching Hospital 1 has traditionally been the cancer centre in the region, as well as a centre of academic power. At the time the Network started, Urban Teaching Hospital 1 had applied for funding for new building and was preparing to become a centre of excellence at a regional and national level. The Network was initially seen as a chance to further this expansion.

Urban Cancer Network is structured in a similar way as County Cancer Network, containing a network management team, multidisciplinary tumour groups—Network Site Specific Groups and generic cross-cutting groups—such as radiology, chemotherapy, palliative care, and pathology. Network Site Specific Groups and generic groups are referred to as the 'building blocks' or 'engine rooms' of Urban Cancer Network in which the development of guidelines, care pathways, and protocols takes place. Relationships within the Urology Tumour group were sometimes strained with urologists from different hospitals competing with and suspicious of each other. Nurses described urologists in Urology Tumour Group meetings being 'horrible' and full of 'aggression' and the Urology Tumour Group was:

> very medically orientated and very medically led. (Clinician-nursing)

The Urban Cancer Network Board provides strategic direction, performance management, and expert advice to commissioners, discussing and endorsing recommendations from specialist network groups. The Board draws its membership from a wide range of NHS organizations across the city (both providers and commissioners) as well as Patients' and Users' groups. The formal purpose of the Board is to provide expert advice to commissioners on cancer services, to inform investments and to drive service improvements. Users' and carers' views are well represented. Board meetings are chaired in a dynamic and friendly way by the Chairman. There are two patient representatives, indeed the chairman promoted one of the patient representatives to the position of vice-chair. Both are fairly active:

> we've got two very good patient representatives but it's very difficult for these people to suddenly be pitch forked into a board. (Clinician-medical)

Respondents described the decision-making process in the Board as transparent.

> The decision making process...tends to be fairly open and transparent...sometimes they're just ratifying other decisions and other working parties.(Clinician-medical)

The Network is led and managed by the Network Management Team. The core team consists of the Medical Director, the Network Manager, the Service Development Manager, and the Nurse Director, as well as various other staff. There is no Network Director and this role is performed effectively by the Medical Director. The Medical Director provides strong leadership at the board but does not 'chair' the session, and his style is less amicable by comparison.

The Network Management Team acts as an expert body interpreting national guidance and developing implementation plans within a local and also wider strategic perspective, providing expert advice both to the local acute sector in the implementation of national policy and local PCT in commissioning services. The Network Management Team interprets national guidance from the DoH and prepares gap analyses or implementation plans and feeds these into the specialized groups to ensure local guidelines and recommendations conform with national policy.

The Network Management Team provides technical information, data, expertise, and promotes communication between the many stakeholders. Each group elaborates a plan or recommendation scrutinized by the Network Management Team and their role is to provide expert advice to the board who in turn 'rubber stamp' recommendations before submitting them to the SHA. The Network also advises on their technical and political viability, so that they are both practical and likely to be approved by the Health Authority. While the technical work is done by the specialist team, the strategic outlook is provided by the Executive, mainly the Medical Director, but secondly by the Chair and Network Manager.

> The structure is that the Network has a core executive team, the professionals who have the knowledge, who link...are the glue who hold together commissioners...and deliverers of service...we are the link that tries to pull them together...[in] intelligent dialogue. (Clinician-medical)

In the early stages, the Urban Cancer Network focused on IOG in the acute sector. It was a newcomer in a difficult field, with little power as a non-statutory body which did not hold a budget. The early Urban Cancer Network board structure was dominated by clinicians and trust representatives, but it was becoming clear they would have to collaborate with PCT commissioners. Consequently, Urban Cancer Network evolved into a consultative role—to acute providers on the implementation of national policy and to PCTs on commissioning services. The Network thus became a broader source of expertise. Data suggest that the role and purpose of the Network was widely understood as providing linkage and facilitation between organizations/groups and also expert support.

Network Management Team

The Network Management Team is led by a Medical Director and managed by a Network Manager, with the role of the Network Director in effect performed by the Medical Director. The Network Management Team includes several other staff with responsibility for specific areas such as service development and improvement. The Urban Cancer Network Chairman was well regarded. As interviewees commented:

> ...warm and careful at allowing people to have their say...shutting people up when they've had their say and very fair, very balanced, and very astute. (Clinician-medical)

> You need to have a certain gravitas as well as a chair because you've got a bunch of clinicians to handle as well. (Clinician-medical)

The Medical Director has been with Urban Cancer Network since its inception, providing strategic direction for the Network. His medical background—in a high-status speciality—provided respect among clinical peers:

> He is a haematologist and not an oncologist or a surgeon, that helped hugely. (General Manager)

> He had a lot of clinical credibility as…a real pioneer in the use of chemotherapy…among other cancer surgeons. (General Manager)

He is described as being highly focused on achieving targets:

> not in the world to find friends…hard as nails, very objective, doesn't get diverted from the evidence. (General Manager)

Some clinicians, particularly those from Urban Teaching Hospital 1, which was negatively affected by the changes that Urban Cancer Network facilitated, questioned the Medical Director's impartiality.

The Medical Director described his network role as:

> …being the clinical face of the Network, bringing clinical medical respectability to what is often seen by doctors as being imposed by managers…cancer networks, indeed I don't think medical management can succeed, without doctors being involved, because doctors need to see that doctors will also sign up to the commitment [and] is clinically important for patients…my role is [to]…shape the direction of travel we are going in. To make sure…the team deliver on the objectives that we have agreed and I am quite strict about it being objectives that deliver change to patients. (Clinician-medical)

The majority of our respondents were extremely positive about the Medical Director, his role in the Network, and his dedication:

> It's an enormously difficult position…the present incumbent has performed an enormously difficult role with immense skill and has shown…the degree of steel that's necessary to take on interest groups…you've got to have a genuine commitment to trying to improve the care of the patients with cancer (Clinician-medical)

The three key members of the Network Management Team (Chair, Medical Director, and Network Manager) appeared to make up a good team, with good interpersonal dynamics. Criticisms came through conflicts of interest between the Network and local hospitals and inter-hospital dynamics, in particular alleging partiality towards the Medical Director's own hospital:

> We've certainly got a very strong chair and medical director, who work very well together as part of that team with the manager, so there are three people there leading. (Clinician-medical)

The Network Management Team's external relationships with the DoH were seen as beneficial:

> a good part of the Network Board was the fact that messages could be taken back to the Network Board to go back up to the Department. (Clinician-nursing)

Reconfiguring urology in Urban Cancer Network

As in County Cancer Network, implementing the urology Improving Outcome Guidance involved: (1) the centralization of services; (2) developing MDT; and (3) the standardization and development of joint protocols. The centralization of services was again the most challenging element because guidelines suggested a single urology centre for specialist procedures, whereas historically they were carried out in five hospital units within Urban Cancer Network with no single unit doing enough to become the centre. Essentially, there were two major players, Urban Teaching Hospital 1 and Urban Teaching Hospital 2, both competing to be the urology centre.

The reconfiguration of urology was influenced by a previous reconfiguration of gynaecological services, eventually resolved by an independent external panel deciding where the services should be. None of the organizations had been happy with this process, so they wanted to avoid going to an external review again.

There were initially lengthy discussions among consultants in Urology Network Site Specific Group meetings with little progress initially. Urologists:

> ...prevaricated and hoped the guidance might go away...we don't like the guidance...or there's no evidence base to say that you should have this number of cases...they rubbish the information, then they deny its existence, then they argue against it and I can see that cycle happening so many times. (General Manager)

> As I say, it is a slightly vague process about how the IOGs were formed...there's no actual author to it, it's just attributed to NICE. A lot of urologists were upset that their practices were going to change. (Clinician-medical)

There was:

> considerable acrimony, particularly between Urban Teaching Hospital 1 and Urban Teaching Hospital 2 because the view from Urban Teaching Hospital 1 that they should be doing all of it. (Clinician-medical)

These fruitless discussions lasted about a year until affected by the intervention of the local Strategic Health Authority which was:

> ...unwilling to say all specialist surgery is going to be based at Urban Teaching Hospital 1...[which was] going through...[Private Finance Initiative] negotiations for [a new site]...it wanted it to be very big and the Health Authority was trying to keep it smaller...The Health Authority could look across the whole of [region] and say the trend overall for beds is decreasing...they didn't want Urban Teaching Hospital 1 to be any bigger. (General Manager)

The Network invited the hospitals to present business cases to be the centre after which a 'common sense' decision was taken. An interviewee noted:

> Everybody wanted to host the unit and there was a panel, an arbitration, and eventually a decision was made to host that unit at Urban Teaching Hospital 3. And it was quite an untidy business and I don't think anybody was terribly happy...[but] common sense prevailed. (Clinician-medical)

This interim stage caused people to focus their minds and recognize that the centre could go to any of the hospitals. So the debate moved on. This pressure led to urgent consideration in Network Site Specific Groups, which first decided to go for two centres instead of one. This decision was based on the number and location of the population so the city was divided along an east–north, south–west axis. This decision was favoured by the Network and had already been put into practice for the reconfiguration of services for the Upper Gastro-intestinal IOG. But even this decision was hard to reach, as other hospitals were hoping to make a claim.

> ...it was made clear over a period of time that...change is not what everybody wants...but everybody knew that it had got to happen, that it was completely out of our hands and we'd just got to make the best job of the task...there was lots of discussion about who was going to be the centres...and it wasn't just presumed it was going to be Urban Teaching Hospital 1 and it wasn't presumed then it was going to be Urban Teaching Hospital 1 and Urban Teaching Hospital 2. So it was a very hard job for [the Chair] to keep that meeting on an even keel and keep everybody focused and not get into personal protection of their patch, if you like...the first thing that was decided was who was going to be the centres and was it going to be two centres...The Network Manager came...the board are getting a bit fed up, you have got to make a decision by such and such, decide on the centres. (Clinician-nursing)

General manager participation within the NHS Trusts also influenced the decision:

> I thought the cancer centre ought to be here...it's just how do you manage the tribal warfare when everyone wants to be that cake...we had discussions about

that and then we took a paper to the Cancer Network to say, well this is what we suggest...that's actually what happened. (General Manager)

The general managers in certain acute trusts acknowledged that they were not doing enough specialist urology surgery to justify being a centre, but their urologists were reluctant to give up this activity:

The amount of very specialist cancer surgery we did in urology was relatively small and so it's not as if there's suddenly a huge hole in the [hospital] Trust's activity but it was the activity that a group of clinicians got a lot of satisfaction out of and saw as an important part of the portfolio...it somehow changed people's perception of everything else the [hospital] Trust was doing in urology, which I think was unhelpful. I mean frankly, in the end, we just weren't doing enough of it to justify keeping it. (General Manager)

One consultant criticized his hospital general managers for conceding too early, who:

dropped us in it immediately by putting our hand up and saying, we haven't got the beds to accommodate your work on our site, so we'll have to come to you, so it was as simple as that. (Clinician-medical)

The same consultant argued that if there had been extra funding the situation might have been different.

A new Chair of the Network Site Specific Groups had a role in one of the minor units, so he was able to facilitate the reconfiguration, as his trust was not competing.

The Network were fed up at the lack of progress that had been made by my predecessor...[but] the majority didn't want this change. I'm sure some people in the bigger centres welcomed it...the previous [Network Site Specific Groups] chairman...certainly didn't want it...but I've accepted that it was inevitable and I think the Network Board's role was to force it through because that was the cancer plan. (Clinician-medical)

This recommendation was passed to the SHA and then upwards to the DoH for approval (which was obtained). It reflected what were seen as much improved local data on epidemiology and changing patterns of patient need as well as bargaining between local interest groups.

The final and least controversial stage of the decision was to select which two units within each part of the divided geographic area would host the primary urological services. The two units selected were the main teaching hospital in each area, which would host the specialist urology services, and consultants from smaller units would travel to work as part of a team in the designated centres. While inconvenient and time consuming, the distances within the area are relatively short. It was then left to the Network Site Specific Groups to arrange the details of centralization.

This process was easier for the east–north centre; consultants at these two units had voluntarily engaged in discussions and decided the way forward was 'a decent meal and have a drink and socialize with your colleagues, get to know your colleagues'.

> we have equal temperament, we have equal skills and we can amalgamate together and we will look at various models of how we can offer a good service based at Urban Teaching Hospital 2...I'm very pleased with the outcome. (Clinician-medical)

A consultant who travelled to work at this new centre noted:

> it's been good for me. I have increased my interaction with my other colleagues...we do interact with each other quite well. (Clinician-medical)

But the second centre at Urban Teaching Hospital 1 did not work so well:

> It hasn't worked particularly well. They [urologists from other hospitals] haven't really been accepted with open arms and I don't think they've enjoyed the experience of going to work there. (Clinician-medical)

One outcome of the main decision was that in the south–west part of the split, two consultants from the smaller unit decided they were not willing to travel to operate at the main site. They were:

> not welcomed at Urban Teaching Hospital 1...there is still tension from the Urban Teaching Hospital 1 end and they see themselves as the people who should be doing all this work. (Clinician-medical)

Some interviewees stated that patients' outcomes had not improved as a result of the reconfiguration:

> There isn't the continuity; there have been problems with follow up...I don't actually think this form of IOG implementation has actually benefited patients one iota. I don't think they're necessarily getting a better standard of surgical [or]...personal care. (Clinician-medical)

Data suggest continuing problems at this site, particularly problems of communication, which have affected patient care:

> And there has been a problem with communication out in Urban Teaching Hospital 1 about when patients have gone home. (Clinician-nursing)

> We don't know what happens, once they've gone over there...if I've got no idea of what's happened to them at Urban Teaching Hospital 1 it can be difficult to sort...problems out for them. (Clinician-nursing)

The theatre staff have been lovely, the ward staff are very obliging...although the cases are being looked after by the junior doctors who are looking after other radical prostates done by the Urban Teaching Hospital 1 consultants, there's no real evidence that it's an integrated team. (Clinician-medical)

These problems were universally attributed to the egos of some Urban Teaching Hospital 1 urologists; their unwillingness to work as a team and collective conviction that they, and only they, should be the foremost cancer centre. A urologist noted that Urban Teaching Hospital 1 had a:

teaching hospital 'prima donna' type attitude...they're excellent at renal transplants and things, they seem to have not realized that over the last twenty years...the skills they had have gone out into peripheral hospitals. (Clinician-medical)

So the Network's approach was to agree to a process by which decisions could be reached and then to maintain pressure and use influence to retain progress. The Network Management Team played an important although subtle role in moving events forward; while the main forum for discussing reconfiguration was the Network Site Specific Groups, the Network Management Team ensured that relevant information and data were available so that decisions could be reached; the Network Management Team also exerted pressure by constantly reinforcing the need for local hospitals to conform with IOG requirements. Some quotes exemplify this point:

Their role, if anything, was to speed the process up and make sure that we'd done things and things had been achieved in the timelines that we stated. (Urology Tumour Group Chair)

They were facilitatory...[but] they had a very set agenda. (Clinician-medical)

In general, in Urban Cancer Network, the data suggest that ICTs played a minor role in the Network; Information Technology (IT), data storage, and accessibility simply underpinned the Network's ability to share and exchange information. There was little online exchange of information or video conferencing for example (although there was a good network website with downloadable information). This evidence supports the view that much information exchange is face to face in small groups, where individuals can debate the data.

Concluding remarks

We see the Management Cancer Networks as two 'high performing' networks. Both networks were broadly successful in brokering complex evidence-based service changes in urology over a period of five years within large-scale geographical patches. What were the facilitating factors behind these large-scale service reconfigurations? We suggest that they did this through providing expert advice to different parties and rebuilding systemic capacity. The provision of evidence-based guidance from NICE was another important positive force, reinforced by increased local clinical audit activity to gather more local data. The Network Management Teams brought a key group of clinical-managerial hybrids into their cores, demonstrating energy and enthusiasm for the ambitious service improvement agenda they were required to undertake. The Network Management Teams were effective in generating clinician support and indeed reshaping Urologists' clinical practices through involving them intensively within the Tumour Groups.

We see some interesting parallels between the two Managed Cancer Network cases. An interesting feature is effective leadership of both reconfigurations by small mixed teams. The reconfiguration of urology services was successful in terms of organizational process, despite initial resistance of powerful urologists to changes in their practices. Yet, as noted, Managed Cancer Networks had no direct statutory, managerial, or financial power over the NHS organizations within the Networks. However, these NHS organizations are obliged to comply with national guidance and targets, and face financial and managerial penalties if they do not. The Network Management Teams successfully influenced organizations in their patches to reconfigure urology services through a combination of persuading people that they would improve patient care by changing ('chatting behind the scenes') and also highlighting national guidance, targets, and local data showing local organizations were not in line with national guidance which might put them in a dangerous position. This reflects Nye's (2008) description of leadership as the combined soft/hard use of power; soft power links to persuasion but in this case the use of hard power is the credible invocation of structural sanctions such as failure to get accreditation.

Key elements shaping the process in these cases can be seen as: (1) clear and legitimate evidence-based national guidance, including sanctions for non-compliance, namely loss of accreditation for service provision; (2) the development of an agreed local process, which once participants had agreed to they were unable to contest; (3) transparency provided by enhanced local data collection which challenged urologists' accounts of their practice and argument against the need for reconfiguration; and (4) the involvement of the Network Management Teams in bringing these different elements together.

These four elements seem to map well on to Dean's (1999) four dimensions of 'governmentality'. In Chapter 3, we suggested that a particular pattern of high energy and internalized leadership might help enact a governmentality project. In both cases, key Network Management Team members were clinical-managerial hybrids who passionately believed in the power of evidence to improve patient care, socially reconstructed local clinical practices, and did so on the basis of high energy and commitment. We explore the extent to which the governmentality framework fits the two Managed Cancer Networks in Chapter 11 in more detail.

ICTs appeared to play a relatively minor role in both networks. In County Cancer Network, video conferencing facilities facilitated and speeded the development of MDT meetings across all the hospitals involved, which might otherwise have been problematic given difficulties travelling between sites in the county. In both cases, the development of enhanced databases containing local data were important—but this is more a facet of the change process rather than a major technological push.

In terms of organizational learning, we see evidence in both cases of network management teams learning from earlier and problematic reconfigurations of cancer services and then the development of novel processes through which reconfiguration decisions would be made. We also see some evidence of the diffusion of best practice in both networks, although this appears more related to top-down standardization and evidence-based working rather than inter-organizational learning.

Is the improvement of cancer services a 'wicked problem'? The prevention of people getting some forms of cancer (e.g. smoking and lung cancer) might well be seen as such, but the particular reconfiguration of urology services was more a managerial problem which mainly involved bargaining between teaching hospitals (Addicott et al, 2007). Prostate cancer, for example, has little preventive component when compared to other forms of cancer such as (say) lung cancer, although early diagnosis can still be important.

More widely, however, the changes in behaviours required to reduce the incidence of many other cancers (smoking, diet, exercise) in an ageing population do reflect aspects of a 'wicked problem'. There are in these cancers major behavioural elements which require the 'co-production' of health with affected populations. There is a large number of stakeholders involved (e.g. food companies in the case of cancers caused by poor diet), with different interests and agendas. There is a need to involve primary care more, speed up complex pathways and achieve earlier diagnoses, so as to improve clinical outcomes further. Fundamental biomedical research is developing new drugs and treatments which can improve the outlook for some cancers (e.g. leukaemia) substantially but there remains a challenge to get them into routine clinical practice across health care quickly.

Finally, and with the implementation of much of the IOG, which had been the managed cancer networks' initial task, what might their future role be? Should they now be disbanded? Some have argued that Managed Cancer Networks should continue to play a modernizing role in facilitating and maintaining complex care pathways across large geographical patches. There is still service improvement work to be done because agreements between competing provider organizations to collaborate might fall apart without Managed Cancer Networks, and the new Clinical Commissioning Groups operate on too small a scale. On this basis, there is a case for their continued existence.

6

Sexual Health Networks: Working with problematic human behaviours

History and recent policy

Prior to the advent of antibiotics in the mid-twentieth century, 'venereal diseases', causing chronic ill-health, disfigurement, and death, and having a strong relationship with socially stigmatized forms of human sexual behaviour, had been feared for hundreds of years. Sufferers were shunned and services neglected, with medical staff seen as low status and hospitals and clinics often isolated from other services and poorly equipped. The recent availability of effective treatments, however, did not solve underlying disease transmission. The possibility of rapid cure, along with the development of reliable contraception in the 1960s, perhaps encouraged a greater sexual freedom among the general population. As Shilts (1987) put it, controlling the spread of Sexually Transmitted Infections (STIs) became 'a Sisyphean task' with some people becoming serial attenders at Genito-Urinary Medicine (GUM) clinics 'with infection after infection', to be given the curative 'magic bullet' to allow them to continue their lifestyle.

Despite this increased sexual freedom and the concomitant rise in STIs, GUM continued to be a 'Cinderella' specialty. As late as 1980, the specialty's first UK professorial chair, Professor Michael Adler, in his inaugural lecture (Adler, 1980), highlighted elements of what continued to pose a 'wicked' problem for society as a whole.

> Poor facilities in dark corners and notices about clinic hours in underground lavatories are some of modern society's ways of trying to avoid the realities of a major health problem which at the same time stigmatises patients. The 'terrible peril' is no longer represented by the disastrous clinical consequences of suffering from inadequately or untreated syphilis and gonorrhoea, but by the positions that we, as society, adopt towards educating the young for the realities of sexual life and towards those that are diseased or at risk—so much so that they are left ignorant, ashamed, and stigmatised, and they fail to seek help.

The particular characteristics of services for people with STIs did not, therefore, augur well for effective networking. Even as Adler spoke however, massive service change was waiting in the wings. In the early 1980s, a new STI, Human Immune Deficiency Virus (HIV), emerged and the government was suddenly alerted to a major health problem. As the HIV/Acquired Immune Deficiency Syndrome (AIDS) issue climbed up the policy agenda in the mid-1980s, support and political attention grew rapidly and money poured in to these services. Here was a rare opportunity to develop a new service system from scratch, involving health professionals, public health experts, and a vocal consumer lobby in a novel policy and planning process. The report of the Commons Social Services Committee on AIDS (November 1986) was explicit about the issue's cross-sectoral implications and the need for coordination (Bennett, 1992). Genito-urinary services (at least for HIV) began to look outwards rather than inwards, other specialties and professional groups became involved, and HIV coordinators were employed to build links between different professional groups and service users. Indeed, developing services for HIV provided a 'best practice' template for future networking, notably in cancer services, as in the 1995 Calman–Hine report with its similar emphasis on multi-agency working and a 'patient-centred' approach. For a decade, service development and policymaking for STI was prompted and defined by the response to HIV (Berridge and Strong, 1993; Bennett and Ferlie, 1994; Berridge, 1996).

However, such development was achieved with ring-fenced funding and through firm service planning. Other sexual health issues took a backseat for almost two decades. The public health White Paper, *The Health of the Nation* (DoH, 1992), did not refer to sexual health. It was not until the end of the 1990s that *Saving Lives: Our Healthier Nation* (DoH, 1999) acknowledged it as 'an important public health issue'. A report mainly focused on reducing teenage pregnancies (Social Exclusion Unit, 1999) noted the importance of sexual health, and its proposal for multi-agency committees to produce strategies for local service provision was an acknowledgement that networking had become a key component of goverment policy. This was a sector where previously dominant quasimarket models had always been difficult to apply, given the focus on health promotion and behaviour change rather than simple consumer 'choice'.

In 2001, the National Strategy for Sexual Health (DoH, 2001a) kick-started new service developments, announcing more money for sexual health in general and a final end to ring-fenced funding for HIV. While it was a national strategy, it was not a formal National Service Framework (NSF) and no National Service Director was appointed (unlike cancer services). The development of local service networks and networking was central to the Strategy (DoH, 2001a—Summary, p. 4; Chapter 4, para. 4.5), mirroring earlier developments in cancer services and enjoying strong professional support. This policy direction was reinforced by the White Paper on public health (DoH, 2004a), identifying sexual health as a key area and calling for inter-agency working and Multidisciplinary Teams (MDTs) 'to break down the boundaries between primary and specialist services' (p. 145). In addition, the Health and Social Care Standards and Planning Framework (DoH, 2004b) included sexual health within the National Health Service (NHS) national targets, with one standard being the development of managed Sexual Health Networks.

Network-based working was supported by the main professional bodies, BASHH (British Association for Sexual Health and HIV), MedFASH (the Medical Foundation for AIDS and Sexual Health), and BHIVA (the British HIV Association). The MedFASH report in 2008 argued for managed services networks and recommended that sexual health and HIV networks should be rolled out countrywide. It extolled the benefits of local networking and suggested 'bolder partnerships...brought together by a shared understanding about why improving sexual health is a priority, clarity about what each partner can contribute and why it matters' (MedFASH, 2008, p. 68).

A critical House of Commons Health Select Committee report on sexual health, published in 2003 (followed by a similarly critical report two years later) referred to a 'crisis in sexual health', ensuring not only that money (over £200 million during the last decade) continued to be made available, but also that sexual health remained on the policy agenda. These reports also implied recognition of the need for networks to deliver sexual health services, with the lack of networking seen as a key weakness.

By 2008, from being an isolated and stigmatized specialty, sexual health was now, in theory at least, fully signed up to the new networking approach. Could this approach assist in dealing with a 'wicked' public health problem which had long resisted all efforts to ameliorate it and addressed fundamental aspects of human behaviour?

The two Sexual Health Networks

Our sexual health case studies examined the provision of network-based services in two urban areas, Metropolitan City and Cathedral City, using the same methods as the other case studies, namely semi-structured interviews, attending meetings, and collecting documentary evidence. Around twenty-five interviews were carried out at each site with Network managers and a mix of other people involved in service delivery. A selection of 'tracer issues' reflected local priorities for service development. Services for HIV in ethnic minority groups, of high importance at both sites, were selected as tracers for both studies. In Metropolitan City the other tracer was the implementation of the 48-hour national target for referrals to GUM clinics, while in Cathedral City the key focus of activity and the second tracer was reduction of the high local rate of teenage pregnancies.

Metropolitan City Sexual Health Network

The Network—context, formation, structure, management, and governance

The Metropolitan City Sexual Health Network (the Network) was based in a deprived area of Metropolitan City, with a relatively high prevalence of STI in general and of HIV in heterosexual members of ethnic minority immigrant communities. This large and complex geographic patch contained almost two million people. The Network included five hospitals and seven Primary Care Trusts (PCTs), all involved with provision of sexual health services. The Network linked with the broader sexual health agenda through an Expert Advisory Group, as well as a consortium which directed funding and provision of healthcare for people with HIV.

Three of the five hospitals forming the Network served an inner-city population. These were: Teaching Hospital, a large and long-established hospital linked to a medical school and with many leading experts in medical science; Foundation Trust, established in the 1980s and historically linked to Teaching Hospital; and New District General Hospital, also founded in the 1980s on a new site and affiliated with Teaching Hospital's medical school. The other two hospitals were less centrally situated; one operated from two sites and the other from a single site. The Network's seven PCTs all had a stake in improving standards of sexual health. The two Outer Metropolitan City PCTs did not have as high a prevalence of STIs as those in the Inner City, but their residents were likely to travel to Inner Metropolitan City to be treated. The financial penalties for not meeting waiting-time targets meant the activities of sexual health services in Inner Metropolitan City impacted on the performance of all PCTs.

Sexual Health Clinical Consultants had been informally networking about clinical issues here since the 1990s. However it was not until 2002, after the publication of the National HIV and Sexual Health Strategy (DoH, 2001a), that discussions began among medical consultants and commissioners about developing a formal managed network locally to provide a 'lobbying force' for more support and resources for sexual health services.

A multidisciplinary 'away day' in May 2003 established local support for the development of a network. It was chaired by the then Chief Executive of a PCT in the area—'It's more likely to happen if you've got a PCT Chair...it is their money at the end of the day'. At the inaugural Network meeting held in August 2003 funding was pledged from the seven PCTs to pay for the Network Coordinator and some of the Clinical Director's time. Although a small sum compared with the overall sexual health and HIV budget in Metropolitan City, this pump-priming money was important in getting the Network off the ground.

Initially there were three main structural components to the Network: a Stakeholder Group, chaired by a PCT Chief Executive, containing represent-atives from the different organizations involved in sexual health and HIV in the area; an Operational Group to manage and direct the Network, and Subgroups. Later, the Stakeholder and Operational groups merged into a sin-gle Executive Board to which the Subgroups reported.

The Executive Board comprised a Chair, a Clinical Director, a Vice-Chair, a Network Coordinator, a lead clinician from each trust, an HIV specialist com-missioner, a sexual health commissioner from each PCT, two user representa-tives, and single representatives from other groups including nursing, health advisors, psychology, pharmacy, social services, managers, and the voluntary sector. This illustrates the range of different groups and agencies involved. The quarterly meetings were designed to provide a democratic forum and this collaborative multidisciplinary approach was seen as 'absolutely vital' by board members.

Subgroups were either issue-focused (GUM, HIV, research, and mental health) or professionally focused (sexual health nurses, HIV nurses, services managers, health advisors, pharmacists, and sexual health commissioners with public health representatives). In 2007 there was a new patient/public involvement subgroup, operating through a patient forum in a local volun-tary HIV organization, and the mental health group changed from an issue-related to a professional subgroup.

Overall, the Network was a combination of a pressure group, enabling members to lobby for more resources, and a support group enabling them to share ideas and communicate in a 'safe' environment. Although the develop-ing Network was supported by many stakeholders, a key influence came from a group of consultants and nurses from Teaching Hospital, whose dominance grew rather than diminished over time. Although initially invited, ethnic minority patient representatives and General Practitioners (GPs) were not involved fully, and public health had less influence than we expected for a Network involved in sexual health.

The Network was officially performance-managed and accountable to its Strategic Health Authority (SHA). In practice, the SHA appeared 'hands-off' and accountability seemed to reside with the Network Chair and the Vice-Chair. Since the Network was seen as effective by its funders, this relationship did not appear to be a problem, and as PCTs and hospitals were accountable for achieving Sexual Health targets (e.g. waiting times), they appeared willing to accept Network advice where it led to concrete service improvements.

The story of the Network following its formation

The formation of the Network in 2003 was an attempt to address the 'wicked problem' of Metropolitan City's increasing levels of STI in general and HIV in particular. As early as 1998, a report for Metropolitan City Sexual Health Commissioners had proposed the establishment of service networks for HIV care, like similar approaches being developed for cancer patients after Calman–Hine (DoH, 1995).

The two tracer issues, services for HIV and implementation of the 48-hour access target for referrals to GUM clinics to reduce long waiting times, were both important to health services in Metropolitan City and identified as targets in its sexual health framework (2004). To understand the impact of the Network, we need to consider the structure and operation of the Network, the political and social context in which it emerged, the influence of some key individuals, and the changes that took place over the period studied.

Firstly, we briefly discuss the context. Three important drivers for setting up a Sexual Health Network were the rising numbers of infections, the National Strategy for Sexual Health (2001) which recommended managed networks and the Government's application of targets to all NHS services from 2001 onwards. This last driver meant that, to avoid financial penalties, GUM clinics needed to ensure all patients were seen within 48 hours, providing a real incentive to consider how clinics could best be organized to meet the target.

> The 48-hour thing perhaps did give the focus we needed, you know, it's like creating a burning platform. (Network member)

What had previously been an informal Network focused on clinical issues needed to transform itself into something more formal which would not only discuss best practice, but agree ways of standardizing its delivery by local clinics and redesigning services both to provide 'equity of care' and meet the 48-hour access target.

Although the 'away day' was set up by the SHA, and its Director of Public Health was seen as 'very useful to wheel in at times' to give the emerging Network 'credibility', the main thrust for forming the Network came from clinicians, in particular a group who had all worked together at Teaching Hospital. Hence the Network was very much a clinical network, founded upon a common interest in providing medical care, especially around HIV, rather than addressing wider social public health issues around prevention of STI in general.

Two individuals, a Consultant in GUM at Teaching Hospital, and an HIV commissioner, were key in getting the Network underway. The Clinical Director described variously as: 'The prime mover', 'an important figure-head', 'a strong character...[who has] a vision and gets things moving' and 'a very forceful person...[who] makes stuff happen', provided clinical leadership for the Network (and in practice leadership overall). The specialist HIV commissioner, whose background included HIV nursing, came from a local PCT and served informally as the first Network Coordinator, becoming the Vice-Chair following the appointment of a paid Coordinator. These two were seen as having a close and effective working relationship, bringing together knowledge of clinical matters and commissioning. The Vice-Chair was seen as providing a good foil to the Clinical Director.

> [The first Vice-Chair]'s experience and...balance made the leadership more meaningful...[the first Vice-Chair] comes up with the idea and [the Clinical Director] enforces it. (Network member)

Once funding was secured and a paid Network Coordinator (previously an HIV nurse at Teaching Hospital) appointed, the immediate priorities were to ensure that sexual health services throughout the Network conformed to standards for best practice and met 48-hour access targets. With a formal organization and a mandate democratically approved by the membership, the organization now exerted collective pressure in pursuit of these goals.

> We shared ideas, innovations. We visited a unit...looking at their patient flow and how they ran their systems and clinics, and then suggested improvements, which they adopted. (Network member)

One mechanism used to achieve change was an audit of practice across the Network.

> [There was] huge resistance to the idea of the target, you know, 'this is an outrage!', real variances in practice....We had a...detailed questionnaire looking at practice...four out of five units are doing this, why are you doing that...peer pressure...definitely I think the Network had an impact there. (Network member)

Services were redesigned to be 'walk-in', avoiding the delays inherent in an appointment system. The audit provided evidence that one service which had previously been resistant to change was failing, and the later resignation of the key clinician enabled it to be merged with another. This reportedly led to that service moving from less than a fifth to almost all patients being seen within 48 hours; though some respondents suggested that changing to walk-in clinics meant that those seen were recorded, but if the clinic was full, there was no way of documenting anyone who was turned away (see Chapter 8 for a more general discussion of targets and instances where the (mis)use of statistical information may mask continuing problems).

The Network's efforts led to it achieving some of the best 48-hour target results in the country.

> We were ahead of the country for quite a long time because clinicians really did sign up to it and we had workshops and we invited all the great and the good to share best practice, and we developed a timetable for rolling out whatever this best practice was. (Network member)

The emphasis on clinical standards and meeting the access targets meant that much Network activity was focused on achieving these goals. Aspects of their wider remit, notably addressing less accessible aspects of sexual health, including prevention and engaging with patient groups, were less prominent. The second tracer issue looked at the impact of the Network on HIV care for ethnic minority communities, and some community representatives from an ethnic group containing a relatively high proportion of HIV positive individuals were interviewed. Although those approached had heard of the Network, they had little contact with it and were unclear about what it did. Comments included 'we're not involved', 'I don't think they are targeting...[our community]' 'I heard of it...[but] I don't know how often they meet'. There was a perception that, while they might be seen as interesting clinical cases, there was little understanding that the needs of the group might be different from the indigenous population:

> Within the...[ethnic minority communities], they are worried about their day to day needs. They don't have a roof over their head; they don't have enough food to eat, so maybe they are running here and there to get extra income...that's why people in the end just come at the last minute when they're almost collapsing...we have to start thinking outside health, to address the other surrounding social issues. (Ethnic community representative)

The other side of the coin was that within the Network it was perceived that ethnic minority representatives often failed to turn up, even when invited to meetings. So there was a mismatch of expectations. This relative neglect of public health issues and community groups may have occurred partly because it was easier to achieve visible results when focusing on targets and standards of care, rather than addressing wider and less visible social determinants of sexual health. Certainly, one Network respondent supported this view:

> The 48 hour access target gave a real impetus and drive to the Network but it's been achieved...the next challenge is around truly developing integrated level one and two sexual health family planning services but there isn't a target attached to that. How do you provide the drive for that? (Network member)

At the time of the research, the Network appeared to be entering a new phase in which progress towards Network goals was slowing and achieving objectives might present greater problems than before. Furthermore, the impetus seemed to have diminished:

> I think at the beginning it was good. I think everybody was on side. I think there was a general commitment but that's waned a bit. (Network member)

Other changes were also impacting on the way it worked. The first Vice-Chair, Chair, and Network Coordinator, who had worked closely with the forceful Clinical Director and had provided a counter-balancing effect, all moved to new posts. Their replacements were more junior and less experienced, leaving the Clinical Director, the only remaining member of the original Network Executive team, in a powerful position. This shift, coupled with new national policy initiatives such as dehosting (sexual health services could be provided on an existing site but managed by a different organization) and payment by results, led to increasing competition and suspicion between hospitals.

> There is... a tension between interests of the Network and the interests of the individual Trusts... So interests are quite often different.... The way that I see the NHS at the moment is that all the different Trusts are basically competing with each other for everybody else's business. (Network member)

It also fuelled previously suppressed feelings about the dominance of Teaching Hospital and its influence within the Network.

> The problem is there is a conflict of interest. Not only is... [the Clinical Director] the Head of the Network but... [the Clinical Director] is also lead for the sexual health services at [Teaching Hospital]... people have their own agendas... as everybody does [and I am] suspicious of [Teaching Hospital], I personally don't trust them. (Network member)

> the tendering of... services, I think that has been... counter productive to the Network functioning because the Network had a view that we didn't believe the tender should... have gone ahead, we expressed that view very strongly,... [Teaching Hospital] was one of the tender competitors... against the current providers and that's certainly... affecting that relationship. (Network member)

Despite these comments, effectiveness in the leadership role and lack of any obvious alternative candidates brought the Clinical Director re-election for a second term, though by the end of the research period in 2009 succession issues were giving some concern:

> Perhaps one of the weaknesses... if you've got such strong personalities that drive, when they go it all falls apart. (Network member)

> And if you look around the Network at the people who are strong leaders, [the Clinical Director] comes to the top... absolutely, without any question, and it's very hard to see another person who matches that. (Network member)

> Who within the Network has the clout and also the energy that [the Clinical Director] has got who can take over the role?...I can't think of anyone. (Network member)

Cathedral City Sexual Health Network

The Hub Committee—context, formation, structure, management, and governance

Cathedral City and its surrounding local area is a Unitary Local Authority (a large town or city which formally functions independently of county or other regional administration) with a growing population and a relatively high proportion of immigrants from various African, Asian, and Middle European ethnic groups (including both economic migrants and asylum seekers). Local official documents state that its citizens are not as affluent as others in its NHS Region. There is relatively high unemployment and overall life expectancy is lower than average. The City has identified four areas for health improvement at a population level, including sexual health.

Cathedral City's Sexual Health Network, the Hub Committee, was formed in 2002 in response to the National Strategy for Sexual Health and HIV (2001). It was the key formal structure for planning and implementing local sexual health services according to national guidelines. The Hub Committee met every month. Tasked to work at the strategic level, its invited membership of over twenty people comprised senior staff from all the statutory and non-statutory organizations involved with different aspects of sexual health services locally.

Cathedral City PCT, which hosted and provided the Chair for the Hub Committee, was established (2006) through the national reorganization of PCTs by the Department of Health (DoH). With the important addition of the local council's Adult Social Care Department, it was essentially a merged organization between the original two PCTs set up locally in 2001.

At the time of the research, the PCT employed the very small Network management team comprising the Chair, an Assistant Director of Public Health, and a part-time middle-ranking Public Health Manager. Two other members of the Hub Committee, the head of Contraceptive and Sexual Health Services (previously Family Planning) and the head of the School Nursing Service, both based at a city centre clinic, were also PCT employees. Other Statutory sector members included: the sexual health consultants, senior nurse, and a manager from the Department of Sexual Health Medicine situated a mile away from the city centre in one of two acute hospitals run by the local NHS Trust; and three City Council employees, including the Teenage Pregnancy

Coordinator. Members from the non-statutory sector included the Chief Executive Officers (CEOs) of three voluntary organizations: Cathedral City HIV Services, the Alcohol Advisory Service, and the Drugs Advisory Service. As in Metropolitan City, GPs were notable by their absence.

The Hub Committee received reports from various other groups and committees in the city involved with sexual health, operating mainly at the practitioner level. In addition it had links with various professionalized networks (clinical, nursing, and social work).

Technically, the Hub Committee was a subcommittee of the PCT's Professional Executive Committee to which it copied minutes and progress reports. It reported to the Strategic Health Authority's *Sexual Health Commissioners' Network*, attended quarterly by the Hub Committee Chair. Although members were encouraged to contribute to the agenda, decisions about priorities tended to be made by the PCT.

The story of the Network following its formation

The story of Cathedral City Sexual Health Network and its key structure, the Hub Committee, only makes sense within its political and social context. The wider political climate was, of course, the same for both our cases, with a relatively new Labour Government trying to implement a wide-ranging set of NHS reforms of which the National Strategy for Sexual Health (2001) was only a part. Both Networks were developed against a backdrop of huge structural changes which formed, and then reformed, the commissioning bodies (PCTs) and merged regional health services (SHAs). In addition, the public health function was dispersed among the individual PCTs, causing concern about loss of strategic capacity (Jessop, 2002).

Following rapid expansion in the 1960s and 1970s, Cathedral City cultivated an independent and progressive self-image and identity. Priding itself on being in the vanguard of change, it rapidly developed transport systems, shopping centres, and other modern facilities less readily taken up in other areas. This entrepreneurial culture appeared to extend to its health services. The local hospital was early to achieve Foundation Trust status and had successfully acquired Private Finance Initiative funding for a complete rebuild. The city's PCT (created from the original two established in the initial 'pioneering' (Denham, 2000) tranche of PCTs, completed an innovative merger with the city council's adult care services in 2003; was early in joining the National Primary Care Contracting Collaborative in 2004; and, in 2006, successfully fought off proposals to merge with other local PCTs (seen as less successful and more indebted).

However, a downside of frequent macro-reorganization is turbulence at the operational and network levels.

> [The service is] working within a wider organisation that's been through constant change and ... [there has] probably been ... change in terms of management, probably every two to three years and there is very little consolidation of that change ... and then it will change again. And it's very difficult to keep on top of what's happening. (Hub Committee member)

On the other hand, some changes which helped amalgamate service provision within the city (achieving so-called unitary authority status) sustained existing, if informal, service networks at practitioner level.

> The beauty of having a unitary authority is that you're not a million miles away from each other, you don't have to travel half way across the country (Local Authority respondent)

> [look] at the number of meetings that are held in Costa's ... if there are issues [people will] try and meet together and sort it out and see what the problems are. (Hub Committee member)

Despite traditional informal networking, before the advent of the Hub Committee there were gaps, notably between hospital and other local services. Clinicians from the Department of Sexual Health Services attended two long-standing medical networks sharing clinical knowledge, one concerned specifically with HIV and one discussing general sexual health issues, but these operated outside Cathedral City and intra-city links were less good.

> [Looking] back five years ... [there wasn't] any kind of dialogue or communication between [some] providers of services. For example, the old traditional family planning service didn't talk to GUM. (Hub Committee member)

This lack of communication between the hospital and other services directly influenced both the tracer issues: HIV services for ethnic minority groups and teenage pregnancy, which had been identified as problems locally for many years.

HIV services in Cathedral City were mainly focused on a voluntary organization. Like many others in provincial cities, it had been created in the early 1990s to meet the needs of a small number of gay men. However, there was a rapid increase in heterosexual clients from ethnic minorities, particularly asylum seekers, during the late 1990s and the charity was now coping with the different requirements of more than 150 people from this new client group. With eleven members of staff and a yearly expenditure of more than £200,000, mostly from the statutory sector, it was well-integrated at operational level with some of the sexual health service provision in the city. The local authority HIV social worker was based in their premises and several staff worked in conjunction with the city's education services to offer prevention advice to schools. On the other hand, and in contrast with other HIV voluntary sector services in the surrounding area, there was no direct referral to or from, and little dialogue or coordination with, the local GUM department.

Teenage pregnancy was also an important issue, with local rates well above the national average and rising. Local sexual health and contraceptive services for young people were not entirely user friendly. The school nursing service, unlike many in other areas, did not offer contraceptive services, and although the GUM clinic was open access, teenagers were more likely to use the city centre based Contraception and Sexual Health Service, not always open at convenient times. In addition, speedy termination was difficult to achieve. The local pregnancy advisory service was not allowed to take direct referrals and early medical terminations were not available at the local hospital. Prompted to tackle the teenage pregnancy issue by a directive from the government's national Social Exclusion Unit (1999), Cathedral City formed a large multi-agency action group. This published a strategy later incorporated into the 2004 Implementation Plan. However, no new money was available to implement the called for action and the group lacked strong leadership— 'meetings were bumbling along and people were talking but nothing was really happening'. So little progress had been made.

Formed in 2002 and amidst massive and concurrent organizational change, the Hub Committee got off to a slow start. However, a newly arrived Assistant Director of Public Health, with a background in health promotion and experience elsewhere of developing a sexual health strategy, took over as Chair (2003). The new incumbent was energetic and pro-active, with a 'warm', inclusive and facilitative leadership style, and set about invigorating the members. By late 2003, the Hub Committee had taken the first steps in strategy development by organizing a successful conference which:

> Brought together...the sexual health community of...[Cathedral City]...people of all ages, ethnicities, service providers, service users. (Hub Committee member)

With a draft strategy document out for consultation, the Chair gained approval for much-needed service development, utilizing some new government money now available. First, there was a successful application to join the National Primary Care Contracting Collaborative to involve primary care in providing sexual health services. This created new links and cross-boundary working between GPs, the Contraception and Sexual Health Service, and GUM, with some GPs being trained to provide contraceptive services at the city centre clinic. In addition, ways were found to speed referrals from primary care to GUM services, crucial to achieving the 48-hour referral target. Another initiative established a medical terminations service in the NHS unit which had previously only offered surgical terminations and improved communication with that department. Also important was the appointment of a full-time Public Health Manager (at middle-management level), specifically to lead on implementing the strategy, once finalized.

Production of the strategy (2004) marked a high point for the Hub Committee and during a visit from NHS Regional Officers in early 2005 the PCT was congratulated on the quality of its sexual health work. However, the speedy progress made in 2003/2004 was followed by three years in which the pace of strategic change and decision-making slowed. Although development continued at the operational level and some national sexual health targets were met, notably chlamydia screening and 48-hour referral to GUM services (as noted previously for Metropolitan City, such figures did not necessarily indicate patients seen, merely referrals recorded), there was a substantial period of time (estimates varied as to its exact length) when the Hub Committee did not meet at all.

This apparent hiatus in the Hub Committee's grip on strategic service development coincided with a further round of organizational change at both regional and local level. Although the Cathedral City PCT fought a proposed merger and finally remained a single organization, there were major changes at management level, including the loss of the Chief Executive, and the Professional Executive Committee, which oversaw the work of the Hub Committee, was disbanded.

Management input to the Hub Committee had always been limited and the Chair's many other responsibilities increased further during the reorganization. The Public Health Manager was now the key resource for most practitioners and the person accessed in the first instance for help or advice. At first a full-time post, when the original manager left in 2006 the position remained vacant for a year and was then replaced by a part-timer. This downgrading of the post reduced the time available for service development. It also adversely affected the Hub Committee, as the Manager would deputise if pressure of work prevented the Chair's attendance. Since the membership comprised very senior people, this was a problem.

> If you've got the right seniority leading these groups, that's fine, but if the seniority is devolved. It's not always as robust as it needs to be...the Chair [should] be a strategic leader at senior level because those of us going are coming with that brief. (Hub Committee member)

During this period local teenage pregnancy rates were still increasing, and geographically and sometimes ideologically separate services for young people continued to encounter difficulties.

> What would be an ideal would be to bring services together under one roof, a one stop shop...it's not just about...[pregnancy], it's bringing everyone together,

to work together for that young person...[which] is really important'. (Hub Committee member)

Another practitioner-based initiative, set up and headed by the voluntary sector, offered a new approach to providing sex education in schools. It seemed to be effective, despite some resistance to introducing programmes designed by people other than teachers.

> The people from [the prevention group]...[should not] come in and deliver everything...[they should] work with the teachers...[Also] they must deliver what the teacher wants them to deliver...because some of the agencies have set things that they want to deliver, which isn't always what the school or the students need. (City Council respondent)

Despite all efforts, the national statistics suggested that teenage conceptions in Cathedral City had fallen by only 0.5 per cent between 1998 and 2005. A new, dynamic Teenage Pregnancy Coordinator came into their post in 2006 and analysis of the data from a comprehensive review showed a few schools at high risk. The prevention focus changed radically from an all schools approach to targeting 'hot spots', a policy change about which many had reservations, feeling that the situation in other schools might deteriorate.

> They had this big consultation and big research project...whereas before...[the prevention group] would go into any school and do, you know, as much or as little work as need be...now...[it is] being told you can only be allowed to go into high priority teenage pregnancy schools and you can only go into hot spot areas...it's upset quite a few people, some people have even been disgusted that services will actually be pulled from green or amber schools and, you know, moved across to red ones. (City Council respondent)

Difficulties persisted in providing suitable services for HIV in ethnic minority populations, given the weak relationship between the voluntary and statutory sectors and the relative isolation and inflexibility of GUM services. Achieving the 48-hour referral target was relatively simple, once a speedier system for making GP referrals had been agreed, since the clinic already ran a walk-in service and many patients referred themselves. However, reducing the time between referral and being given a first appointment was one thing; ensuring attendance at appointments was quite another. The GUM clinic, previously in the city centre, was now situated a bus ride away in a different hospital, and its HIV services were not well matched to its new client group.

> If you are socially excluded most people become low and depressed. If you are taking medication, and you've got appointments, and you are very low and depressed, things kind of get left behind, ...so if you've got an appointment at 10 o'clock, [you] might not arrive until twelve. And the GUM will say 'well we can't see you'. (HIV Worker respondent)

By late 2007, Hub Committee activity began to pick up again. With the PCT reprieved and the Professional Executive Committee re-established, it was time to update the Cathedral City Sexual Health Strategy, and in March 2008 a review signalled the Committee's formal renaissance. A revised strategy document, covering 2008–2011, was published in July 2007.

Further impetus was provided in the spring of 2008, when recently published data compiled locally and submitted to the Office for National Statistics appeared to show that teenage pregnancies were still increasing, rather than diminishing, making Cathedral City one of the worst perform-ers in the country '[Cathedral City is] on the naughty list for teenage preg-nancy'. Surprisingly, no-one seemed to recognize that the 2008 figures related to data collected two years previously and did not necessarily reflect the cur-rent situation. This apparent poor performance drew unwelcome ministe-rial attention and prompted a visit by the National Support Team, set up by government to help local authorities achieve their Public Service Agreement to halve the under-18 conception rate by 2010. It also, perversely, served to increase resources for and interest in the issue.

> It is like they are signed up at the top now . . . teenage pregnancy is now high prior-ity, high visibility, monthly Assistant Director level meetings. Things are happen-ing, decisions are being made. (Hub Committee member)

In 2009, when 2007 figures were published, they showed the much awaited downward trend, suggesting that prevention efforts had begun to impact before the 'crisis' of 2008.

When the research was completed in 2009, it seemed that momentum was being maintained. There were further initiatives in prevention and educa-tion services for young people; the appointment of a specialist nurse for HIV looked likely to improve communication and service delivery; and voluntary sector HIV services had a more certain future as they merged with a large national charity. The Hub Committee was meeting regularly, with a new style of agenda designed to allow in-depth discussion of particular issues, rather than covering all areas superficially, so members might opt out if a particular topic was of little personal interest. Some felt that three-monthly meetings were not adequate to maintain awareness of the strategic position.

With such a small management team, however, the Network appeared vul-nerable to future disruption. In particular, the Chair was very important to its functioning. During restructuring, when the Chair's attention was diverted, the Hub Committee did not meet; it was the Chair that reconvened the group to update the strategy; and it was the presence of the Chair which deter-mined attendance at meetings by senior people. For one person to have such a central role in the Network must raise questions about how such leadership might be replaced, if required.

Concluding discussion

Two contrasting Networks

Both case study Networks were based in cities containing areas of relative deprivation, with higher than average rates of teenage pregnancy and substantial numbers of people from immigrant ethnic minorities affected by HIV/AIDS. However, these problems were more acute and on a bigger scale in Metropolitan City.

When the National Strategy for Sexual Health and HIV (DoH, 2001a) required the development of managed networks to coordinate and improve services, Metropolitan City responded rapidly, acquiring funding from local PCTs to staff and manage an informal clinical network already existing amongst staff from five GUM departments, all linked to the same major teaching hospital. Their Network had a complex structure with an Executive Board which included three key decision-makers (latterly one; the Clinical Director), and sub-committees. Membership included representation from all local stakeholders including service users.

In contrast, Cathedral City's Hub Committee was a single structure comprising senior staff from local organizations. The committee was hosted by and reported to the local PCT and was chaired by an Assistant Director of Public Health with a non-clinical health promotion background. Although clinicians from the single GUM department were represented on the committee, their professional networks operated outside the city. No service users attended. Although a managerial post was created in 2004 to service the committee and act as a resource for practitioners, in 2007 this was downgraded and became part-time.

An important difference between the two Networks was that Metropolitan City tended to focus on clinical issues, whereas Cathedral City's Hub Committee had a stronger public health perspective. One possible reason was that both Networks were largely constructed from pre-existing local organizational templates. For Metropolitan City's Network, the impetus for development and much of its membership came from an existing clinical network. In Cathedral City, with more restricted input on the medical side, many members came from organizations already involved in prevention and sex education through the Teenage Pregnancy Action Group.

Local priorities were also different. The key issue in Cathedral City, teenage pregnancy, seemed invisible in the Metropolitan City case study. Yet, if current national statistics for Metropolitan City's inner city area are compared with Cathedral City's figures, a very similar pattern emerges with both showing a high rate (around 58 per cent) in 1998 and both currently showing an achieved reduction of around 8–9 per cent. These figures must either indicate a general trend which would have occurred without intervention, or that there are effective public health initiatives in both places, possibly existing separately from the clinically based Network in Metropolitan City.

Governance

The 'managed' network ideal type supposedly exercises internal control through shared meaning and joint commitment (Boltanski and Chiapello, 2005) and should not require much external regulation (Rhodes, 2007). As these two NHS Networks demonstrate, however, there may be considerable variance in governance in different settings.

Metropolitan City's Network, a stand-alone organization with funding from several sources, had relative autonomy protecting it somewhat from pressure to perform or the penalties of failure. Thus Metropolitan City's Network was an example of what may be the 'ideal' for the managed network form in healthcare, lying somewhere between the NPM style quasi market system and traditional tacit professional networks and, as argued earlier, potentially well-suited to the clinical governance model envisaged by Flynn (2004), where control is exercised in large measure through internalized self-discipline and organizational norms (Reed, 1999). It was a specific organization, set up to deliver national policy objectives and run as previously suggested by 'ener-gised clinical professionals'. There was a cycle of information sharing and debate (particularly at the '5th Wednesday' research days), which fed into discussions of best practice and service planning, fitting well with Hood et al's (2001) conceptualization of governance, and delivery of the 48-hour access target was achieved largely through peer pressure. Thus it closely followed the Foucauldian idea of social control through developing norms in line with accepted and acceptable standards set by legitimated and expert authority (Foucault, 1991).

However, the agenda set out in the National Strategy included a large public health/health promotion and education component, which was not addressed to any significant extent by the Network as it focused primarily on narrower clinical issues. Goodwin (2008) suggests that members of a network could 'develop a provider cabal that forces purchasers to conform to their ver-sion of network requirements'. Since the original instigators and most active members of the Network were predominantly clinicians, maybe their domi-nance skewed the governance process towards their norms and hampered consideration of wider strategic perspectives. Certainly when our fieldwork ceased in 2008 there was some uncertainty about how to maintain momen-tum without an obvious clinical target to address.

Cathedral City's Sexual Health Network presented a different picture. Here there were no clinical product champions, indeed the clinicians made little effort to integrate and preferred to use their existing professional networks.

Instead a managerial initiative utilized a collective city-wide history of joint working to bring together a multi-organizational membership not dominated by any one professional grouping. Unlike Metropolitan City, which developed a separate organization, the Hub Committee, as its name suggests, had only a virtual existence. Embedded within the governance structure of the PCT and with no dedicated funding, this Network was susceptible to various forms of local and national control, ranging from the 'soft' power exerted by legitimated standards of best practice (Courpasson, 2000; Flynn, 2002; Courpasson and Dany, 2003) to the more coercive power (French and Raven, 1959; Raven et al, 1998) of direct performance management buttressed by threats of financial penalties for unmet targets. This case demonstrated clearly that in the NHS the centre does not disappear but rather seeks to 'steer from a distance' though indirect means, with the surveying centre monitoring the performance of the remote localities and retaining the capacity to intervene if things go wrong, as when senior figures were summoned to Westminster and interrogated by government ministers about their apparent failure to meet teenage pregnancy targets.

Another difference was that the membership composition of the Hub Committee made it less likely that a particular viewpoint or interest would dominate. While there was not such a strong bias as that towards clinical issues in Metropolitan City, there were cultural, professional, and organizational leanings towards public health deriving from the city's long history of concern with social deprivation, the inclusion of professionals from education and other organizations with a prevention and/or health education remit, and its leadership and location within the public health directorate. Arguably, this 'epistemic community' (Knorr-Cetina, 1999) was predisposed towards addressing the parts of the National Strategy that pertained to public health. This contrasts with the position in the Metropolitan City Network where the public health function never gained prominence in terms of influencing the agenda for change.

Leadership

Leadership in Metropolitan City's Network came initially from three teaching hospital colleagues who set up the Network and latterly from the sole surviving member of that group, the Clinical Director, a senior consultant in GUM who was forceful and directive, also inspiring admiration and loyalty from colleagues. The Cathedral City Network's Chair had a warm and facilitative leadership style, helpful in cross-boundary working. These very different personalities were both successful in their role, supporting Hogg's (2001) suggestion that effective leaders fit the groups they direct. Both were charismatic and inspired confidence and both were highly performance orientated; however the powerful leadership exerted by the Clinical Director of the Network was more suited to running a group composed mainly of high-ranking doctors, while the Chair of the Hub Committee's more persuasive approach befitted someone trying to encourage collaboration between very different organizations.

It might be thought that the philosophy of a network better suits joint rather than individual leadership, and indeed the initial tripartite leadership of the Network was an effective format, with the different styles of two of the individuals complementing and providing a useful 'counter-balance' to the dominance of the Clinical Director. When they were succeeded by others without the same degree of influence and rapport, leaving the Clinical Director in control, this led to suspicion that the powerful teaching hospital faction might manipulate the Network's agenda in its favour. Some felt this had had a deleterious and fragmenting effect on the collective drive and ethos of the Network. However, collective leadership may not be essential to developing a sustainable network. Cathedral City's Hub Committee always had a single leader, but in this instance the Chair's personal leadership style was inclusive and less dominant, giving active individual support to all members' interests. This, in addition to the Chair's lack of any obvious competing interests from those of the group as a whole, tended to foster trusting relationships, a key role for a network leader (Ferlie and Pettigrew, 1996), and probably helped maintain network cohesiveness, even when meetings were infrequent.

Organizational learning

Both Networks had systems to promote organizational learning. In Metropolitan City, Network sub-committees tasked with exploring different aspects of service delivery met regularly. Run by clinicians and reporting back to the Executive, these appeared to be useful fora for sharing profession-specific knowledge and best practice, though diary constraints meant they were not always well attended. In addition, the large biannual research meetings promised to strengthen existing ties and create new relationships through informal networking, as well as promoting learning through exchange of ideas.

At the three-monthly Hub Committee meetings in Cathedral City, information about progress and current plans was exchanged between senior members of the different organizations involved. Respondents spoke of it as a forum enabling them to share practice and be 'ahead of the game'. Since the process was partly designed to provide information to the PCT in relation to funding decisions, this could have led to the information exchanged being subtly manipulated to give the best possible gloss. The new format for Hub Committee meetings in which regular agenda items and updates were followed by a presentation on a particular topic had the potential to improve in-depth understanding of problems and did so in some cases. However there was some evidence to suggest that an individual organization's lack of interest in that particular issue might have the perverse effect of reducing attendance.

The extent to which learning and dissemination of best practice was promoted outside the main Network organizations was less clear. The research meetings run by Metropolitan City's Network drew a wide audience, including some service users, but were mainly focused on clinical topics. The Hub Committee excluded users and more junior practitioners, who were thus dependent on the (admittedly close) informal networking between organizations to keep up-to-date. In addition, sharing information at the strategic level does not necessarily equate to greater understanding of problems at the operational level and feedback was reduced when the dedicated manager post became part-time.

Information and Communication Technologies

Part of the argument for network management is that it is fuelled by the ready availability of new Information and Communication Technologies (ICTs), seen as allowing better and more timely data collection as well as enhanced ability to share information across a wider spectrum of stakeholders. Indeed, the influence of ICTs is clearly visible within our sexual health cases, though they did not always achieve the intended service improvements. An obvious example is meeting the 48-hour access targets for GUM services, supposedly a way of ensuring patients were seen without undue delay. In Cathedral City, where the flaw in the process was identified as tardy primary care referral and patient numbers were not particularly large, the target system worked well, prompting the introduction of telephone or fax requests for immediate appointments. On the other hand, in Metropolitan City, although the target was apparently met once all the clinics offered open access, there was no way of recording those who were turned away. Here statistical data appeared to mask a continuing problem, questioning the validity of collected data. Exactly the opposite happened in Cathedral City, where published figures apparently showing rising teenage pregnancy rates became a major political issue. Here there was a problem with how valid data was interpreted, since the statistics for the year in question, published two years later, showed the rate was already falling.

Accessibility of information was another issue. Various technical problems with software caused difficulties at both case study sites. As anticipated by Currie and Suhomlinova (2006), knowledge-sharing across organizational and professional boundaries was not straightforward. Even where systems were compatible there was often resistance to making data available to all within the Network. This was noticeable in Cathedral City, where a key voluntary sector organization, though open with its own data, considered that there was no chance that it would ever feature 'on the list' of those to whom the health service would give free access to its data.

The 'wicked' problem of how to improve sexual health

The National Strategy for Sexual Health and HIV (DoH, 2001a) identified two major problems, the rising rates of STIs and a high rate of unintended pregnancies, particularly amongst young people, and suggested 'managed networks' at the organizational level. Its Implementation Plan (DoH, 2002) tasked PCTs with achieving this end by bringing together 'an inclusive part-nership involving local stakeholders and commissioning organisations'. However, six years later the Independent Advisory Group of the Medical Foundation for AIDS and Sexual Health (DoH, 2008) suggested progress was 'patchy' and criticized the 'medical model' of sexual health services 'failing to address the wider determinants of sexual health'.

Evidence from these two cases suggests that the mandated network may well be an effective mechanism in principle for addressing 'wicked prob-lems' in sexual health. However, it is difficult to avoid the conclusion that (as with HIV in the 1980s) much progress was dependent on available new money. Such resource dependency (Pfeffer and Salancik, 1978) provided the 'glue' which kept the Hub Committee together, and indeed kept the sexual health programme intact at an operational level through periods in which the Committee itself was barely functioning. New funding was critical in pro-viding management input to Metropolitan City's Network, without which re-organization would have been even more challenging.

Both case study sites were aware of areas which needed improvement, with Cathedral City needing to develop better integration and dialogue with clinical services and Metropolitan City concerned to develop a wide-ranging perspective on public health issues. Respondents in both cases identified continuing difficulties in addressing the needs of unconventional lifestyles which differed markedly from those to which the NHS currently responds. Nevertheless, both Networks developed functioning multidisciplinary organ-izations and achieved considerable changes in service provision. In Cathedral City, this was done with little extra resource and during considerable struc-tural turbulence. In both organizations there was optimism and some evi-dence that foundations had been laid for increased effectiveness in the future, suggesting, not unexpectedly, that managed networks dealing with 'wicked' problems require time and sustained effort to succeed.

7

Networks for Older People's Care: A really wicked problem

Introduction—A brief policy history of Older People's Care

The health policy arena of Older People's Care has, over the last two decades, become increasingly politicized and important as the proportion of people living to over 80 has grown; yet it seems incapable of ready resolution. The recent Dilnot Commission (2010) concluded (yet again) that the current system of funding care was in urgent need of reform and put forward proposals for radical reform which require some new public resources (at a difficult time for public spending). At the time of writing, the Department of Health (DoH) is still considering its response.

The issues associated with Older People's Care represent major issues for society as a whole and have multifarious dimensions—in other words, a really wicked problem which includes behavioural elements. Contemporary attitudes towards older people are frequently negative and display ageist stereotyping. For example, though the older population is clearly diverse, we often refer to anyone over the age of 65 as an 'older person', thus grouping together in an (implied) homogeneous group those aged 65 and those aged 90! This stereotyping may also have practical implications for the way we attempt to meet the needs of differing age segments. Crucially, for health care, as predicted life expectancy increases from 4.7 million over-75-year-olds in Britain in 2007 to 8.2 million by 2013 (Office of National Statistics, 2007), we note that those over 75 and 85 constitute the highest proportion of health users. Those between the ages of 65 and 95 have more long-term conditions and co-morbidities than other parts of the population. This is problematic for a health care system traditionally orientated towards 'cure' and rehabilitation, which may not be the only relevant goals for the over-75s. As we shall illustrate, throughout society there are now significant concerns over the quality of care provided to older people and a growing public concern to combat ageism and discrimination against older people.

Older People's Care is a highly multi-sectoral arena. It has long involved local authority social care and voluntary agencies (such as Age UK) as well as health care. While care in the National Health Service (NHS) is free; social care is means tested. To a greater extent than other cases, the Older People's cases include private providers of nursing and residential care as a major stakeholder. Services for older people consume major public resources and budgets and demand is growing. There is frequently a pattern of physical and mental co-morbidity (e.g. falling, plus Parkinson's, plus dementia) which is complex to manage.

The sector has been reshaped by the long-term privatization of nursing and residential care. So unlike cancer care, Older People's Networks need to embrace the public, voluntary, *and* private sectors. In the two decades preceding the last Labour governments (1997–2010), there was a dramatic growth in private and voluntary sector provision (mainly still funded, if not provided, publicly) and a drastic decline in NHS beds. Publicly funded residential care is means tested so that the costs of care for people with even modest levels of capital falls on them or their families, with the possibility (at present) of considerable sums being required. The private and not-for-profit nursing home industry has grown as a proportion of the sector and now provides the majority of nursing and residential homes. In 2010, there were 13,418 privately run homes and 3,517 run by voluntary organizations out of a total of 18,255 homes (Age UK/J. Rowntree, 2011). However, funding pressures are now leading to the closure of homes, despite the increase in demand (National Care Homes R&D Forum, 2007). The increased privatization of the sector also creates issues of governance, exemplified in the recent financial collapse of the Southern Cross private chain of care homes, with the potential closure of all 750 care homes (BBC News, 11 July, 2011). Within healthcare, specific concerns focus on the spiralling costs of acute care for older people and the impact of prolonged hospitalization (or 'bed blocking' as it is sometimes labelled), leading to initiatives to facilitate earlier discharge of older people. The social care sector may in turn resent perceived 'cost shunting', leading to revolving door readmissions to hospital.

There has been a long history of policy initiatives, without evidence that the major problems have been resolved. Over twenty years ago, a joint report by the Royal College of Nursing, the British Geriatric Society, and the Royal College of Psychiatrists (1987) criticized poor standards of care for older people in acute hospitals and this remains a core concern today (Patterson et al, 2011). The Royal Commission on Long-term Care (Cm 4192,1999) (enacted in the NHS Plan (Cm 4818, 2000)) assigned lead responsibility for community care to local authorities to energise the social care sector and rebalance care away from health. New regulatory mechanisms were established, given the growth of private sector residential provision. The Care Standards Act (2000) set the regulatory framework by which the National Care Standards Commission (created 2004) had jurisdiction over care services and homes, taking over registration and inspection functions. It was merged in 2009 to create a 'super regulator' (the Care Quality Commission, or CQC) which now acts as the independent regulator of health care and adult social care in England. In 2011, the CQC in turn came under criticism for allegedly failing to spot abuse in homes for people with learning disabilities which it should have regulated and which was exposed in the media, leading to possible further institutional reorganization.

In terms of establishing national standards, the National Service Framework (NSF) for Older People in 2001 (DoH, 2001b) represented a step forward. It announced itself as: 'a comprehensive strategy to ensure fair, high quality, integrated health and social care services for elderly people'. The NSF set out standards and models of care to improve the quality of support in health and social services, building around four themes: respect for the individual; developing intermediate care; the provision of evidence-based specialist care; and promoting healthy, active lives. Two of these themes are picked up for more detailed study in our case studies, namely intermediate care and specialist care for end of life.

The NSF set out a number of standards, for example on person-centred care and falls. One key to implementing person- (and not service-) centred care was the Single Assessment Process (SAP) to coordinate assessment, data collection, and service availability among local health agencies and social services. The objective was to produce multidisciplinary, inter-agency assessments of needs and therefore holistic, individualized care packages. The NSF shared many of these institutional features with the Cancer Plan: a proclaimed evidence-based approach (using a conventional hierarchy of evidence approach); an External Reference group and task forces; the construction of milestones and a performance management system; and the appointment of a senior academic as National Service Director. However, some of the standards can be seen as relatively 'soft' and not based on Randomized Control Trials (RCTs) meta analyses: for example, Standard 1 is essentially attitudinal rather than scientific: 'rooting out age discrimination'.

In terms of local implementation, the NSF contains strong user involvement with the designation of Older People's 'Champions' as collective change agents, including at the attitudinal level. While it does not mandate the formation of formal networks, it calls for strong leadership to cross agency boundaries and an inclusive and whole-systems-based approach consistent with network-based working. The question of whether the NHS or social care should chair such bodies was left open, perhaps reflecting the high resource power of social services in this field.

The NSF represents a major progression in government policy for the care of older people. And since NSF publication, there have been a series of further developments, such as the Green Paper 'Independence, Well-being and Choice' (Cm 6499, 2005) on adult social care, followed by the White Paper 'Our Health, Our Care, Our Say' (Cm 6737, 2006) which set a new emphasis on prevention, effective integration, and a proposed shift of resources to primary care. And also there has been strategy development around specific issues, for example a national dementia strategy (2009). There has certainly been an attempt to take forward a more holistic, preventative agenda. These developments have been supported by local experiments with pooled budgets and merged organizations (Hultberg et al, 2005; Henwood, 2006). However, the Wanless Review (2006) reports that care management and an SAP are still far from being routine. The report concludes that while a range of policies and guidance support integration, these are mainly incremental, based on past performance, and it is questionable whether this approach will be sufficient to achieve the required shift from partnership to integration. The review also recommends attention to financial arrangements. Mechanisms in place are often facilitative and passive and more active encouragement is required, such as incentives to pool resources. Our national-level policy interviews reinforced this, indicating that in many areas an SAP was either not operating, or was operating unsatisfactorily. More recently, a report (Age UK, 2012) highlights the growing funding gap and the decreasing provision of publically funded care. So, whilst there is evidence of some progress being made since the NSF in improving quality of care (Philp, 2004), the picture is variable and there continue to be criticisms of the standards of care in both acute hospitals (Patterson et al, 2011) and the community (Lewis et al, 1994; Young et al, 2003). Crucially, in a flat economy, there are still inter-sectoral tensions in both the funding and provision of health and social care to older people.

Finally, in terms of policy development at the national level, there has been increased emphasis on palliative care and end of life care. *The End of Life Care Strategy* (DoH 2008) built on earlier end of life reports (Help the Aged, 2006). The National Institute of Health and Clinical Excellence (NICE) Quality Standard (2011) underlines the need to improve end of life care in the last six months of life and sets out specific standards to improve working practices.

So there has clearly been a proliferation of policy development in respect of older people's services in the 2000s. However, all quality standards currently in place and the newer targets require increasing coordination of resources and joint responsibilities across public agencies, in health and social care but also with the private and voluntary sector providers who are major players. Whilst financing Older People's Care has been identified as an increasingly critical issue (Wanless, 2006; Dilnot, 2010), to date there have as yet been no firm government proposals. Thus the dysfunctional incentives which exist within the system continue. For example, it narrowly appears more cost-efficient for the health system to prioritize rapid hospital discharge of elderly patients which shifts further costs back to social care (or private individuals), even if such discharges require greater social support. Additionally, the NSF for Older People sets standards, but has not set any timescale for their achievement. It assigned the 'lead' responsibility for improving care to local authorities, but the government has not committed extra resources to support this objective. Consequently, the issue is whether these developments have made a substantial difference on the ground, given the long and disappointing history.

These prolonged difficulties in tackling inter-agency, inter-professional, and also resource issues mark Older People's Care as an intractable 'wicked issue': a national system of high-quality, affordable, integrated community-led care seems as far away as ever, despite a history of promising local innovations going back to the 1980s (Davies and Ferlie, 1984; Challis et al, 1991; Patterson et al, 2011).

Case Study 1—Regional Older People's Network

Network site

The Regional City network (hereafter called 'Regional') was located in a major regional city and was set up in 2005. The proportion of the population between the ages of 60 and 90 was less than that of the average population for the rest of England and Wales. The average age of the total city population as a whole was also less than this average age. During the last few years, the size of the various ethnic minority communities in the city, already extensive, has grown considerably, but not as much as earlier anticipated (Office for National Statistics, 2007).

The constitution of the Network: History and membership

There had been much reorganization of local authority services between the city and the neighbouring county locally, with Regional city becoming a so-called metropolitan council with full responsibility for all services in 1997 (acquiring functions previously exercised by the county, notably Social Services). In addition, there were mergers of local Primary Care Trusts (PCTs) in 2006. Until this date, there was more than one PCT working with each of the local authorities to achieve common goals. The changes resulted in a single merged PCT serving the whole city. These factors might prima facie be seen as helpful in promoting co-terminosity and cross-boundary working. But the process of dividing up services between Regional city and the county was complex and remained a key factor in the slow development of the Network.

> Senior managers of the organizations...had to change their whole relationship and dialogue on several occasions in the last few years in order to get the same work done. And I suppose it's easier now because there are fewer people to talk to in theory, but equally the organizations that they're talking to are more defused and have separate cultures within them. (Doctor)

Interview data revealed that the reorganization of services had disrupted pre-existing relationships:

> The complication is, in addition to the major unitary authorities, we have boroughs and the boroughs have independents [care homes] and have, as far as older people are concerned, quite a lot of the services that are delivered to older people by the boroughs not the county or the city. And it is quite a complex mix, developing relationships with all these people, has been, well it's been a challenge but it's getting better. (Manager, Local Authority)

As a result, many staff belonged to more than one network, depending on their remit and the local geography:

> Yes, I am a member of a couple of networks but I am kind of, sometimes an official member of the Network, sometimes an invited member of a Network. (Manager, Local Authority)

Some respondents held a positive view of multidisciplinary planning, despite some inter-professional barriers to networking:

> I think if people have a positive experience, if you have a positive experience of working with colleagues and you achieve your outcomes jointly, I don't think you're going to worry too much about what their professional background is. I think when there are difficulties, then thoughts might start to occur as well. They're thinking like that because they are a doctor or whatever, yes, and that's where barriers and obstacles can start to appear. (Manager, Local Authority)

Within this network, there was a complex range of varied stakeholders, including social care, health care, private sector residential and nursing home providers, charities, and voluntary sector groups. To understand the Regional Network, it is imperative to offer some detail on these stakeholders. The local authority, Regional city council—rather than the NHS—was designated as responsible for leading the development of services for older people including working collaboratively with other parties (as proposed in the Older People's NSF). Its Department One supported adults and older people in need of personal care services and was most actively involved. In healthcare, there were four main sub-sectors involved in the Network. These were Regional City Primary Care Trust, Regional Hospital NHS Trust, Regional City Community Health Services, and Regional City Mental Health and Learning Disability Trust. This meant that in healthcare alone, there were four separate organizations involved with older people. There were many privately run nursing homes in the area and the private sector had a Trade Association from which a single representative sat as a member of the Network. There were also a number of voluntary and charitable organizations represented in the Regional Network which included a large specialist charity, which ran day centres for older people, and a Voluntary Action Group.

The structure of the Network attempted to reflect this variety of stakeholders. It was a tiered structure, reporting at the apex to Regional City Executive, through the Regional City Health Unity Group which was responsible for a particular stream of strategic activity, overseeing work done by more focused Networks, such as the Older People's Network.

The Regional City Health Unity Group was:

> One of the delivery blocks of the Local Area Agreement, although that reporting mechanism had still to be established.

> [The Group] is relatively new and has focused to a great extent, at the moment, on actually getting the Local Area Agreement written. So it's now beginning to move into a phase where it can start determining who reports to it and how it wishes to receive updates. (Manager, Local Authority)

So the group itself was in a formative stage during the period of fieldwork and had not fully established all its systems of accountability.

The Older People's Network consisted of two core groups. The Executive Group was a multi-agency partnership designed to develop strategy within the city and oversee its implementation. It included senior personnel drawn from the health and social service organizations and reported to the Regional City Unity Group. The key individuals included the Chair as a senior manager in the local authority; other local authority directors; and a Clinical Director that is a doctor from the acute hospital, with a broad policy remit to improve care for older people. This doctor held his post because of his extensive management experience, even though he was not a geriatrician by specialty. Other attendees included managers from mental health, intermediate care, and housing services. There was also participation from the Regional City Primary Care Trust; the Regional City Hospitals NHS Trust, and public health. It was described during one interview as 'very much an officers' group' (Manager, Local Authority), implying that elected representatives take a secondary role.

The group met for two hours every two months, indicating either the low level of resources available to the Network, or the relatively low priority it had among participants. So the lack of time devoted to the Network emerged as a key problem.

The second group, the Older People's Group, was broader and more representative, comprising elected members and officers from the local authority, voluntary sector, cultural services, pension services, tenants and residents associations, and independent provider representatives. Representatives from other interest groups as well as individual older people could also attend. The purpose of the Older People's Group was seen as primarily 'consultative', helping to set direction for the Executive Group. The group met for two hours every four months, again indicating the lack of priority and/or resources.

At a lower organizational level, Project Planning groups tied in with the work of the Regional Network. The use of Project Planning groups as a mechanism to manage larger scale changes pre-dates the setting up of the Regional Network and was a standard mechanism within the local authority. The intention of the Regional Network was to work collaboratively with project planning work streams to ensure that account was taken of the interests of older people and if necessary to institute new mechanisms to take action on identified issues.

One prominent constituency within the city whose members were represented on both the core groups discussed earlier was the 'Older People's Champions', though the group was not a formal part of the Network. This set of people had high interconnectivity in many of the support groups and Networks in the city working to improve services for older people. It was suggested that the Champions had the capacity to raise the profile of issues affecting older people and supporting their cause. The Older People's Champions, therefore, could be described as underpinning the process of improvement of services for older people. It represents an unusual and distinctive approach towards securing social and attitudinal changes across the City, linked to an attempt to stimulate a collective social movement.

As part of the NSF for Older People, a 'toolkit' for Older People's Champions was developed (DoH, 2004c). The National Director for Older People's Services commented in a personal message that:

> ... the role of champions has grown in importance when set within the context of wider policy, decentralising the management and decision making from central government to the NHS and social services. (Philp, 2004, p. iv)

The Older People's Champions could be described as a voluntary, mass social movement where individuals committed to the cause of improving care for older people set out to promote changes to attitudes and practices. The movement is educative and cultural. The Champions group had extensive membership across the Regional Network:

> Many of them are senior level but quite a lot of them are very, very, very, straight-forward, hands on, doing the job people. So everybody, from the chairman to the porter. (Doctor)

It was noted that the main gap in membership were staff in residential and care homes.

Some personal development and general training is provided centrally by one support individual and there are centralized events and an annual celebration event.

Within this complex and inter-sectoral network, we selected two particular strands of work as our 'tracer' issues, to explore their operations at greater depth. These two issues were intermediate care (an NSF priority) and end of life care.

The narrative of intermediate care in the Regional Network

Within health and social care policy, the term 'intermediate care' has a specific definition. It refers to a temporary package of care, identified as the result of an individualized assessment, limited to six weeks. The care package is designed to either provide support for a vulnerable person to avoid their admittance to hospital or to provide rehabilitation and extra support after illness or a hospital stay to enable the individual to fully recover. Thus intermediate care is a time-limited bridge which is designed to enable people to stay in their own home with extra support or in a local nursing home. Whilst many people who receive intermediate care are older, individuals of any age are eligible for the service. Clearly, the concept of intermediate care has an economic as well as quality and support dimensions.

> Intermediate care in itself is avoidance, to keep people out of hospital, look after them at home because a lot of them don't want to go into hospital. I don't think the elderly, they don't want to go in, unless it is actually dire necessity. So we try and maintain them at home, with up to four visits a day from nurses, physios etc. and Occupational Therapists, for up to two weeks and then we refer on. (Nurse)

Within the Regional Network, the development of intermediate care made a slow start. Partly, due to the reorganizations previously described, there was no prior history of coordination and collaboration between the Regional city local authority, who were leading this work and the primary care sector, the PCT, and the local acute hospital. So these activities were starting from scratch. The Clinical Director from the acute hospital was leading developments with the health care sector in an attempt to extend collaboration between the community-based and the hospital-based clinical staff and developing outreach services to support older people in the community. The leadership of the Regional Network had worked hard from its initiation (2005) to set up network structures and to develop inclusiveness within its key groups, across the varied range of stakeholders. But progress was slow and by 2008 when the fieldwork was underway, there had still been limited progress, no strategy had been agreed, and the Network members had not agreed work priorities.

> There's the beginnings of strategic work for older people...some really good things. We have ideas about what the strategy for older people should look like, we need to pay someone to write it up because I don't think anybody's got the time to do it. So there will be a shared older person's strategy in the near future and that will form the basis of the commissioning strategy, so yes, moving forwards that is quite good. (Manager, Local Authority)

At this point, three years on, the initial enthusiasm of some members of the Network had waned. There were problems with meeting attendance and continuity of membership:

> I think one of the main problems is getting the same people in the seats each time we meet because if they only come haphazardly or don't get the minutes, minutes don't actually tend very much to give the full picture, they largely are just decisions reached. You get one or two...and there are good attendee's but there are a lot of people who only come very spasmodically. (Member, PCT)

Within the Regional Network, there was a degree of acceptance that improvements to intermediate care were necessary. There was a question of the adequacy of the provision for the size of the city's population, given the relatively high levels of deprivation. There were mixed views as to whether the current provision was adequate or not. Some unsatisfactory aspects of the current arrangements related back to the original shared services between city and county that were now split:

> Since...Regional City Primary Care Trust formed in Nov. 2006, I think there was acknowledgement that intermediate and, well particularly intermediate services, weren't as good as they could be in the city. We've got patients that are in intermediate or rehabilitation care in the county, which we don't think is acceptable in the long term and we want to address that balance. (Representative, PCT)

But limited action was taken to explore the adequacy of current services. During the fieldwork, there was no evidence of data search or the use of local authority statistical services to explore current provision and perhaps compare this with comparable cities. So no one sought to build an evidence-based case for change.

A project group addressing the issue of intermediate care had existed 'in some guise' since 2003 and before the setting up of the Network. Originally, it was established to examine differences in quality between two parts of the structure. At the time of the fieldwork, an Intermediate Care Project Planning Group existed, led by the PCT and focusing on implementation and planning. This project group had members from Regional City Hospitals, from social services, and from the PCT provider teams. It envisaged seconding others including experts in Information Technology (IT) to deal with data-sharing issues. Members of the project group were represented on other Networks, including as members of the Executive Group in the Regional Network. The Project Planning Group, meeting monthly and under the review of the Executive Group, was perceived as the driving force for this development.

It was apparent, by 2008, that there was slow progress on developing services for intermediate care. There are several reasons which account for this slow pace. Firstly, there was the issue of leadership and resources and perhaps the perception of a slight partisanship in the leadership process.

> Well, the City Council govern it. We have our terms of reference and work to that. (Older People's Group Chair)

The Chair of the Executive Group was a senior manager from the local authority and was a prominent and central figure in the operation of the whole network, as well as functioning as a member of other groups. In addition to various other job responsibilities, the Chair also functioned part-time as the Network Coordinator. It is important to note the absence of an appointed network manager and that this work was additional to the Chair's normal full-time role. There was no committed administrative support either. Clearly, the lack of resources was a factor influencing the performance of the Network:

> So I feel I squeeze in what I can, on top of the day job, in terms of getting the stuff actually prepared for the Network meetings but when I see other Networks, they appear to be better organized and they have this kind of project officer whose job it is...to kind of pull that together and make sure the Network operates effectively. (Executive Group Chair/Local Authority Manager)

A further difficulty in performing the role was a need to exercise leadership without direct power. Effectiveness was therefore dependent on diplomacy and very good interpersonal skills, linked to the ability to persuade:

> So I have no...leadership, no responsibility, if you like, for making sure that things are done within the PCT, other than trying to get them to work in partnership with me. I can't direct somebody to do something, not likewise with all of the other organisations. (Chair, Local Authority Manager)

Network members broadly agreed that the Executive Group Chair was effective in their role:

> ...an excellent chair and very sort of driven and knows where he is going, I think sometimes the participation of others in the meeting aren't necessarily there. It's

not the chair's fault, [Name] is good and very ambitious to an end but sometimes I think it's tough to do that. (Manager, NHS Hospital)

[Name] is the lynch pin. (Manager, Local Authority)

Despite this apparently effective part-time leadership, the Chair faced some daunting issues. In particular, as a local authority manager he did not have the perceived credibility with professionals to 'carry' difficult decisions.

... there's definitely a professional, a huge professional discipline that's called management, managerialism, strategic management, and a group of people of which I'm a kind of a usurping member, a group of people believe that they have consensus and I think that they understand needs in a similar way. We formulate understandings of the situations that we're faced with and share, so that kind of works. When trying to take those understandings and formulate actions and then implement them more broadly amongst the mainstream of proper work in the organizations, social work, nursing etc., then you certainly do get really quite glaring differences in organizational culture and approach. That can thwart developments, yes. And within the Regional Network, there are definite huge power anomalies and relationships of power. (Manager, Local Authority)

This interviewee stated that clinical medicine 'definitely considers itself to be of a higher status and is more powerful'.

Alongside the Chair of the Executive Group there were other key players, such as the local elected councillor (an interesting but rare example in our study of politically based leadership) who chaired the Older People's Group and the Clinical Director from the NHS acute trust. But there was no shared leadership arrangement agreed within the Network.

Secondly, and associated with the issue of credible leadership, the Network had not developed agreed processes of decision making and/or conflict resolution.

I suppose, I guess the not having the strategy and this hiatus that hasn't really enabled us to kind of really pin our activity onto something tangible. It's been a bit haphazard and a bit issues-based. (Manager, Local Authority)

Initial work had focused on relationship-building and information-sharing. Various respondents spoke of 'cascading' information and cross-germination. The cascade effect was viewed by some interviewees as representing a practical way of filtering and disseminating information, both vertically and horizontally across the complex organizational structures.

... on my project team I've got people from [Hospital Group], for example, and I've got people from social services and I've got people from our provider team. So I assume they will have had an involvement in other Networks and Groups. (Assistant Director, City PCT)

Communication and other processes within the Network made only limited use of IT. Paper, telephone and e-mail were all important in disseminating policies or practice development, as was face-to-face networking.

Thirdly, the NSF for Older People set out some broad generic targets but did not specify processes for their achievement or timescales.

> In a much longer time, we still struggled to develop intermediate care services because there hasn't been any kind of national legislation. We've got a generic legislation regarding the National Service Framework and care in the community, but they're not specific enough in a directorate. I think national legislation ultimately focuses people's minds, it gives managers a structure to work within, it gives the person campaigning for change a business case and that's basically [why] I think it's vital to have the national legislation. (Doctor)

So, in 2008, developments within the Intermediate Care Project Planning Group appeared to be at an early stage:

> So we're in the process of producing a project initiation document, like a brief, and we've got structures in place. We've got terms of reference and then we've got a link back to the Health Unity Group, although we've not formally sent anything through to them yet because it's fairly early stages. (PCT Representative)

A pathway plan had been formulated and agreed. Some members of the two core groups were part of the project group (although intermediate care does not relate exclusively to older people). Money has been committed by the city council and the health care provider organizations. These organizations stated that the development of intermediate care in the city was a priority, but delays were still being caused by organizational difficulties as outlined by one respondent:

> So, for example, the agreement to do a capital development for intermediate care, which we've, you know, the council's just agreed £3.5 million capital money to develop an intermediate care site, alongside the commitment of some resources that were already being held by the PCT and held by ourselves.... Much of the difficulty, well I suppose the things that have had an impact on how fast things have moved have been around individuals' capacity and people having been in the right, been in the job, so they're actually having the post filled or the right person identified or that person having the capacity to do what is necessary. So it's as much about people and time as it is about money to buy things. (Manager, Local Authority)

The project manager was anticipating substantial development within six months:

> If we don't do it this year, then it will have to wait to go into the investment round for next year. But certainly within the next six months I would hope to be very clear about where we're going. (Representative, PCT)

However, the Project Planning Group had not reported by the end of the fieldwork for this research.

End of life care

Our second 'tracer' issue was 'end of life care', also one of the specialist areas of care in the NSF. Here the local picture of progress was bleak.

A senior member of the Executive Group was involved with other major groups addressing 'end of life care'. These include a combined city and county group. The provision of services and anticipated developments had been outlined and there was speculation about how services might develop, given what were, at that stage, possible changes in the NHS commissioning function:

> Practice-based commissioning will definitely want to stop people coming in simply to die, it will place an emphasis on identifying people who are in the last few days, weeks, months, however you like to define the last period of someone's life and create a system, which actually supports them at home and so on. We've already got a private project funded by the Department of Health. (Doctor)

The role of the Regional Network was not specifically emphasized in relation to these developments although the Network provided a platform to share information with colleagues from health and local authority services.

A specific development which formed part of the new guidelines from the DoH on end of life care was the setting up of 'living wills' and this project was in the pipeline:

> We have some work involved in living wills. Living wills, the work that's gone on around that has been more outside of Regional City Hospitals Trust than inside and not therefore my kind of view particularly, but yes, there are pockets of living will work. (Doctor)

Other groups that focus on end of life issues and were active within the county, but not the city, were mentioned by one interviewee. Respondents were sceptical about progress:

> I imagine that they link into the cancer network, the Liverpool end of life care pathway that we have adopted within Regional City Hospitals Trust and that is rolled out within the county and forms part of that, but I know that there's a greater Gold Standard framework in primary care that links in early to that process for it. I just wonder how it is coordinated because what I hear about it, there's patchy elements of opaque, of response to it in primary care and there doesn't seem, there seems a lack of coordination. So I would imagine probably there isn't a network or if it is, it's not visible, it's not delivering what it should be. (Manager, Hospital)

This manager uses the word 'imagine', expressing lack of actual knowledge in relation to end of life care. Similarly, the manager quoted below was not confident of progress:

> To my knowledge, not hugely, but that's not to say that it hasn't. I can't say, you know, with confidence there's been work in any way comparable to what's gone on in the county, for example, as far as the end of life stuff is concerned. (Manager, Local Authority)

A private care home manager reported very limited involvement with end of life care plans from the city:

> We did have one lady that had a will, like a living will, who came from Regional City Hospital. Now that was discussed with me before she came in, was discussed at nurse level as in the hospital discharge nurse and my team here and also district nursing lead within the area. The GPs were informed about that before she was transferred to us. (Home Manager)

To summarize, our analysis was that the Regional Network had, to date, primarily provided a platform for discussion and the exchange of information, but no action on end of life care.

In conclusion

So this case demonstrates a highly complex network, which is cross-sectoral as well as cross-organizational and cross-professional. Management faced daunting issues in terms of differences of views across a range of professionals, with divergent incentives for action across the public and the private sectors. The management resources committed to the Network leadership were extremely limited. Moreover they were all located in the local authority. As a result, slow progress was made in developing intermediate care and there was very limited attention paid to end of life care. It was proving difficult to translate the burst of policymaking activity nationally into jointly agreed action at ground level.

Case Study 2—Metropolitan Older People's Network

Network site

In contrast to the Regional Network, the Metropolitan Network was an organic network, focusing entirely on 'end of life care'. So this was an informal, clinically led, inter-organizational network. The Network was situated in a mixed area of 'Metropolitan City' containing a diverse ethnic population and some deprivation. Most residents' care in the homes under study was funded by local authorities.

The constitution of the Network: History and membership

This is a smaller and simpler network, with all the member organizations within healthcare. The organizations involved in the Network included: the local PCT which was involved in running an NHS Hospice; an NHS General Practitioner (GP) Practice run by four GP partners, which was contracted to provide care to two care homes; Big Home, which was a nursing home run by a housing trust that had operated on a 'not for profit' basis since it opened in 2003; and New Home which was a residential and nursing care home, opened in 2008. It was funded as a private finance initiative by the local authority, replacing what was described as a 'crap' or 'nightmare' local authority-run care home.

The intermediate tier of NHS management (the Strategic Health Authority (SHA)) funded a local pilot project to promote higher-quality end of life care. Of the two nursing homes within the Network, Big Home with 125 beds had been established longer, whilst New Home was still establishing its procedures and protocols when fieldwork was undertaken (2008–2009).

The narrative of end of life care in the Metropolitan Network

With funding awarded by the SHA, the project was led by a Lead Coordinator, a former palliative nurse, seconded for two years (and working for the PCT). She was supported by another palliative nurse, who worked in the Hospice, and had recently been appointed as the Coordinator to lead the project.

So this network was enabled to start work with some specific objectives:

- To educate/reeducate staff in the care homes and GP practice on end of life care;
- To reduce inappropriate admissions to hospital when patients were dying:

  It is about reducing people's inappropriate admissions to hospital...that's one of the core things that they measure...the perception is, from listening to some of the GPs talk, that the system is geared towards, there's no disincentive not to admit people to hospital. (Lead Coordinator)

- To develop a Register of Palliative Care;
- To develop the work practice of living wills.

The first aspect of the project involved getting people within the Network talking about end of life, educating them, and normalizing the dying process:

  When I first started, end of life care was just a kind of nebulous thing, the [Lead Coordinator] role has been there to get interested parties together, get people talking about end of life...Gold Standard is very much about empowering care homes from within, it's not from without. (Lead end of life care Coordinator)

> We have educated and really taught the nurses with regards to end of life and the fact that it's not wrong to die in a nursing home because nurses do panic when a patient...[is] deteriorating and clearly they are dying and they quite often call for an ambulance if it's out of hours, because they feel if they don't do something, they've been a failure. (GP)

> Nurses going to work in care homes just want to do basic nursing, I've seen nurses absolutely petrified about palliative care. (Palliative Nurse)

The two end of life care Co ordinators led this work:

> I hugely believe in spreading the word of palliative care...the Liverpool care pathway and the Gold Standard Framework....(End of life care Coordinator/Palliative Nurse)

Within the core settings, there were some other important figures involved. Within Big Home, the Nurse Clinical Director was the key person involved in end of life care—she was praised as highly effective by most interviewees. A Patient Liaison Coordinator responsible for updating the end of life care register on a weekly basis supported her. Within New Home, both the Home Manager, who was praised as a good manager and a newly appointed Nurse Clinical Director were key to the Network and both were thinking about rolling out the end of life care standards. Then among the general practitioners, there was the General Practice lead for end of life care and care homes, a GP who chaired the PCT professional committee and a GP leading the end of life care audit project.

To address their concerns, all staff in New Home (including cleaners and those in the kitchens) watched an educational film about end of life care and attended a talk by the Lead Coordinator, with the aim of making staff more confident when dealing with the dying. In addition, nurses who 'are in the job of curing rather than dying' (Nurse Clinical Director, Big Home) went on a three-day course.

Families were included in the project too as relatives were often uncomfortable or in denial about the death, so a second strand to the project was to 'prepare the patient and family early for death' (Nurse Clinical Director, Big Home).

As a GP commented:

> residents are often very, very sick...a lot of times the family are not really on board in terms of knowing that it's really close to the end.

Similarly a nurse in New Home commented

> Patients and relatives sometimes don't want to discuss death, others do.

A third strand of the work involved inclusive planning for death. In both homes, there was a form to be completed about making arrangements for death and dying, but staff often avoided completing it. So in Big Home completing the death and dying form was made mandatory;

> [mandating completion of] the death and dying form is very useful...it forces you to have that conversation. (Patient Liaison Coordinator, Big Home)

> I used to be afraid to ask it. And when I do ask them they [patient and relatives] said they don't wish to talk about it...but we explain it is part of the procedure, we have to do that because someone can die tomorrow. (Senior Carer, New Home)

Sometimes problems with such 'prognostic coding' produced clashes between GPs and home nurses over the condition of patients:

> there is often a clash...the nurses could come to me to say, we really think this lady with dementia is dying, she's deteriorating but the GP says, she's got dementia, she's not deteriorating. (Lead end of life care Coordinator)

The Lead Coordinator suggested that nurses were learning to influence how GPs made end of life care decisions:

> nurses...learn how to play the game...there is stuff written on the nurse/doctor game isn't there...who really makes the decision? Is it the person who thinks they make the decision or perhaps they've been guided into making that decision by somebody else?...senior nurses...shape the decision in terms of how that information is put forward or put in a subtle suggestion and get a decision that's from the doctor.

The end of life care project appeared to have improved the way decisions about end of life were taken.

Although relations appeared good between the care homes, the general practice, and the hospice, the Network's links with wider organizations less centrally involved in end of life care were more problematic. Agency nursing staff, working at weekends and at night, felt 'vulnerable' when dealing with dying patients. As a consequence they were 'bouncing' people into hospital unnecessarily, often 'because relatives didn't understand a patient is dying' (GP).

> ...in the evenings and weekends, often there's not regular staff on, there's agency staff or night staff, there's the out of hours service and sometimes that's where things fall apart a little bit. (GP)

The handover of dying patients from the hospital to care homes could be problematic. The Nurse Clinical Director at Big Home commented that hospital consultants often failed to tell patients who were discharged from hospital that they were dying:

> the biggest problem...when the patient is discharged and comes to us, the hospital is not able to do anything further...they need someone like a consultant...to

sit and explain that this person is dying instead of leaving it for the nursing homes to explain that.

However, palliative nurses in the end of life care project developed sounder relationships between healthcare and social services:

> People have never traditionally commissioned for end of life care...the commissioners for the social services side have been very open with me and very receptive and that's helped me develop links...The social workers, I've done lots of teaching with social workers, again all very, very interested and they are very key people, continuing care is incredibly key. (Lead Coordinator)

So the end of life care Co ordinators focused on building relationships within their network and with those professionals in close alliance with their work, such as social workers. But we found limited evidence that they developed their external relationships with SHA and more pertinently with the local authority. Since the project was funded for a time-limited period of two years, any resources required to sustain or develop this work would come from the 'lead' organization for Older People's Care, namely the local authority.

An interesting, specific, feature of the case were the high levels of ethnic diversity of the staff within the Network, in particular in the care homes:

> We have a lot of African, Nigerian staff...residents can be racist...[but] if it wasn't for these people coming into the country, nobody would be looking after the old people...maybe eight out of 70 people [staff in New Home] who actually come from Britain, who were born here. (New Home Manager)

As part of the end of life care pilot, palliative nurses trained overseas staff about appropriate ways to deal with death and dying in the UK:

> Certain places in Africa, nurses, I think culturally if someone is dying or has died you don't speak to the relative initially and that did happen here and then relatives...got a bit upset...So a lot of communication has been done about that. (Palliative Nurse)

> I think it's a cultural thing and a lot of Nigerian staff are really, really emotional. I had to actually speak to them about the way they were behaving when a resident died, like weeping in front of all the other residents. (Care Home Manager)

Another unusual and unexpected feature of the case was that many staff interviewed, particularly staff from overseas in care homes, spoke about Christianity as an important part of their identity:

> I'm a God-fearing lady, I am a born-again Christian...staff, the majority are Christians. (Nurse)

The final major development relating to end of life care was a register of palliative patients, between care homes and general practices, which contained a list of patients who staff 'would not be surprised if they died in the next six months' (GP).

In Big Home, the register was updated on a weekly basis, with nurses making a judgement about how ill residents were and coding them A–D accordingly. The register was shared with the general practice. Some staff in Big Home had found moving towards prognostically diagnosing these patients challenging:

> How do you...prognostically code your care home?...It's about getting their thinking processes around, do they think this person has days to live, weeks to live or months to live...Training them also to be aware of prognostic things but also it's ok for them to use their gut feelings, their intuition, their nursing instincts or whatever. GPs might not think that was appropriate...that's such a big issue identifying when people are dying...from a GP's perspective there's lots of fear around litigation and Shipman, if I don't send someone in [to Hospital], am I going to get complaints?...It's a big ask of care home staff. (Lead Coordinator)

Within the project, we traced various new developments occurring around end of life care. These developments were evidence-based on the most up-to-date guidelines (and indeed, foresaw the NICE guidelines). Persuasion was based on these principles of Evidence-Based Medicine (EBM) and the desire to achieve high standards of quality. Most staff such as New Home's Clinical Director described the Liverpool Care Pathway/Gold Standard Framework as 'brilliant guidelines...because it forces that conversation'.

We see a pattern here of passionate and respected hybrid clinicians (such as the end of life care Coordinators) involved in the implementation of national policy (legitimately developed by respected clinicians), softly persuading people to adopt new standards of best practice:

> The national [Liverpool Care Pathway] programme is led by...a GP and the care home project by...a district nurse. So it is very primary care led, which is good, although they clearly do have very strong links with specialist palliative care...It's not about dying...it's about living well and at the end of that process you will die...hopefully you will die well. (Lead Coordinator)

The two core Coordinators were backed by a large and diverse, active group of people, committed to end of life care. The Lead Coordinator commented on the distributed nature of good leadership within Networks:

> Good people...make a difference and it isn't all about money...people working towards a common goal.

Several problems persisted. Here there was little evidence of Information Communication Technologies (ICTs) contributing towards the functioning of the Network. Big Home had been faxing information to the General Practice, more recently e-mailing information because faxes were getting lost.

> We're not able to have a system over there, that's a real pain because...you go there, they fax us who they want to see, we print out reams of paper, take it with us, then we have to write in their notes, then we have to come back and write in our notes on the computer, it takes hours. And we can't get a way round it...there's no, we can't have a system over there because...they only need access to their patients, they don't need access to the rest of our patients...the PCT won't fund it either, so that's a second problem. (GP)

> We don't have an IT system in the home which is a constant bugbear. (Clinical Director, New Home)

Interviewees also perceived issues of competition, which impeded sharing and networking. The manager of New Home believed that Big Home saw New Home as competition, not only for residents but also for staff, particularly as New Home had 'nicked virtually all their [Big Home] staff' when it opened. So relations between the two homes were distant, and Big Home was unlikely to directly share what it had learned about end of life care with New Home. Learning was channelled between the homes through GPs and the Hospice and knowledge about end of life care was transferred by individuals moving between care homes:

> Before I came here I was working for [a national private health care provider]...I have worked in different places...before [that] we were using the Gold Standard one and then when I joined [national private health care provider] we were using the Liverpool [care pathway]...I bring that. (Clinical Director, New Home)

This case study is of a local and organic network, smaller in scale than the Regional Network. We saw it as effectively developing improvements in end of life care, achieved through an active and passionate group of professionals working to an evidence base. The danger is that these positive developments may not be sustained without continuing project leadership, or remain as a small-scale project which does not spread.

Concluding discussion

These two cases raise some interesting comparative points, both when contrasted to other Networks and within the pair. To begin our concluding discussion, it would be tempting to dismiss the failings of these Networks as merely due to a shortage of financial and/or personnel resources, but this would be a partial analysis. There are some significant features which differentiate these cases from our other Networks.

Firstly, we see a high degree of inter-sectoral and inter-organizational complexity, exacerbated by the many professions in each network. These Networks contain organizations which are public sector, voluntary, or charitable organizations and significantly sized private sector organizations, all of whom operate with differing incentives and priorities. The Regional Network, in particular, engages across public sector agencies (health and local authorities), voluntary and charitable sectors, and the private sector, (though the views of the latter were largely excluded). This strong inter-sectoral basis contributes to the 'wicked problem' of collaboration.

These inter-organizational differences also exist in the cognitive and intellectual arenas. There is no common shared knowledge base between health, social care, and general management (especially in the private sector). Compared with the cancer cases, there is no common currency, no accepted knowledge, as the evidence base for decisions and developments. This presents enormous issues in building collaboration and shared action. In particular, the credibility of the senior managers in the Regional Network was fragile. They faced a credibility challenge from the medical professions, exacerbated by perceived issues of status and power. Unlike the directors of the cancer networks, they could not use their personal and professional knowledge base for credibility but had to build and 'earn' this credibility over a longer period.

These problems are compounded by the diffuse quality standards in the NSF for Older People. Whereas the national standards for cancer care specify unequivocal targets and processes, this is not the case in the Framework for Older People. So it is essentially more difficult to focus and prioritize managerial actions by using Framework standards. As a result, we observe that in the Regional Network, the leadership is not able to invoke the authority of the national standards to urge agreement, collaboration, and action. Thus the Network tends to flounder and experience difficulty in selecting priority tasks on which to commence work. In the smaller Metropolitan Network, this was less of an issue since the Network was set up to focus on end of life care only. In this specific area, there were useful concrete guidelines and the Network members selected specific and factual components of the guidelines for end of life care upon which to work.

Next, these two Networks operate in an arena which has a low political profile but also large resource and financial needs. Despite the urgent societal need to improve the care of older people, unlike cancer care this topic has still not risen to the top of the political agenda. Historically, the older people's care issue has not had the support of powerful pressure groups, unlike cancer care. There is an embryonic alliance between strengthened advocacy groups (since the merger of Age Concern and Help the Aged into Age UK) and middle-class families horrified at the costs of residential and nursing home care for their relatives, which may change the political agenda. Will this policy arena hit a crisis before (expensive and complex) policy changes can be agreed and enacted at local as well as national level?

In terms of our analytic framework around Foucauldian governmentality, the Older People's Networks represent interesting examples of partial or incomplete transition. Some core elements of a possible macro shift to governmentality are in place, but there is limited evidence of a shift in micro practices. This is accounted for in several ways. Government, through the DoH and NICE, as an 'arms length' agency, have set quality standards for the care of older people. But these standards are deficient as a steering mechanism for two reasons. Firstly, as the geriatric specialty is under-researched, the care of older people is less susceptible to the dominant paradigm of the RCT, and also because many older people have multiple conditions. So in this field, the conventionally defined evidence base is weak. Secondly, there is no distinct professional group who are charged with implementing the standards; rather the 'professionals' are a mixed group of clinical professionals, social workers, and general managers. Each profession has differing views on the available evidence and there has been little prior history of sharing either evidence or practice. With a weak knowledge base and diffused leadership and power, the power/knowledge nexus is disconnected. The smaller-scale end of life care network was less affected, having a more established evidence base accepted by the Network's largely clinical membership. These conditions are substantially different from those in the cancer networks.

In the Regional Network, there was the opportunity for shared or collective leadership between the managers in the local authority and the Clinical Director in health care and this could have led to more effective progress. Prior research suggests that in health care organizations (Denis et al, 2001) and in other networks (Ferlie et al, 2011a) collective strategic leadership may operate effectively in such complex, professionalized settings.

The issues relating to the power/knowledge nexus are compounded by the lack of technology to manage across the organizations within the Networks and to communicate accountability upwards. Both Older People's Networks demonstrate poor ICT systems. The members of the end of life care networks complained about the difficulties of communication, but were at least improving their recording of standardized data. In the Regional Network, there was no evidence over the study period of developing a basic database on care provision and standards, making it difficult to judge if improvements were being made. Nor do the respondents note or complain of the poor use of ICT for inter-organizational communication. This is strange in this context, since within months of the fieldwork finishing the Estates Department of the local authority, with government incentives, implemented remote monitoring of falls by older people in their own homes.

Finally, partially as a result of the disconnect between those in power and the accepted knowledge base *and* the lack of underpinning communication technologies, there was only limited evidence in these cases of shared learning and exchange (despite this being clearly needed!). In the Regional Network, respondents frequently acknowledged the need for sharing and working together, recognizing differences of perspective, knowledge, and organizational cultures. But in reality, shared learning only occurred regularly in the Older People's Group. With the exception of the Older People's Champions, there were no fora for staff from health care, social work, and the residential and nursing homes to discuss care standards and concerns. Within the end of life care network, the situation was more positive. There were individuals in 'bridging' roles who regularly carried information across the organizational boundaries and mitigated the competition (and suspicion?) between Big Home and New Home. There were workshops and training events organized by the Lead Coordinator and others. But the sharing did not extend outwards or crucially, upwards to the PCT.

We now proceed with some comparative reflections between these cases, which further explain their different trajectories. Significantly, in the Regional Network, there was no prior history of cooperation or established understanding between the various stakeholders upon which to build. In the Metropolitan Network, there were basic Cooperative relationships prior to the inception of the Network. Thus, the end of life care coordinator could build relationships and engage with professional staff. In the Regional Network, the Executive Group saw their first tasks structurally, designing inclusive structures and establishing fora for sharing ideas.

One difference between the Regional and Metropolitan Networks was that the Regional Network was a mandated and 'top-down' Network, led by a general manager, whilst the Metropolitan one was more organic and 'bottom-up', driven by two hybrid professional project leaders. Clearly, there were substantial differences of scale between the two networks. Whilst the Metropolitan Network had a strong core of likeminded health care professionals, the core group in the Regional Network was more diffuse.

So the characteristics of the leadership group itself were different between the two Networks. Furthermore the engagement and leadership processes in the two Networks varied. In the Regional Network, there was a clear initial plan to build an 'inclusive' network and attention paid to enabling all stakeholders to contribute to the strategy. This resulted in much discussion of options, but a waning in enthusiasm when no immediate action resulted. In the Metropolitan Network, the engagement was professionally focused, which led to early engagement on tasks, but at the expense of building Networks with potential longer-term commissioners.

Decision-making processes in the two Networks differed. In the Regional Network, a well-intentioned and well-respected general manager in the local authority largely led the Network individually. Even when apparent that a single leader did not have the resources to drive forward the substantial agenda, they did not shift towards joint leadership. In the Regional Network, there was no evidence of distributed leadership to enable the implementation and delivery of changes once tasks were agreed. In the Metropolitan Network, by contrast, we see a shared—if not collective leadership—process between the two end of life care Coordinators, supported by distributed leadership via active clinicians across a range of palliative care nurses, general practice, general nursing staff, and key senior managers.

Finally, we note that in both Networks strategic intent and operational implementation were poorly linked. In the Regional Network, implementation had not been adequately considered in terms of the resources, commitment, and skills required; whilst in the Metropolitan Network the project managers did not sufficiently consider the upwards link to future sustainability and the spread of the improvements achieved locally.

Having presented our case study data across the four pairs of Networks, we now move to a more thematic set of chapters. We explore (in turn) the role of leadership processes and the extent of inter-organizational learning across these eight cases.

8

The limited role of Information and Communication Technologies in managed networks

ICTs in the NHS—a brief history

Initially, investment in new Information and Communication Technologies (ICTs) in the National Health Service (NHS) had been concentrated on devising systems for management and administration, and it was not until 1992 that a broader view was taken with the development of a strategy which included clinically relevant information (Leaning, 1993). The goal was 'better health for the nation' to be achieved by 'supporting care and communication through IM&T'. (DoH, 1992). However, although several fundamental steps were achieved, including creating an NHS-wide data network and issuing a unique identity number to every patient, by the mid-1990s progress had stalled (Cross, 2006). The new Labour Government of 1997 issued a revised ICT strategy document (DoH, 1998b) with the aim of providing 'accurate and reliable data to support: local clinical governance; National Service Frameworks, local care pathways and clinical protocols; Health Improvement Programmes and the National Framework for Assessing Performance'. It also aimed to provide 'every NHS professional with on-line access to the latest local guidance and national evidence on treatment, and the information they need to evaluate the effectiveness of their work and to support their professional development'. This ambitious programme was given greater impetus in 2002 when the Wanless review of NHS Finance recommended that the NHS double to 4 per cent the proportion of its budget invested in information technology (Cross, 2006).

ICTs and networks—the vision

As we highlighted in the earlier literature review, there has been considerable interest in the potential of new ICTs in moving organizations towards network forms and in transforming the way in which networks function and are governed. Some have argued the use of ICTs may move us closer to Foucault's vision of governance through electronic Panopticons (Foucault, 1977; Zuboff, 1984). The many difficulties which may be encountered in sharing knowledge across agency boundaries (Currie and Suhomlinova, 2006) could be partially alleviated by strongly developed public sector networks using effective cross-organizational ICTs and databases to share information. New ICTs (e.g. desktop computers, e-mail, the web, electronic databases, and templates) are potentially available to support network-based forms of working but it is an open question whether these radical new technologies will be adopted. Some streams within the knowledge mobilization literature suggest cooperative networks are an organizational form better able to diffuse knowledge than either markets or hierarchies (Ferlie et al, 2010). We argue that the ability to share electronic information easily across agency boundaries and the development of shared and locally meaningful databases will underpin any substantial move from stand-alone agencies to a functioning network. More ambitious networks might go on to develop a network-wide knowledge management strategy.

However, despite massive extra funding, the last decade of the NHS ICT programme has not yet delivered the seamless system envisaged. As we shall see, many of our network cases reported difficulties with computerized data collection and information systems and Greenhalgh et al (2010) found that large scale, centrally driven models for innovation in healthcare Information Technology (IT) systems are associated with multiple competing perspectives, complex interdependencies, inherent tensions, and high implementation workloads. Indeed, it has been suggested (Raymond, 2012) that greater collaboration between government, industry, and clinicians to create an evolving set of standards and promote dialogue across sectors is required. Thus, paradoxically, the technology required to support and maintain networks may itself need to be supported and maintained by them.

While we focus on NHS-mandated and -managed networks, it is important not to ignore the existence of informal, or what Braithwaite et al (2009) term 'natural', networks. These may be either pre-existing or form concurrently with (possibly stimulated by) a formally constituted network. New ICTs are often just as, if not more, important in developing and sustaining such networks, with e-mails, websites, and blogs providing platforms for large groups of people to interact. Such informal networks 'exert powerful and pervasive influences on how systems actually perform and function' (Braithwaite et al, 2009), so we need to consider their 'behind the scenes' role in shaping the performance and output of formal structures and systems.

Webster's (2006) review of the organizational literature on the impact of new ICTs on work practices notes various authors and contested positions. Castells (1996) sees new ICTs acting as a radical technological driver which actively constitutes network-based forms within a new epoch of informational capitalism. Complex network-based firms would be impossible to manage without powerful computer networks which store, process, and transmit information. Similar arguments may well apply to the public sector partnership-based forms suggested by the network governance reform narrative. While Castells (1996) does not specifically analyse the dynamics of e-government, Margetts (2005) suggests that the new ICTs may 'hollow out' traditional middle management, creating virtual networks of inter-organizational relationships within e-government. Dunleavy et al (2006) argue that the effects of ICTs on public organizations have been understudied. They suggest that one scenario is that public agencies move into a brave new post-New Public Management (NPM) world of 'digital era governance', where 'many agencies become their websites' (although they studied social security and taxation agencies which deliver more bounded services than in health care).

However, in looking at new ICTs we should not to get too focused on the *how* of communication, which is arguably less important than the *why*, the reasons behind its use, and the *what*, the quality of the data transmitted. As far as the *why* is concerned, authors are divided in their assessment of the motivations behind introducing new ICTs, with optimists pointing to their potential role in enhancing local democracy and interactive policymaking (Snellen, 2005). Examples include processes of electronic consultation and dialogue on agenda setting, determining priorities and drafting proposals, as well as feedback on implementation which could all help build the co-production needed to tackle 'wicked problems'. From a more bottom-up perspective, user-driven e-based groups and chat rooms could build a critical voice amongst citizens against a purely top-down government agenda.

By contrast, pessimists see new ICTs as contributing to a 'Surveillance State' which builds up sophisticated electronic databases on its citizens (Webster, 2006), tracking and storing e-mails, routinely monitoring online activity, and merging databases across agency boundaries for security purposes. Data on aspects of social life—especially among deviant or problematic sub-groups— may be recorded on an ever-escalating number of registers or risk management systems, then stored and if need be transmitted electronically. This is a dystopia of state-directed electronic surveillance with the new ICTs acting to 'delocalise' information (Miller and Rose, 2008) previously physically stored in localized written records.

These arguments about the purpose and usage of information, important as they are, only tell part of the story. We need also to ask questions about, and critically examine, *what* is being communicated. Of paramount importance here are the hoary old issues of reliability and validity of data. However efficient communications are, or could become, they are at best useless and at worst harmful if the information they contain (a) is not accurate and (b) does not appropriately reflect the reality it purports to illustrate. Thus Pronovost et al (2011), reviewing a major study of an organizational intervention by the NHS to promote patient safety (Benning et al, 2011a, 2011b), point out that some clinicians resisted the interventions on the grounds that they were using weak evidence and measures the doctors considered were invalid; a recent report into child protection issues (Cm 8062, 2011) criticises a new computerized system for recording information on the grounds that it 'does not support professional judgment and often inhibits efficient working'; and former government ministers talk about ending 'bean-counting' (Kenneth Clarke, reported in the Guardian, 27 July 2011). On the other hand, although the 'tick-box culture' (not invented for, but made simpler to utilise by ICTs) has become a pejorative term, it is important to remember that valid and reliable computerized information underpins safety measures such as pre-flight and pre-operation check lists as well as facilitating comparative data for statistical purposes, without which it would be difficult to govern complex organizations and societies.

Of course, however ubiquitous, new ICTs may play a minor role in practice. Zuboff (1984) suggests that new technologies in 'informating organisations' may interact with existing organizational forms, so that partial change is as likely as ICT-driven organizational transformation. We therefore looked at some 'old' communication technologies, such as written material, telephones, and faxes, and the extent to which they were still used within the networks studied alongside e-mail, the Internet, and the world wide web. So we probably lean towards the body of scholarship identified by Webster (2006), which sees ICTs more as 'informatisation', a continuation and enhancement of established systems of communication, rather than as something completely different from what has gone before which could usher in an 'information society' with radically different ways of working.

Evidence from the cases

We now consider how information and communication technologies impacted in our network cases. Our assessment of the overall picture across the cases is summarized in Table 8.1.

Examining this picture in more detail, we will firstly look at respondents' views of the technical aspects of the electronic systems in use for collecting

Table 8.1. The role of ICTs and databases across the networks

Network	Role of ICTs	Database Issues	Commentary
Genetics Translation Network 1	Limited—NHS and University systems remain incompatible.	None.	New forms of virtual and template-based reporting upwards; not actively used.
Genetics Translation Network 2	ICTs not a major theme.	None.	As above.
County Cancer Network	Slow development of teleconference-based Multidisciplinary Team meetings. Good website.	Proactive work on local audit.	Management Team used local data to achieve local service changes in line with Cancer Plan/IOGs.
Urban Cancer Network	Minimal use of novel ICTs. Good website.	Proactive local audit; good data storage and accessibility.	Information seen as a source of expert advice which adds value to the network.
Metropolitan City Sexual Health Network	Cross-hospital IT systems slowly emerge; 'joined up auditable data'; Dated website.	Inaccurate and misleading national GUM databases; issues of confidentiality.	
Cathedral City Sexual Health Network	Future plans to develop a learning platform at school level.	Inaccurate and misleading national GUM databases; issues of confidentiality; useful local data on teenage pregnancy rates.	
Regional Older People's Network	Major IT problems with Single Assessment Process; inter-organizational barriers; duplication of notes.	None.	Failure of inter-agency ICTs a major block.
Metropolitan Older People's Network	Primitive and incompatible IT systems across the agencies; duplication of notes.	New register on end of life care but filled in manually.	Failure of cross-organizational IT systems.

and sharing data and then at the influence of ICTs on two key themes: governance and organizational learning, as discussed in previous chapters. The case material varied considerably in the extent to which ICTs emerged as a significant theme, dependent in part on the tracer issues selected. Hence in the genetics networks, where tracer issues focused on the success or otherwise of specific workpackages (Genetics Translation Network 1 (GTN1)) and developing public health genomics, ICTs were not particularly prominent, whereas in the sexual health cases two tracers demonstrated important aspects of how ICTs may affect network performance.

Technical systems and their use in the networks

As suggested earlier, the concept of managed networks as a system for delivering integrated health care across professional and agency boundaries placed considerable reliance on the ability of new ICTs to facilitate the flow of information between themselves and between the networks and central government. For this concept to be translated into practice accurate and reliable clinical and statistical information needed to be available and useable. The reality for most of our case study networks was rather different.

All case study sites delivered statistical information to central collection points to allow monitoring of progress against agreed standards and targets, or to provide 'evidence for inspections', and the technical systems set up to do this on an annual basis worked reasonably well in most cases.

> We do annual returns that feed into the Department of Health publications. So you can compare yourself nationally against all your outcomes and your outcome data, so that would all go back in centrally, yes. They do regular audit returns on that.

While the requirement for annual returns was generally accepted as standard practice, the GTN, perhaps because there was a perceived need to justify the expenditure of large sums of money on this new initiative, were asked to report back on a three monthly basis. This 'box-ticking exercise' was seen as unnecessary and was widely resented by those involved.

However, taking the example of annual returns, the length of time between collection and publication of such information clearly limited its usefulness as feedback. For instance, respondents commented that National Cancer Registry Data were not particularly valuable as they were 'three years out of date'. A similar time lag in the publication of nationally collected statistics on teenage pregnancy rates led to misinterpretation and overreaction in our Cathedral City Sexual Health Network (see Chapter 6) when data appeared to show little progress, and a ministerial reprimand followed. Another instance from the same case illustrated both difficulties which may occur in marrying up technical systems and the pitfalls possible if percentage data is accepted uncritically. Here the Genito-Urinary Medicine (GUM) department apparently failed to meet the 48-hour target.

> GUM failed to meet their 100 per cent appointments offered in 48 hours reporting in April, simply because they'd upgraded their software system in April and

there was a problem with it. So in fact they had offered 100 per cent but the data looked as if it was 95 per cent and it was the assessment month, the healthcare assessment, so, you know, really terrible. The SHA have been crawling all over us.... [The Primary Care Trust (PCT) has] just served an improvement notice on the Trust as a result of them not achieving that target and... [there have been] discussions with the General Manager about what happened.

The fact that this apparently large percentage failure, even if accurate, related in this small department to only a single patient did not make any difference to the magnitude of the reaction.

One patient out makes above point 8 per cent of... [the figures] and then all hell lets loose... You know, a difference of point 8 per cent. Its only one patient, and... [that can involve] days and days and days trying to back track and see where the errors were... [Department of Health] staff can't understand why,... just for one patient it causes... 'we'll get fined!' and all this goes on and then it goes to the Strategic Health Authority.... 'why has this happened, what's going on here'.

Setting aside problems with local/national audits, networks reported that the availability of clinical and practice data at local level was a persistent problem. Lacking an integrated national system to enable clinicians to share patient data, many hospital trusts attempted to establish their own IT systems with very mixed success. Problems with sharing information were particularly evident in the sexual health cases, where GUM clinics had traditionally been particularly resistant to computerization, maintaining paper filing systems long after other specialties had transferred to electronic record keeping. A respondent from our Cathedral City Sexual Health Network remembered:

The main thing that would always get in the way, in terms of sharing information, was this whole issue about information from a service like DOSH [the Department of Sexual Health Medicine]... there's so many rules and regulations about how or how not information can or cannot be shared... and there was often a perception of, 'we can't, we can't and the legislation says we can't'. And... [sometimes it might be found] that you could do more than perhaps was thought, but overall... it still felt... as if it was a barrier.

Eventually even these records were computerized sufficiently to allow feedback of 'non-patient-specific data' (i.e. statistical data) to managers within the hospital, who would then share this with the PCT, but this was a long way from making clinical information available in a format that could cross professional and organizational boundaries. Even within the health service this could be a problem:

[If we could] just share data,... actually be counting the same things, you know, that would be a great start,... but at the moment we're not counting the same things. So, for example, … GUM … [can] now count the 48-hour targets of offered and seen appointments, that's not being counted in community-based services.

I find the communication [about cancer patients] is a one-way system into … [X hospital]. We communicate in and you never get anything back out and that can be a big problem if you're getting patients who have had surgery and they're back out again … I find that very concerning, you know, at a patient level. We don't know what happens, once they've gone over there, we never find anything out although they're back in our area. And if the patients, often when they are diagnosed, I'll become their key worker and they'll often phone me and if I've got no idea of what's happened to them at … [X hospital] it can be difficult to sort that sort of problem out for them really.

The Metropolitan City Sexual Health Network, facing similar problems with the five GUM clinics within its remit, decided to implement a common IT system with the aim of providing 'joined-up auditable data'. There was some resistance, with one member hospital insisting its current system was adequate, but the Network was able to overrule the doubters and persist with the plan, though views about its effectiveness were mixed.

The decision was made by the Network several years ago that it would be good to be able to share information and that … [a new IT system] was the best way to do that. And so a deal was brokered so that if a certain number of Trusts, I think it was five, went ahead and got it, that everybody would get a big discount … [there was] a lot of pressure from the Network to just go with it.

Difficulties in harmonizing data collection systems within the NHS paled into insignificance beside those encountered in trying to network with outside organizations. Some of the problems were illustrated by Cathedral City Sexual Health Network's efforts to share data with the local authority and voluntary organizations.

It's … really important … and it's been one of the biggest frustrations …. The network per se is dependent entirely on the participation of everyone else and their contribution. And that can be a weakness in terms of, all of our IT and information management systems are different, you know, there's no set data set as such … And it's not anything about the commitment of individuals around the table but it's about where different organizations are. And when it's such an inter-agency group, you know, the systems aren't talking to each other.

One voluntary sector respondent felt that struggling for uniformity might not always be the best way forward.

A lot of information technology has ruined partnerships because … what's going on is that people are trying to formalise some networks into something that they can't be and others are trying to shake them into uniformity ….(the) best way that partnerships can work is accepting what is standard between you but with that can also be accepting difference and I'm afraid information technology doesn't accept that.

Similar problems in introducing and marrying up technical systems were encountered with the Regional Older People's Network. A Single Assessment Process ((SAP): introduced in the National Service Framework for Older People, 2001) was a new integrative measure meant to coordinate assessment procedures across agencies and services. It was decided that this should be implemented using an electronic, rather than paper-based, system but at the time of the fieldwork this had yet to be accomplished.

> We've been talking about SAP for more than five years now and nothing has happened.

Respondents pointed to the massive changes required,

> Yes, for the tape, I have a pained expression. Yes, well there's a lot of good intention. I don't know—is SAP working anywhere?...I don't think...the full implications of the suggestion were thought through really....[it requires] quite fundamental developments in infrastructure and IT and equipment and all of those things.

There had been piecemeal development:

> All of the community nursing staff are trained, they have the IT, they'll have the capability to use SAP. The local authority position is slightly different, in that we have got an IT system that does all of our reporting and we were not prepared to use SAP as a mainstream assessment tool until we had got a way of linking the two IT systems.

This led to duplication of work for some clinical networks.

> Not only are we having to write notes manually, we're having to input it on...[the IT system].

The Metropolitan Older People's Network presented a similar picture. As a small informal network of care homes and a hospice it was only just beginning to use ICTs, but members were already recognizing the need for an integrated system to enable ready access to clinical data.

> The biggest hole is the IT I think. If we could all share one IT, so we all had access to the same records in the nursing home, I think that would make a big difference.

Where electronic systems were not available, or perceived to be inefficient and unreliable, respondents in all our cases placed considerable reliance on communication through older technical systems, such as fax, phone, or letters, though this could be a complicated process. A respondent from

Urban Cancer Network reported ringing ward nurses to get information on discharged patients.

> It comes down to, literally, phoning one of the nurses at...[X hospital], for them to find out what's happened to those patients.
>
> [X service] haven't got any kind of IT systems, they're totally paper patient .records and that's a nightmare. Then getting any kind of performance data management out of...[Y organization] is incredibly complex and a nightmare and if I didn't have...[Z] as my link into...[Y organization] it would never happen. She is pretty good at hunting down the right person to get that, but yeah it's really difficult.
>
> We're not able to have a system over there,...they fax us who they want to see, we print out reams of paper, take it with us, then we have to write in their notes, then we have to come back and write in our notes on the computer, it takes hours. And we can't get a way round it...there's no, we can't have a system over there because...they only need access to their patients, they don't need access to the rest of our patients...the PCT won't fund it either, so that's a second problem. And then, I suppose the only other thing is if we had a laptop and could dial in but that would only, again, make it better for us, it takes one path of the loop out but they still won't have access to all of the results and everything that goes on over here...we do write everything in their notes but, for example, if they phoned me here, on a non-ward day, and I gave them advice, I mean they might write that in the nursing notes but they won't write that in the doctor's notes but it will go on here. So should [an out of hours] doctor come later on in the evening, when we're not here, he's not going to necessarily see that, especially if that nurse has gone off-duty. I mean hopefully the nurse would read what, but you can just see it going wrong and we're often phoned about the people who are really not well...can't have our system up there with only their patients...I don't know how to get round that one.
>
> We put it on [the computer] but social services can't access it, so we fax it over.

Indeed there seemed sometimes to be almost a hierarchy of communication systems. In Cathedral City Sexual Health Network, for instance, patient referral for General Practitioners (GPs) by fax was seen as a huge advance over a letter-based system, enabling the GUM clinic to meet their 48-hour referral targets; while in the Regional Older People's Network, in the absence of an effective computer-based system, the telephone had been important in establishing a single point of access system for intermediate care.

> I use the phone and then somebody else does the single assessment. So there's a single access point for all intermediate care and there's somebody who picks it up at the other end and then they, well I think they use a single assessment anyway. And I appreciate it is meant to be like an electronic thing and it didn't really take off.

Of course, online data transmission is not the only use that can be made of new ICTs. Two networks had their own websites. County Cancer Network's site contained up-to-date information about the Network, as well as cancer and cancer care more generally, and was considered to be very successful. However, the website hosted by Metropolitan City Sexual Health Network was not working so well and at the time of our study information about the Network was a year out of date.

> The website's just been a joke...it's got no utility at the moment, so no one uses it. We can make it function better as a provider website...it should...signpost you to services and it doesn't do that.

There was talk within the Network of an Inner Metropolitan City PCT funding and taking over the website management.

Although there were no plans for Cathedral City Sexual Health Network to have its own website, there was talk of creating a sexual health website as a learning tool.

> If we're looking at schools,...what we have in...[the city] is what we call learning platforms and...the idea is that everyone in school...will have their own pin and everybody can access anything anywhere in...[the city] through the school system....There's a real potential there for having signposting, all of that kind of thing around sexual health actually on that learning platform so you don't necessarily have to go and see someone down the corridor but can access information through your own platform. So although that's in its infancy,...there is potential for ICT to be very very useful.

Interestingly, an idea which is just in the early stages of development in the statutory sector was already up and running in a local voluntary sector organization which was a member of the network.

> [The voluntary sector service organization] also built an online web space so...[clients] can interact on there because the sexuality survey which was done in Cambridgeshire in...possibly 2005, said that most young people find out information about sexual health and sexuality by accessing it through the Internet.

The Regional Older People's Network developed a website for consultation on further rises in the standards of care provision and prevention of abuse of older people. It was seen as a resource to coordinate action towards that aim. By 2008 over 4,000 people had joined the Campaign and signed up as 'Champions' for the improved care for older people.

Teleconferencing was another technology with potential for increasing interaction amongst network members. This was a particular issue for the cancer networks as their 'hub and spoke' design meant that clinicians needed to travel to different hospitals for Multidisciplinary Team

(MDT) meetings, which was hugely time consuming. In the County Cancer Network £33,000 had been invested in teleconferencing facilities which, after some initial teething problems, appeared to be working well; while the lack of such equipment in the Urban Cancer Network was bemoaned by respondents.

> We haven't set up a special MDT time, it's merely slotted into...[X hospital's meeting], which is very nice for them because it's at a time that suits them and it's down there. At the moment, we do not have active video conferencing, which means that Mr XX and myself have to travel to...[X hospital].
>
> I don't feel that the problem of how you set up a specialist MDT has been seriously addressed...it is the logistics of it and a lot of my time is taken up and wasted when I can do better, be doing more useful things. And if we at least had video conferencing active and live, that would relieve a lot of the unnecessary timewasting.

For communicating informally many people said they preferred more traditional technologies or indeed talking face-to-face.

> The ability to actually pick the phone up and get to the—quickly without all of the campaigns, procedures, and all the rest of it, by just knowing about people in the NHS, in the local government, in the voluntary sector, to actually lever things along or say, 'this isn't working very well', whatever.
>
> I think it is just somebody rings somebody and they have a meeting or a discussion beforehand so that by the time it comes to the Board the decision has been made.
>
> If you're interested in networking, you should just spend a day just looking at the number of meetings that are held in...[the coffee shop next door] because that's a classic example of informal networking, 'well let's have a coffee' or, you know, it provides a setting where people can actually communicate in different ways...[so there are] those sorts of methods of communication,...[to] go and meet people and talk to them, you know, if there are issues [people will] try and meet together and sort it out and see what the problems are.

The role of ICTs in governance

Whether viewed through an optimistic or pessimistic lens, commentators often consider ICTs as a key medium through which network governance can be conducted and our case study material would support this view. Governance of networks may be external to the organization or organizations within which a network exists, as when managed networks are mandated by government policy and monitored through regular progress reports. Cancer networks, for instance, send annual returns to the National Cancer Registry and in our sexual health sites statistics on specific and high-profile health issues such as GUM waiting times, chlamydia testing, and teenage pregnancy were collected at national level. The networks were, at least potentially, kept under direct supervision from central government or its agencies as Reed (1999) suggested. Some data were ranked hierarchically and we found at least one instance (Cathedral City's teenage pregnancy figures) where apparent poor performance led directly to government intervention.

In other cases, however, the content of progress reports produced little feedback, either welcome or otherwise. In the Genetics Translation Networks all sites had to report progress on an electronic template to the Advisory Group on Genetics Research every three months. This unusual frequency may well have been to help ensure that the large sums invested in this highly visible project were justified, but amongst the scientists involved such reporting was resented as excessive and pointless as the centre did not appear to use the data reported in any active way. It was treated as a 'cut and paste' exercise, absorbed by the Network Director in GTN1. If this were an attempt to construct an 'electronic Panopticon' observing the six GTN sites, then it appears to have been ineffective.

With the exception of the Metropolitan Older People's Network, which was informally constituted, all our networks were subject to internal governance processes from their host organizations. In some cases these were notional. Metropolitan City's sexual health network was officially performance managed by and accountable to its local Strategic Health Authority (SHA). However the SHA appeared 'hands off', and in practice accountability had devolved to the Network Chair and the Vice-Chair. Similarly neither of the GTNs was closely monitored by internal means. This left the networks fairly free to organize themselves as they felt best. The Cancer networks were also driven more by national guidelines for cancer services than local interests. In contrast, Cathedral City's sexual health network, embedded within the PCT and run by an assistant Director of Public Health, was notably responsive to the PCT's performance targets; while in the Regional Older People's Network, run by the local authority and seen as 'very much an officers' group', local governance was exercised by people with many different organizational and political interests. Such internal governance was clearly influenced to some degree by ICTs; for instance in Cathedral City suggested meeting agendas were circulated by e-mail, giving people the possibility of easily transmitting possible additions or revisions in advance, and regular feedback of progress on local targets was more realistic than before the advent of electronic communications. Combating such potential, however, was a rapidly developing resistance to the burden of (particularly) group-circulated e-mailings, and the impossibility of coping with the large volumes of information often transmitted leading in some cases to deletion without reading. Since effective networking was seen as depending on members being fully informed this overload could cause major problems: 'you just physically don't have time to read through all those papers before one of those meetings. It is a constant battle not to overload people with emails'.

As well as formal governance, were there signs in any of our cases of ICTs affecting the development of 'governmentality', where individuals and groups become convinced of the value of a particular point of view or mode of operation and thus become in effect self-governing? Six of our networks showed some signs of governmentality. This was probably most developed in cancer services, where the recommendations of the Calman–Hine report in the mid-1990s had been widely accepted by clinicians as best practice; but in both sexual health services and services for older people clinicians and others involved were clearly aware of and working towards implementing professional standards, whether or not these were, or were likely to become, mandatory. There was evidence that readily available data helped convince those who doubted their peers' assessment that local services were not meeting acceptable standards. In the County Cancer Network, for instance, we saw that intra-professional battles about which hospital retained cancer surgery were shaped by wider rational evidence-based structures, standards, and measures for practice, though data sets were acceptable only when presented by those they saw as their peers as the following quotations from respondents demonstrate.

> The main reason we decided on...[Hospital X]...[was] surgical activity data...showed a reduction in...[Hospital Y] activity and increase in...[Hospital X] activity....there were probably three times as many operations at...[Hospital X]
>
> There are huge issues about data collection...consultants are very clear that they remember how many patients they have treated...when someone from the data side of things says, 'excuse me but you have only done such and such', they...say 'Excuse me, but I know my practice!'
>
> We had to do all the number crunching to demonstrate to all the clinicians actually if you look at our numbers versus what this guidance is recommending we can't sustain four teams doing all of that work.

Similarly, clinicians in the Metropolitan City Sexual Health Network used computer-generated clinical statistics and questionnaire data to influence their less-convinced peers that achieving 48-hour access represented best practice.

> [There was] huge resistance to the idea of the target, you know, 'this is an outrage!', real variances in practice and we got bunches of clinicians together in rooms, you know, ran workshops, and...[had a] detailed questionnaire looking at practice...shared all that...four out of five units are doing this, why are you doing that...peer pressure...I think they got there quicker...definitely I think the network had an impact there...Peer pressure, about modernising practice, allowing people to make and facilitating earlier change of clinical practice, earlier

efficiencies in service, so you need to follow up ratios, you know, bringing in tex-
ting and all that sort of stuff.

In the Cathedral City Sexual Health Network it was harder to tell to what
extent we were seeing 'governmentality in action' at network meetings where
the heads of different organizations met to discuss how to achieve agreed
practice outcomes; or simply 'resource dependency' (Pfeffer and Salancik,
1978) with the PCT-employed Chair holding the purse-strings, thus keeping
member organizations focused on figures showing whether or not they were
meeting national targets. A mixture of the two seems most likely.

The Older People's Networks were also resource dependent, but there were
definite signs of ICTs encouraging governmentality in the Regional Network's
'Older People's Champions' where people were encouraged to debate, consider, and sign up to policy through the organization's website.

In contrast, in the GTN there were no signs that the elite scientists were
enrolled into a governmentality project. On the contrary, they largely continued with their academic research, insulated by the Network Director from
having to consider policy and practice within onerous reporting requirements. Where there was some success in translational research (as in the cardio vascular project), it appeared to be due to an energised cluster working in
a bottom-up way rather than a product of national electronic surveillance or
its internalization by scientists.

The role of ICTs in facilitating organizational learning

Part of the rhetoric behind the development of networks was to encourage
collective learning by the organizations involved. There is potential for ICTs
to facilitate this process, but to what extent was this realized? There were
some examples of new ICTs enhancing access to knowledge.

In the Urban Cancer Network, video-conferencing MDT meetings proved
to be one way of improving attendance and hence learning opportunities.

the [MDT] meeting is a good idea, it can be very educational and quite fun.

We have also mentioned the use of websites, such as the 'Older People's
Champions' website in the Regional Older People's Network which was specifically designed to be a learning tool.

We use it as a cultural and education training tool and when we believe that
there are certain types of skill or certain areas of new, information is the wrong
word, it's not particularly information because you can simply tell people
that by sending them a letter, but new understandings, new interpretations of
things.

Shared statistical data in the Cathedral City Sexual Health Network had enabled an in-depth study of just where the problem lay following heightened concern about teenage pregnancy:

> the data people have drilled down. Drilled down into all the information we have on each pupil. They have actually identified actual young people through looking at the risk categories and it's flagged up a group of pupils in four schools in particular, that have the highest potential teenage pregnancy sexual health rate…what that has enabled them to do is to put these specific programmes, tailor made programmes into those particular schools

and played an important part in presentation of the findings to local audiences.

> (ICT) has been crucial in finding all of the data and recording it and [in producing] all the visual aids…to demonstrate [the findings].

However, while 'learning' is often seen as unequivocally 'good', the issue of providing access to knowledge which people require to learn is rarely addressed. Our cases suggest that ICT systems, even between different NHS facilities, are frequently incompatible, and this is even more so in interfaces with local government and voluntary sector organizations. The problems may appear technical in origin, but comments from some respondents hinted at a possible lack of willingness to share, hiding behind surface technical problems.

> Facilitate, the common goal, if you can identify a common goal and you can talk the same language and you can agree that you can pool your thinking and pool your sovereignty and even maybe pool your resources…. Why don't we all pull some money out, plop it into a big pot and we will administer it separately but there again, there's a stop isn't there, I would think. The organizational system rears its ugly head.
>
> Cross party agency working, could be much, much better, should be encouraged, pooling of sovereignty, pooling resources, but it doesn't often happen. So one of the major barriers is quite clearly, we are very, very loath to give up our own authority on behalf of our organization and I sense we should.

Voluntary organizations in particular may see themselves considered less than full partners in service delivery. Thus on the one hand they see themselves as willing to share with the statutory sector.

> [This voluntary sector service organization is] very open to sharing…information, you know, it's about learning together and…[we are] well used to managing huge amounts of data,…and if people are doing any sort of needs-led assessments, then…[we] will share…information.

However, on the other hand, they may fail to profit from available information because they assume, rightly or wrongly, that they are unlikely to be given access to it.

[ICT makes] absolutely no difference to...[this voluntary sector organization] because...[we] would not be on the list of people that...[health services] could communicate with....It took...six months...[and] a requirement audit...for them to be able to email...[us] and for...[us] to be able to email them back...[We] wouldn't get close to [sharing performance data]...[we] wouldn't get a look in.

Concluding discussion: The modest role of shared ICTs

Our cases provided little support for the argument (Castells, 1996) that new ICTs were a major driver to new network forms. Overall, we found continuing obstacles to transfer of information electronically across agency boundaries and only incremental moves to shared ICTs or databases. There were few if any explicit knowledge-management strategies found in operation across the networks. In practice, existing organizational forms had regrouped around jurisdictions to blunt the potentially radical impact of new ICTs (Zuboff, 1984; Dunleavy et al, 2006).

There were some incremental changes. The networks often set up their own websites, but they were sometimes poorly maintained (although the cancer networks' websites were better and did upload documents on new care pathways which providers and patients could access). There was some growth of video conferencing (e.g. County Cancer Network) which helped MDTs to confer remotely. There were some cross-hospital IT systems emerging (e.g. the 'joined up auditable data' in the Metropolitan City Sexual Health Network could develop into a network-wide electronic patient record). The Urban Cancer Network's well-functioning IT system displayed good data storage and accessibility which underpinned its ability to share and analyse information, and hence add value.

However, the need for human support for ICTs and the limits placed on inter-organizational exchange of information by a continuing desire for organizational autonomy—and fragmented information systems—were still apparent. Working practices were not 'transformed' by ubiquitous computing. For example, the slow development of a common IT platform in the Regional Older People's case illustrates the danger of relying on shared IT to drive inter-organizational change. Information here crossed agency boundaries through a confusing mix of electronic information, faxes, and paper and it had so far proved impossible to use shared IT to facilitate SAP. Both sexual health networks showed over-reliance on poor-quality data sets that represented 'noise in the system' and did not add real value.

With the notable exceptions of two of the websites, one run by a voluntary sector organization, we found little evidence of ICTs promoting effective public participation. There were plans to use ICTs more creatively in the future: for example, creating a learning platform accessible by personal pin numbers for pupils in schools to diffuse health-related information to young people (Cathedral City Sexual Health case) but that was for the future. Overall, we conclude that ICTs were not acting as a major driver of organizational transformation towards network forms.

9

Leadership in health care networks: Clinical-managerial hybrid teams and evidence-based identity work

Introduction

In this chapter we discuss leadership patterns found in the health care networks studied. 'Leadership' is prominent as a theme in UK health care policy and often heralded as a panacea for many problems in the National Health Service (NHS), with responsibility for implementing government policy being devolved to energized leaders on the front line (for a critical review, see O'Reilly and Reed, 2011; Martin and Learmonth, 2010). It may also have political and ideological undertones: O'Reilly and Reed (2011) write of 'leaderism' as a discourse of public services modernization in the New Labour period. However, there is considerable debate about what 'leadership' means (Bolden et al, 2011; Alvesson and Sveningsson, 2003), with limited evidence about its substantive impact in public organizations (Hartley and Benington, 2010; Brooks and Grint, 2010) and even less in health care networks (Currie et al, 2011). We need to take a broader view of the leadership wave, examining its pitfalls as well as its promise (Teelken et al, 2012), given the highly institutionalized settings in which such leaders operate which might restrict the scope for agency.

However, it may be that agency is to some extent important as well as structure. Literature on networks and boundary-working in public organizations (Ferlie and Pettigrew, 1996; Sullivan and Skelcher, 2002; Klijn, 2005) highlights the important role of individuals with interpersonal and diplomatic skills that enable them to span boundaries between different organizations and groups within public sector settings. It has to be acknowledged that leadership theory too often takes an individualized perspective, for example, highlighting the effect of a single transformational leader. However, this analysis neglects the extent to which context (here the public and health care sectoral contexts) affects leadership styles (Porter and McLaughlin, 2006; Currie et al, 2009a, 2009b).

Denis et al (2007, p. 452) analyse leadership forms in public services in terms of interaction between leaders and the context, noting that: 'because of the complexity and ambiguity of power in public organisation contexts…research on leadership in public administration needs to focus on processes and skills that may or may not reside in formally designated leaders. Greater emphasis needs to be placed on the complex emergent activity that is dispersed throughout the whole political and administrative context and its effects over time'. Accordingly, our analysis of leadership in health care networks will examine the interrelationship between leaders and their organizational context.

We here describe in particular how network leaders played active roles in reconfiguring health care services by framing and socially constructing their local contexts in terms of wider evidence-based government health policy and targets. Our analysis also responds to a call from Alvesson and Spicer (2012) for leadership scholars to examine more closely the link between leaders' abilities to interpret and construct their context, and wider forms of power shaping their ability to do so.

While the role of individual leaders was found to be a significant part of network leadership in our cases, by examining 'distributed leadership as the unit of analysis' (Gronn, 2002), we also conceptualize network leadership as the (re)framing of context in terms of 'governmentality' (Foucault, 1991, 2007).

Doolin (2002) explains the development of clinical leadership in terms of governmentality. He describes the New Zealand government's introduction of 'enterprise discourse', associated with managerialism and new public management, as an attempt to constitute the subjectivity and identities of doctors in ways that made them more responsible for their expenditure. However, these clinical leaders used a mixture of managerial and professional discourses to construct their identities and subjectivities, which produced complex and varied outcomes.

We also used the idea of governmentality to explain clinical leadership, focusing on how Evidence-Based Medicine (rather than managerialism) constitutes clinicians' identities and subjectivities. We explain governmentality in terms of Dean's (1999) model, in which evidence-based 'episteme', clinicians' 'identification' and 'identity work', 'visibility' mechanisms, and local process or 'techne' are all important elements. Our research also suggested that where these dimensions of governmentality were present, more tangible improvements in health care services—at least according to our assessment—occurred than when absent.

Collective and distributed leadership forms in health care contexts

Denis et al (2001) argue that health care contexts are complex and pluralistic and even beyond the understanding of any one individual. Weick and Roberts note (1993, pp. 357–8), 'agents working alone have less grasp of the entire system than they do when working together'. Therefore 'collective leadership', where different health care leaders who understand different aspects of context work together, may be more effective than individualized leadership (Denis et al, 2001) in these complex settings. Similarly, Pettigrew et al (1992) found that 'team leadership', containing members of the different professional, managerial, and other communities in health care, able both to understand and relate to these different constituencies involved in change, was required to understand context and make complex service changes happen. So it appears a distinctive characteristic of the health care sector may be 'collective' or 'team' rather than individually based change leadership (Ferlie et al, 2005b, p. 118).

There has been recently enhanced interest among scholars examining 'distributed leadership' (Gronn, 2002; Buchanan et al, 2007a) in terms of the interrelationship not only between a constellation of leaders but also between leaders and their contexts (Spillane, 2006; Currie et al, 2009a; Bolden, 2011; Currie and Lockett, 2011). Bolden (2011, p. 262) notes a 'need for increased recognition of the primacy of contextual factors in shaping both how leadership practice occurs'. Grint (2005) argues that while leaders are often constrained by context, they can also socially construct it. He explains how, for example, leaders can frame problems as 'tame', 'critical', or 'wicked' (our particular interest) to legitimate courses of action. Accordingly, leadership involves 'the management of meaning' (Smircich and Morgan, 1982), 'sensemaking' (Pye, 2005), the strategic use of discourse to shape context (Fairhurst, 2009), the structuring or focusing of attention on particular issues (Heifetz, 1994) or indeed 'seducing...followers into accepting what may not be in their interests' (Martin and Learmonth, 2010, p. 2).

Martin et al (2009) have recently explained the operation of leadership within NHS cancer genetics pilot projects as the 'making of meaning'. This is 'a relational perspective that views leadership as a process of social construction through which certain understandings of leadership come about and are given privileged ontology'. (Uhl-Bem, 2006, p. 654). Like Alvesson and Spicer (2012), we argue that such leadership can be both potentially problematic but also beneficial.

Leaders in health care, universities, and schools have been found both to be affected by and able to manipulate positive or negative aspects of their context (Wallace and Tomlinson, 2010). Newman (2005) describes how local government leaders packaged local initiatives to fit with national policy, so leaders can be seen as both agents and objects of change. Currie et al (2009a) see school leaders as creatively playing with contradictory policy pressures to enact leadership based upon their own visions, values, and ethics. However, Currie et al (2011) found that a context of performance management focused on individual organizations and the tendency for public organizations to create bureaucratic processes rather than (necessarily) make changes mitigated against effective network leadership. In their study of public sector collaborations, Huxham and Vangen (2000) describe a form of 'contextual leadership' involving the interrelationship between local participants, processes, and structures imposed by policymakers and funders. We suggest that one important contemporary factor affecting healthcare is the local impact of national evidence-based guidelines and targets.

Leadership, an evidence-based context and governmentality

As already indicated, a major development in health care is the rise of EBM, which increasingly frames healthcare professionals' understanding of their practices and contexts. EBM has been described as the 'standardization of medicine' (Timmermans and Berg, 2003) or a 'scientific-bureaucratic' model of medicine in which expert scientists produce standards of best practice, which are then implemented in a bureaucratic manner to guide the practice of rank-and-file clinicians (Harrison et al, 2002). The implementation of such standards is 'inherently political because their construction and application transform the practices in which they are embedded' (Timmermans and Berg, 2003, p. 22). Clinicians may resist EBM because it changes the nature of their practice, in particular undermining its 'indeterminate' (Jamous and Peloille, 1970) nature and challenging their autonomy by making what they do more manageable and governable.

Professionals have historically dominated health care organizations and organized themselves to resist organizational changes which undermine their autonomy (Ackroyd, 1996). Professional administrators running 'professional bureaucracies' such as health care organizations traditionally needed to share the background of the professionals they manage, and cannot deviate too far from professional norms, to retain their credibility and influence. Accordingly, there has been much interest in 'hybrid' medical professionals in managerial roles and how and whether they enact their roles in ways that change health care services (FitzGerald and Ferlie, 2000; Montgomery, 2001; Kurunmaki, 2004; Spurgeon et al, 2011). Hybrids may function as 'critical bridges' (Denis et al, 2001) or 'two-way windows' (Llewellyn, 2001) between medicine and management, appropriating and using managerial and clinical discourses and concepts to mediate between them (Cohen and Musson, 2000; Doolin, 2002; Iedema et al, 2004). Accordingly, such clinical-managerial hybrids may play key leadership roles in healthcare networks, arbitrating between professional stakeholders and the evidence-based contexts in which they practice.

Svenningson and Larsson (2006) explored leadership as a form of 'identity work'. Identity work can be defined as 'anything people do, individually or collectively, to give meaning to themselves or others. Identity work is thus largely a matter of signifying, labelling, and defining. It includes creation of the codes that enable self-signifying and the interpretation of others' signifying identity' (Schwalbe and Mason-Schrock (1996, p. 115). For Sveningsson and Alvesson (2003, p. 1165) identity work refers to people being engaged in 'forming, repairing, maintaining, strengthening, or revising the constructions that are productive of a sense of coherence and distinctiveness'. We will suggest that the way hybrid clinical-managers enact their leadership roles in networks is associated with such 'identity work'.

Alvesson and Willmott (2002) note 'the construction of knowledge and skills are key resources for regulating identity...knowledge defines the knower: what one is capable of doing (or expected to be able do) frames who one is' (p. 630). They add: 'establishing and clarifying a distinct set of rules of the game...establishing ideas and norms about the natural way of doing things in a particular context can have major implications for identity construction' (p. 631).

Furthermore, 'By describing a particular version of the conditions in which an organisation operates...identity is shaped or reinterpreted' (pp. 631–2).

Sanders and Harrison (2008), for example, described the 'occupational legitimation talk' of clinicians involved in the treatment of heart failure as identity work. Similarly, Pickard (2009, 2010) described the development of medical sub-disciplines (General Practitioners (GPs) with special interests and geriatric medicine) as aided by support from central government concerned about the important health policy problems these sub-disciplines addressed.

On this basis, we suggest that the development of evidence-based guidelines and new network-based organizing may require network leaders and other network members to engage in 'evidence-based identity work' as a form of 'subjectification' in which they make sense of themselves individually and collectively as professionals in relation to new evidence-based forms of knowledge, increasingly framing the context in which they operate.

We theoretically frame our analysis of network leadership using the notion of 'governmentality' (Foucault 1991, 2007). Specifically, we draw upon Dean's (1999, p. 23) description of governmentality as an 'assemblage' of four interrelated dimensions within the 'analytics of government':

(1) 'Episteme': Ways of thinking and questioning, vocabularies and procedures for the production of truth—like evidence-based guidelines and mentalities.

(2) 'Visibility': Ways of seeing and perceiving, for example, clinical audits which make clinical practices visible and comparable against national guidelines and targets.

(3) 'Identification': Ways of forming identities, which we link to 'identity work'. Dean (1999, p. 32) points out that: 'Regimes of practice...elicit, promote, facilitate, foster and attribute various capacities, qualities and statuses to particular agents...[which people] come to experience themselves through'. As Chan (2000, p. 1064) notes, 'power invests individuals in these institutions and raises their consciousness within these structures of recognition constitutive of their own subjectivity...[and] bring about new ways of identifying with and handling their roles'. Thus clinicians and clinical leaders may identify with and construct their own and others' identities and roles in relation to evidence-based guidelines and targets.

(4) 'Techne': practical rationalities ('expertise' or 'know how'), mechanisms, techniques and technologies, specific ways of acting, intervening, and directing, 'means, mechanisms, procedures, instruments, tactics, techniques, technologies and vocabularies' (Dean, 1999, p. 31).

We suggested earlier that a governmentality perspective provides a useful framework to make sense of new and indirect governance in pluralistic health care contexts and networks. We will now examine these four dimensions of governmentality found in practice, building on earlier work (Ferlie et al, 2012a). We focus here on the 'assemblage' (Foucault, 2007) of these four dimensions at micro-level practice as a form of leadership: how EBM makes health care knowable in terms of a wider governmental episteme; how audit make health care visible; how clinicians' 'identification' and 'identity work' is related to a governmental episteme, in turn affecting modes of practice; and how practical processes (techne) bring together the dimensions of governmentality at local level.

One unresolved debate among scholars of Foucault relates to questions of agency (Smart, 1982; Power, 2011) and its status (if any). Sewell (1992) and Emirbayer and Mische (1998) suggest that actors have 'interpretive agency' if they are situated between competing structures. We are interested in how leaders might use agency to interpret an evidence-based episteme in relationship with more traditional structures associated with medical professionalism. We examine how leaders engage in 'interessement', creating 'allied interests through persuasion, intrigue, calculation or rhetoric' (Miller and Rose, 1990, p. 10) and thus how regimes of government are 'translated into the personal capacities and aspirations of subjects' (Miller and Rose, 1990, p. 10) who change their clinical practices in line with national evidence-based guidelines.

We now move on to explore our theoretical framework on leadership within our network cases, drawing on some of the detail presented in the earlier case study chapters but now moving it up to a more theoretical level.

Managed Cancer Networks

We here examine leadership processes associated with the implementation of the urology Improved Outcome Governance (IOG), seen as an evidence-based 'episteme'.

Network leadership

The County Cancer Network exhibited a 'collective' (Denis et al, 2001) or 'team-based' (Pettigrew et al, 1992) form of leadership, with a full-time Network Director (a former nurse in a full-time management role) and Nurse Director and part-time Medical Director playing key leadership roles in the Network. Their clinical backgrounds were seen to be vital in providing credibility with other clinicians and brought together different forms of expertise, enabling the Network Management Team collectively to understand and relate to the diverse clinical perspectives within the County Cancer Network. Different team members engaged with different roles that played to their strengths, so, for example, the Network Director wrote business plans, which the Medical Director was less skilled at doing, while the Medical Director spent time 'chatting behind the scenes' to convince urologists to change their practice, something the Network Director would have been less able to do. The Nurse Director commented:

> We are all essentially going in the same direction... [Medical Director] will be looking at it from you know the doctors' point. I [Nurse Director]...looking at it from my perspective and [Network Director] looks at it from her perspective...the combination of all those collective expertise...brings it together as a...unified sort of collaborative.

All three leaders identified with County Cancer Network's global mission of using evidence-based standards (regime of governmentality or episteme) to improve cancer services rather than being divided by different professional backgrounds: 'We share a belief that what we do makes a difference and I think we share pleasure in seeing change happen for the best' (Network Director). They were perceived to 'have the interests of cancer patients at heart' (patient representative), reflecting (Stjernberg and Philips, 1993) a model of change leaders with 'souls of fire' and burning enthusiasm to drive change.

The Network Director was described as County Cancer Network's 'driving force', working 'phenomenally hard' and putting her 'life and soul' into the Network. She noted:

My identity at the moment is...a mother...who is lucky enough to have found a job I really, really enjoy that I passionately believe in...I am good at what I do, and I really care about the team I manage and I have a responsibility for all of them and ultimately to...benefit patients. I am a great believer in the NHS...My identity as a person is being all things to all people in the Network.

Her 'vision' and 'passion' stemmed from having had family and friends affected by cancer, which had highlighted to her how complex and potentially problematic cancer care could be. Her enthusiasm for using evidence-based guidance to improve patient care had been infectious within the Network. She noted how the attitudes towards the Network and using evidence-based guidelines had changed among Network participants:

From being sort of like a government thing that has happened, now they are all passionately interested in which people aren't being seen, because they all know, they all recognize that if it was their own relatives they would want them seen on day one wouldn't they, nobody wants to wait.

The Nurse Director was described as 'a work horse', 'focused', and 'passionate' about standing up for patients. Like the Network Director, the Nurse Director's motivation to improve cancer services stemmed from personal experiences of poor patient care. She recalled 'a patient being told their [cancer] diagnosis in the middle of a ward round surrounded by six medical students' and 'I wanted an opportunity, instead of hearing these stories...to see if there is anything I can do [to change things]...that's how I ended up here [in the Nursing Director role]'. She too identified with using evidence-based guidelines to improve patient care and engaged in identity work to legitimate doing so among other members of the network:

What I do is pluck out the nursing and patient implications of those guidelines...so clinical staff and patients...don't have to wade through loads of documents...wading through these massive documents....It's about focusing on and helping other people focus on...the key things that are important in these guidelines...I would like to think that who I am [is]...delivering all the stuff that I should be delivering around nursing and patient-focused improvements, that is what I should be about and should be doing.

The Medical Director was similarly passionate about improving cancer care through multidisciplinary work as outlined in guidelines, commenting:

I am angered by [the previous reconfiguration] more than anything else because it is not good for patients...The patient should not be dictated by personal enmity between individuals [doctors]...I don't see myself as a doctor or a consultant and I have always been a great believer in teams working. You know, doctors, nurses, everyone together...a lot of clinical nurse specialists are far more patient-centred than some of my consultant colleagues, and that has been a great benefit in cancer.

Change tracer: The reconfiguration of urology services

The reconfiguration of urology services (2003–2008) can be seen as a successful example of change leadership, driven by national evidence-based guidance (episteme). National guidance specified that complex urological procedures should only be carried out in cancer 'centres', conducting at least one-hundred of these operations annually. This implied that only one of the five hospital sites (across three hospitals) should do these operations, which were both financially rewarding for the hospitals and interesting for surgeons. Hospitals and surgeons losing these services would be left to do only routine surgery. Urologists from all sites therefore resisted reconfiguration, 'fighting for the politics of it and saving their own individual departments and hospitals...private practice', which initially made little progress.

The Network Management Team had no line managerial authority over people and organizations within the County Cancer Network, so had to 'influence' them to change by framing or constructing their reality in a particular way. We suggest they did so through assembling 'dimensions of governmentality' (Dean, 1999). With the evidence-based guidance (episteme) already in place, the Network Management Team needed to create local processes (techne), visibility, and then affect clinical identification by socially constructing County Cancer Network's local context in evidence-based terms that would legitimate service-level change.

The Network Management Team interpreted and made sense of national evidence guidance (episteme) in their local policy context and then created a local process (techne) to decide where the second cancer centre should be. The Network Director commented:

> You get the process agreed through the tumour group fundamentally to start with, they feel that they own that...if you don't they will spend months and years arguing about who said what and when. By having the processes there with the evidence if anybody challenges it.

The Network Management Team then gathered local audit data (making local practice visible) and benchmarked these data against national guidance (episteme), which suggested that without centralization local clinical practice was less than best practice, in turn affecting urologists' identification as good surgeons. The Network Director noted: 'We had to do all the number crunching to demonstrate to all the clinicians actually if you look at our numbers versus what this guidance is recommending we can't sustain four teams doing all of that work'. The Medical Director commented:

> We showed them [urologists] the house data…I said, OK, you have got two weeks, take the data, go through it…you have two weeks to challenge the data and you get back to me. Otherwise this will be the basis of what we use. And I only had one response.

So the Network Leadership Team actively framed local context in evidence-based terms to legitimate a complex service change; establishing the legitimacy of evidence-based episteme and creating forms of visibility against it at local level. We argue this was not a crude use of directive power (which the network did not have) but more indirectly about changing how network members, particularly urologists who had traditionally resisted reconfiguration, perceived themselves and their practices, so that they adopted the evidence-based episteme willingly.

This social construction of governmentality is not an impersonal and purely rational process, it crucially depended upon network leaders' identity work. The leadership personally identified with the evidence-based episteme and actively undermined the legitimacy of clinical practice that did not conform with evidence-based practice. The Medical Director, as a medical professional, was crucial in this respect, 'chatting behind the scenes' and, when necessary, 'going to see them and saying, look this is not reasonable behaviour…I will have to put it in writing to your medical director and chief executive'. So the network's leaders convinced others that a good clinician's practice should comply with national guidance and even surgeons no longer able to perform specialist urology surgery accepted the legitimacy of related changes. As one put it:

> we swallow a lot more of these things than we did before…we accept that certain things have to be done and that as long as they are reasonably sensible we accept it.

In summary, we see a combination of clear national policy, evidence-based guidelines, and performance incentives providing a framework (episteme) with which leaders in the Network Management Team could overcome resistance from urologists, who had previously dominated local cancer services, so as to reconfigure health care services across the county. The collective leadership in the Network Management Team provided vision, overlapping collective expertise, and mutual support. Clinical and social credibility, high social and contextual intelligence about how to use processes (techne), local audit data (visibility), national guidance (episteme), and identity work (identification) were all key ingredients in the change process observed. The

Network Management Team collectively and passionately believed in (identified with) using evidence-based guidelines to improve cancer services. They made sense of their complex task by drawing attention to particular aspects of local urology services and national policy and thus socially constructing their context in a way that change was accepted as 'sensible' and 'inevitable' for urologists if they wanted to continue identifying themselves as good surgeons.

Having analysed this case in some depth, we now make briefer observations about the leadership processes evident in the other cancer network.

Comparison with the Urban Cancer Network

In the Urban Cancer Network, we observed a similar pattern of a collective hybrid leadership constellation within an even more reconfigured process. Its Network Management Team also contained three key leaders, who believed in (identified with) the evidence-based guidance they were tasked with implementing. They worked cohesively to develop a process (techne) and local audit data (visibility), and enacted changes according to 'a very set agenda' which was 'difficult to argue with' in the context of national guidance (episteme). We see a similar pattern of change in this site. Urologists were initially in 'uproar' at the new national guidance (episteme), 'rubbishing' local data (visibility), and 'prevaricating' over the reconfiguration. Guidance was then adapted to local circumstances to permit two urology centres. The Network Management Team designed and facilitated a reconfiguration process (techne) to decide where specialist urology centres should be, assembling episteme, visibility, and identification/identity work, so that even those disadvantaged by changes accepted their necessity, given national guidance.

Metropolitan City Sexual Health Network

The Metropolitan City Sexual Health Network also reconfigured complex local services across a large urban patch in line with national guidance and targets. Again we explain the change leadership observed as driven by evidence-based national policy and the assemblage of episteme, techne, visibility, and identification.

While the Network had an Executive Board and Chair (Primary Care Trust (PCT), Chief Executive Officer (CEO)) formally in charge of the Network's activities, in practice three people collectively led the Network. These leaders were clinical-managerial 'hybrids', either having worked as clinicians before moving into more managerial roles or continuing to do so.

The Clinical Director was an HIV consultant and head of sexual health services at the Teaching Hospital. She was described as 'the prime mover' within the Network, 'a strong character and good leader' who had 'stopped it from being a talking shop' and was passionate about improving sexual health services, noting: 'What motivates me?...Team working, delivery...On a good day I [as a clinician] can give them [patients] the best service...It's wanting to replicate that throughout the service'. She had a national profile in sexual medicine, had been involved in developing national evidence-based guideline for sexual health care ('writing the standards document, I was involved in that on the steering group...we did have good input into that'), and had written in leading medical journals arguing for using evidence-based standards to improve care.

The Clinical Director appeared to be on a managerial career trajectory, moving from clinical to managerial roles, commenting:

> Education and the research wasn't going to happen, I'm just not good enough or motivated enough. The clinical role, yes, but would that hold my interest?...Then you kind of realise...most medics could do management...[but] lots of people don't want to, have other interests, or don't have the aptitude...I'm not crap at it [management]...I see him [the Medical Director] on a monthly basis...I chew the cud with him...[Medical Director] looks like my career path.

Here we see that the Clinical Director firmly identified herself with the national evidence-based episteme and as a Clinical Manager, with ambitions to rise to more senior managerial roles. Accordingly she was motivated to construct sexual health care in more manageable and evidence-based terms and engaged in individual and collective identity work to do so. Much of her role as Network Clinical Director, like the leaders in the cancer networks, was linked to convincing others, particularly doctors, of the need to change their practice medicine to become more oriented towards national guidance. She noted:

> We should all be working to BHIVA [British HIV Association] and BASHH [British Association of Sexual Health and HIV] standards, each [hospital] Trust should be doing that and they should be monitoring that. We can, as a network, help pull that together and I think we need to do more of that because then again, that's back to that peer pressure and support to help them improve quality.

She added,

> You have to do big selling to your colleagues that we need to use this to our advantage, focus on patient experience, use targets to improve that and your lives

and was seen as 'very good at that, and she will go and talk to people, and try and talk them around' (Vice-Chair).

The second key leader in the Network was the Vice-Chair, a specialist HIV commissioner, who had previously been a nurse at the Teaching Hospital and had also been involve in writing local sexual health standards:

> The MedFASH [Medical Foundation for AIDS and Sexual Health] came out. And so I designed the self-assessment tool for that. I say assessment tool, I just turned the standards into some free text boxes under it, for everyone to evaluate...from that we then identified some priorities.

He commented on his commissioning and network roles: 'I do genuinely believe that most of it is about benefitting people'. He was also seen in positive terms and provided a 'good counter-balance' to the Clinical Director, while the two also worked well together, bringing together their clinical and commissioning (managerial) expertise about sexual health services in a complementary fashion.

The third key member of the leadership team was the 'Network Coordinator', who had good soft interpersonal skills that gave her clinical and social credibility, used to facilitate changes in the Network.

We see here an example of effective 'team' or 'collective' leadership (Pettigrew et al, 1992; Denis et al, 2001), with three leaders using their different expertise and abilities to relate to different stakeholders in a complementary fashion to convince them to change clinical practices.

Change tracer: Redesigning sexual health services

The Metropolitan City Sexual Health Network 'tracer' we focus on is the redesign of sexual health services and the implementation of evidence-based standards (episteme), to meet nationally imposed guidance on a 48-hour waiting time for sexual health appointments. This was seen to create a 'burning platform' for network activities.

The Teaching Hospital had previously redesigned its sexual health services as a nurse-led service provided on a 'walk-in' basis, and as a result was already seeing all patients within the 48-hour target (episteme/visibility). The Network organized a series of workshops (techne) and ongoing support to share this best practice in service redesign with other hospitals in the network, which had 'worked brilliantly' enabling all but one service to meet the 48-hour target.

The one sexual health service within the network that did not meet the target had long been known to provide an unsatisfactory service but was run by a well-connected but change-resistant doctor. The Network's leaders organized a 'network-wide review' of its services, which was implicitly and indirectly aimed at targeting the failing service. The review made the clinic's poor waiting times publicly visible. The Network then made recommendations about how the service could be redesigned to improve care. The consultant concerned then decided to leave the organization. The consultant who took over the service then acted on the Network's recommendations, redesigning the service in line with other clinics within the Network, and as a result the service met the 48-hours target. A sexual health doctor commented: 'The Network had an impact there...peer pressure, about modernizing practice, allowing people to make, and facilitating earlier change of clinical practice'.

In theoretical terms, the Network's leaders can be seen as skilfully socially constructing their local context in evidence-based (governmentality) terms to demonstrate the necessity of change. They created an assemblage involving a local review/audit of services (techne) that produced local data (visibility) comparable with national best practice (episteme) and other local services. They then applied clinical 'peer pressure', engaging in a form of identity work reconstructing and clarifying what a good doctor should do, so that the consultant leading the poor service either had to change or leave; he chose the latter option and a new consultant took over his service and made dramatic improvements to patient care.

However, after standards had been audited, best-practice implemented, and sexual health services redesigned to meet the 48-hour targets, the network appeared to lose impetus. Local sexual health issues such as public health promotion failed to make much progress without an explicit national policy agenda and target or incentives. At the same time the government introduced the policy of 'payment by results' (a different governmental regime), which heightened competition for patients between the hospitals' sexual health services and undermine trust, cooperation, and sharing of best practice between stakeholders within the network. This reflects the findings of Currie et al's (2011) study of health care networks. Thus we see how network leadership often relies upon policy contexts supporting their aims.

Concurrently the Vice-Chair was promoted to a more senior role and withdrew from the Network and the Network Coordinator also moved on to a new role. While the Vice-Chair and Network Coordinator roles were filled, these replacements were younger and less experienced than their predecessors and less able to 'balance' the Clinical Director's influence. The network therefore assumed a more individualized form of leadership, under the Clinical Director, which appeared to be less effective. Thus successful leadership constellations can be fragile and vulnerable to losing key leaders.

To summarize, the Clinical Director, Vice-Chair, and Network Coordinator provided a balanced complementary form of collective/team hybrid leadership. They were all passionate about improving sexual health services and using national standards in order to do so; their identification was affected by governmental/managerial regimes of practice. This trio implemented a review of services (techne), with assemblage persuasion and peer pressure (identity work), involving the national guidance and targets (episteme) and local audit data (visibility) to facilitate service redesign. However, with a changing leadership constellation and policy context, service improvement slowed.

Comparison with the Cathedral City Sexual Health Network

The Cathedral City Sexual Health Network was focused on achieving the national 48-hour waiting target (episteme/visibility), where it made progress, as well as a broader aim of reducing teenage pregnancies, a 'wicked problem' of many years standing where it was harder to demonstrate improvement. Here the Network was led by a single individual, a senior PCT manager, with a participative and inclusive approach, high social skills, and a capacity for hard work. However this leader was overloaded, juggling other responsibilities, and was also hampered by massive local structural reorganization. Leadership was also facilitated by a history of collaboration between local statutory and voluntary agencies. However, although located within the public health directorate, this individual did not have a clinical background and thus was less able to influence local Genito-Urinary Medicine (GUM) clinicians to participate fully in the network than the Clinical Director in the Metropolitan City Sexual Health Network.

Regional Older People's Network

We now examine the Regional Older People's Network, where change leadership appeared less effective.

Policy context

Although there was generic policy (episteme) relating to older people, namely the National Service Framework (NSF) for Older People (2001), the lack of specific government legislation and targets made it difficult to create a focus. As a doctor commented:

> We still struggled to develop intermediate care services because there hasn't been any kind of national legislation. We've got a generic legislation ... but they're not specific enough ... national legislation ultimately focuses people's minds, it gives managers a structure to work within, it gives the person campaigning for change a business case ... it's vital to have the national legislation. (Doctor)

In addition, performance management regimes (visibility) for older people's services were weak. Another doctor commented:

We're required to provide audit and feedback for work we do...I wouldn't say it's...strong...I'm not sure if our...data would be particularly noticed...lip service can be paid to clinical governance and audit. (Doctor)

Local Network context

The Regional Older People's Network was led from a City Council Social Services Department, formally responsible for developing services for older people collaboratively; the Network's purpose was 'enabling multi-professional, multi-agency discussion'. The Network was supposed to play a role in bringing together individuals from different backgrounds and perspectives and enabling them to develop a common understanding of how to improve older people's services. These organizations spanned municipal, healthcare, voluntary, and private sectors, each with different performance management regimes. However, before the formation of the Network there was no formal relationship between these various services in the site. In addition, the PCTs involved in the Network had been through major reorganizations which distracted their focus from improving older peoples' services. Thus the Network was an extremely complex and pluralistic setting, in which previous research (Pettigrew et al, 1992; Denis et al, 2001) suggests change would be difficult to achieve.

Network leadership

The Network was led by a part-time interim Chair, a manager in the City Council who 'inherited the role' when two local PCTs merged. He lacked time and resources, commenting: 'I squeeze in what I can on top of the day job'. The Chair also commented that he had little formal power or authority over Network participants, so that diplomacy and persuasion were key interpersonal skills. The creation of the Network therefore produced discussion about how to move older people's services forward, but little action. Some interviewees commented that, because of its poor resources and situation within a policy void, the Network lacked strategic direction.

Change tracer: Developing a strategy for older people's services

We struggled to find tracer issues exemplifying change processes within this Network because of the lack of policy steer and strategic focus from the Network itself. One possible tracer was the project group looking at intermediate care which had been in existence 'in some guise' since 2003, but this was described as 'a shambles... there has been no leadership, no clinical leadership at all, and that has been the greatest failing of why there is not a strong inter-mediate care service' (Manager, Hospitals). A clinician commented:

> The constricting factors are cash, availability of that and priorities within the [council] and the PCT. I have not felt particularly that intermediate care has been as health priority for [either]. So we make noises, we see changes sporadically but it is not a uniform growth.

We also looked for the implementation of an 'end of life care' strategy, which might have included top-down guidance to drive change, but again there was little evidence of progress. There was a Department of Health (DoH)-funded pilot project 'in the pipelines' but a private care home manager reported lim-ited involvement in end of life care. This Network primarily provided a plat-form for discussion and the exchange of information rather than action.

From its formation, the Regional Older People's Network had been largely preoccupied with developing a Strategy for Older People but this was still a work in process, with the Network still trying to generate consensus between the highly diverse organizations involved. A city council manager commented:

> Not having the strategy and this hiatus that hasn't really enabled us to kind of really pin our activity onto something tangible. It's been a bit haphazard...as opposed to it being more strategic about, well what do we need to talk about, not what we like to talk about.

The manager of a specialist charity noted that there was no shared basis of relating within the Network:

> We come from various different directions. You might have shared visions of where you want to be but...how we get there might be different. (Manager, Specialist Charity)

While managers within the Network appeared to agree on ideas about how to develop older people's services, they struggled to

> implement them more broadly amongst the mainstream of proper work in the organizations, social work, nursing, etc., then you certainly do get really quite glaring differences in organizational culture and approach. (Council Manager)

Crucially, Network leadership failed to engage the medical profession which 'definitely considers itself to be of a higher status and is more powerful' than other groupings. While the medical-managerial hybrid in the leadership team may have been able to help overcoming this problem, without a national pol-icy episteme to identify with as a focus for change, the Network was unlikely to make progress. We see here that members of the Network identified them-selves in different ways and there was little identity work attempting to build a common identity with which to galvanize the Network into action.

Overall, the Regional Older People's Network was under-resourced and without a full-time manager or a complementary team. The key individuals were too widely distributed across different organizations, leading to a sense of drift. More fundamentally the lack of national policy (episteme) and 'ownership' of a strategy for older people, stymied progress within the Network as leaders were unable to do the identity work needed to get people to change.

Comparison with the Metropolitan Older People's Network

The Metropolitan Older People's Network was smaller-scale, which we saw as successfully implementing national 'end of life care' guidelines. Here a top-down evidence-based episteme was more clearly driving change. The Network was formally led by a palliative care nurse (a hybrid clinician in a management role), who played an important coordinating, networking, and teaching role, but it can be seen more as an example of distributed leadership, crucially involving GPs and the Clinical Directors (with nursing backgrounds) in care homes. This leadership constellation was committed to (and identified with) the service changes proposed by the End of Life Care Programme. Network leaders engaged in identity work to associate the new guidance with Network members' sense of self as people caring for patients as well as they could. They were also clinically and personally as respected by their peers, and had effective communication skills, so persuaded others within the Network of their legitimacy and importance of changing end of life care.

Clinical Genetics Networks

The Genetics Translation Network (GTN) policy initiative was described as 'vague', providing a general aim of translating academic research into practice, but a lack of specificity (a clear episteme) hampered leadership in both the genetics networks we examined. There was also a lack of visibility regarding what these networks were doing, in part due to the nascent nature of the genetics discipline. While the DoH recognized this problem and introduced quarterly performance reporting in the GTNs half way through the programme, this was perceived to have been introduced too late with its legitimacy contested by those within the Networks ('changing of the rules').

Genetics Translation Network 1: Cardio Genetics Network

GTN1's leadership constellation was centred on the Network Director (a former research scientist—so therefore a hybrid leader as in other cases) supported by a distributed range of network members, including a prominent medical professor. The Network Director was well-regarded, personable, and focused, and built up influence and credibility, partly as a result of insulating the GTN from DoH performance management regimes, developing expertise in the translation of meaning across epistemic and professional boundaries through negotiating cooperation between stakeholders. However GTN1 contained powerful academic medical professionals, who were more focused on ongoing academic research than necessarily translating research into NHS practice. With the problems of vague policy specification and late and contested performance monitoring, GTN1 struggled with identity work and in motivating Network members to translate research into practice within the five years that the GTN was funded (McGivern and Dopson, 2010).

While GTN1's leadership struggled to translate research into NHS practice within the terms of the DoH policy framework (in large part due to a vague policy episteme and lack of legitimate visibility mechanisms which were not shared by members of the Network), members of GTN1 were eventually able to translate the genetics test into NHS practice. However this was driven by a concern for patients and involved a bottom-up distributed leadership configuration, containing the Network Director and other boundary-spanning clinicians able to span epistemic communities. A key boundary-spanner was a consultant geneticist. He had previous experience of working in the labs linked the scientific and translational worlds, so was able to negotiate between the labs and the university/NHS hospital. He also had excellent interpersonal skills and a passion for patient care and creating the new NHS service, which stemmed from personal experience. He described during interview 'sitting in clinic last Friday with this dad, three kids and his wife who has been diagnosed with [a cardiac condition]' who was 'shaking and in tears' after he had to explain that her 'kids have got something they could pop their clogs with'. He therefore had first-hand clinical knowledge of the benefits a genetic test that could diagnose potentially fatal conditions could have for patients he had met and he engaged in identity work that linked the importance of creating a genetic testing service to clinicians' core identity as people serving patients' interests.

Genetics Translation Network 2: Public Health Genetics Network

GTN 2's leadership was more of an individualized fiefdom, with a strong and enduring founder. It speaks to the impact that a determined, visionary, and entrepreneurial elite actor with high levels of personal social capital, passion, and vision can make in network development and the attempt to develop a new genetics discipline. Influential actors from outside the site had been enrolled in the Network.

The weakness of this leadership style was the limited impact in developing effective partnerships with the local genetics and public health communities: the network remained an enclave. It also had a weakness at the level of operational management which was needed to rebalance the strong visioning. The leadership style did not evolve but remained stable and highly individualized over a long period of time, difficult for juniors to challenge, and the network produced few tangible outputs.

Discussion

Table 9.1 compares the different features of leadership processes and influences in the eight networks. The first column identifies each of the eight networks. The second column describes the networks' levels of complexity, including the number and nature of organizations involved, and whether there were powerful medical professionals supporting or opposing changes the network was trying to achieve. The third column shows the clarity of national policy (in theoretical terms 'episteme') and visibility mechanisms guiding changes. We found that clear policy aims and visibility mechanisms supported effective change leadership. The fourth column describes the nature of local leadership in each network. The fifth assesses the change outcomes achieved by each network within our narratives, including the creation of local processes (techne) and identity work (identification). In some cases, we suggest there were different phases of change which could be seen as more or less effective. On the basis of this comparative table, we make some more general observations.

Small team leadership, including passionate, emotionally/socially intelligent clinical-managerial hybrids, appears the most effective network leadership configuration

Our analysis supports the appropriateness of using 'distributed leadership as the unit of analysis' (Gronn, 2002), given the small team-based forms of leadership found in our network cases. We note that a small mixed team, including clinical-managerial hybrids ('duos and trios in change'), was apparent in the three networks (both cancer networks and in the Metropolitan City Sexual Health Network during its initial phase) we assessed as making most progress. Some of the networks that displayed individualized leadership patterns (Cathedral City Sexual Health Network, the Public Health Genetics Network, the Regional Older People's Network, and the Metropolitan City Sexual Health Network in its second phase), by contrast, were assessed as making slow progress. Collective leadership appears to provide personal support,

Table 9.1. Leadership processes and influences in the eight networks

Network	Local Context	National Policy	Network Leaders	Change Narrative & Outcome
Urban Cancer	High complexity: 3 teaching hospitals; 3 smaller hospitals & PCTs; Fierce inter-hospital rivalry; Dominant & change-resistant academic medics.	Clear & legitimate urology IOG (episteme); All NHS organizations obliged to implement & meet auditable standards (visibility).	Credible & socially intelligent collective hybrids, who strongly identify with improving cancer care using the evidence-based episteme.	Change narrative: Networks leaders developed local process (techne) to decide reconfiguration of cancer services, conducted audit to make local practices visible & engaged in identity work to legitimate changes. Outcome: Successfully reconfigured urology services in line with national best practice, overcoming resistance from urologists (some medics unhappy).
County Cancer	Medium–high complexity: Teaching hospitals, 2 smaller hospitals & PCTs; Inter-hospital competition; Dominant urologists resisting change.		Credible & socially intelligent collective hybrids, who passionately identify with improving cancer care using evidence-based episteme.	Change narrative: Network leaders developed local process (techne) to decide reconfiguration, conducted audit to make local practices visible, & conducted identity work to legitimate changes. Outcome: Successfully reconfigured urology service in line with national best practice.
Metropolitan City Sexual Health	Medium–high complexity: Teaching hospital, 4 smaller hospitals & PCTs; Powerful teaching hospital, consultants driving change.	Phase 1: National Sexual Health & HIV guidance; 48-hr GUM waiting target. Phase 2: Lack of clear policy guidance.	Phase 1: Credible & socially intelligent collective hybrids strongly involved in developing & promoting using the evidence-based episteme to improve sexual health care. Phase 2: Individual hybrid (in effect).	Phase 1 change narrative: Network leaders organize a 'network-wide' audit/review (techne) making local practices visible, ran workshops sharing best practice (techne) & engaged identity work to legitimate changes. Outcome: Service redesign to meet 48-hr target & implement national best practice. Phase 2: 'A talking shop'.
Cathedral City Sexual Health	Medium–high complexity: Representatives of local sexual health organizations (PCTs, hospitals, council, HIV/AIDS, drugs & pregnancy agencies).	National 48-hr GUM waiting target; Vague intention to reduce teen pregnancy.	Committed, credible, & socially intelligent individual manager.	Change narrative: Individual leader lacking support & overloaded with network responsibilities; lacked clinical background & associated credibility to convince people to change sexual health services. Outcome: Met 48-hour target; teen pregnancy reduction remained 'a talking shop'.

Cardio Genetics	Medium complexity: Network spanning elite university & NHS hospital; Complex ascent genetics discipline; Elite powerful medical academics focused on academic research rather than translation.	Unclear Genetics Translation Network policy specification; Contested performance reporting introduced halfway through the programme.	Phase 1: Committed, credible & socially intelligent collective hybrids. Phase 2: collective/distributed clinicians.	Phase 1 change narrative: Academics capture jurisdiction & develop genetics test not translated into practice; Dept of Health withdraws programme funding. Phase 2 change narrative/outcome: Collective clinicians develop genetics testing service in practice.
Public Health Genetics	Medium complexity: Network attempts to link university & NHS; Complex nascent genetics discipline; Powerful medical academics.		Committed, 'astute & political' individual hybrid.	Change narrative: Network director pursues his own agenda to develop new genetics discipline, inc. running topic conferences. Outcome: Little engagement with wider university or translation into practice; Dept of Health withdraws network funding.
Metropolitan Older People	Low complexity: Local informal clinical implementation network: GP practice; 2 care homes; PCT hospice; End of life care project funded by & accountable to PCT/SHA.	Clear 'End of life care' guidelines; GP Quality Outcomes Framework audit incentive; Care-home accreditation & inspection for end of life care.	Credible, committed, socially intelligent collective clinicians who identify with the evidence-based 'end of life care' episteme.	Change narrative: Leaders engaged in identity work to legitimate the evidence-based episteme. Outcome: Implemented end of life care plans across network.
Regional Older People	Medium–high complexity: Plural health, social services, voluntary, & private organizations with 'huge power anomalies'.	Generic older people policy; End of life care 'in the pipeline'.	Overstretched individual manager from social services without clinical leadership.	Change narrative: Leader lacking time & credibility to convince network members to change; little progress overcoming complex contextual constraints. Outcome 'a talking shop'.

as well as wider complementary expertise, which enables the leadership to understand different aspects of context and have the credibility and expertise to relate to different stakeholder constituencies effectively.

Having members of network leadership teams with hybrid clinical/professional backgrounds appeared important in terms of their credibility and effectiveness. Individual non-professional managers appear least effective in network leadership roles. Effective leaders also appear to be committed to and passionate about the changes they are making in order to convince others of their benefits. They appear to display an energized and value-led 'post-bureaucratic' style (Reed, 2011). They also appear to need clinical and personal credibility, 'emotional and social intelligence' (Goleman, 2006). So we suggest that network leaders should be selected on the basis of having an appropriate clinical/professional background, passion, and enthusiasm for the role and high emotional/social intelligence.

Highly complex contexts make network leadership more problematic but can be overcome

As Pawson and Tilley (1997) and Pettigrew et al (1992) argue, it is important when studying organizational change to consider the impact of context and whether it supports or undermines the change process. Changes in complex contexts involving multiple and plural stakeholders, particularly powerful medical professionals and teaching hospitals, have been found to be more challenging (Pettigrew et al, 1992). Accordingly, we see the Regional Older People's Network operated in such a complex and plural context that leading change proved particularly difficult. However, we also assessed the context of the Urban Cancer Network as highly complex; yet the network was able to progress strategic change effectively. This suggests that other factors may be in play which can act to neutralize the effects of high contextual complexity. While leadership is both framed and constrained by contexts (Bolden, 2011; Currie and Lockett, 2011), both national (evidence-based guidelines) and local (particularly the presence of powerful stakeholders) leaders may also have some agency in how they construct context, which they can use to make changes happen: the discretion accorded to the managed cancer networks about which evidence base they used (as long as they used one) is a case in point.

National policy and guidance focuses minds: 'Burning platforms' and 'talking shops'

Performance management and target-setting regimes in the NHS have had their critics, including from some of the present authors. Currie and colleagues (2011) found pressures on health care organizations to achieve their individual performance targets rather than invest in network activities, and also public organizations' tendency to create more bureaucratic processes (rather than engage in network activities and changes) undermined network leadership. Our previous research (Addicott et al, 2007) on cancer networks also found that top-down pressures could 'distort' networks in an unhelpful way; focusing them on meeting top-down performance targets in a way that undermined inter-organization and inter-professional learning, collaboration, and sharing of knowledge and best practice.

We found some evidence of this pattern in this new study, for example in the later phase of the Metropolitan City Sexual Health Network. However in our new cancer and sexual health network cases, and also the Metropolitan Older People's Network, evidence-based guidelines and targets provided a 'burning platform', which focused network leadership and drove forward service improvements. The Metropolitan City Sexual Health Network later became more of a 'talking shop' without a clear policy focus and a target to meet. Likewise, the Regional Older People's Network was seen as a 'talking shop' and struggled to make any progress because of a lack of specific policy to 'focus minds'.

Only in the Cardio Genetics Network (GTN1) did we see effective service development which was not driven by top-down guidance and targets. In this case a distributed constellation of clinical leaders created an NHS service driven by the personal desire to improve patient care. Lacking a clear national policy focus, network leadership may depend upon motivated collective clinical leadership to make changes happen. So we suggest that top-down evidence-based guidelines and targets may be one key driver of desired service change in health care networks.

Network leadership as the social construction of governmentality

Most of the networks in our study can be seen as top-down implementation networks rather than networks characterized by organic or bottom-up learning (Addicott et al, 2006). Perhaps by definition, therefore, these networks were charged with implementing national evidence-based policy epistemes to achieve their officially stated aims. Other scholars have previously described leadership as 'the management of meaning' (Smircich and Morgan, 1982) or as a form of social construction (Grint, 2005; Pye, 2005; Fairhurst, 2009; Uhl-Bem, 2006), including in health care (Martin et al, 2009). Doolin (2002) has explained the introduction of 'enterprise discourse' associated with managerialism as a form of governmentality intended to constitute the identities and subjectivity of doctors in leadership and managerial roles. We suggest effective leadership in the health care networks studied can be explained as the social construction of governmentality.

We draw upon Dean's (1999) four dimensions of governmentality, as explained earlier, to identify correlates of effective network leadership. In the absence of any of these dimensions, networks appeared to produce more talk rather than activity. We suggest that examining leadership as the successful construction of governmentality at local level may be a useful and novel perspective on network leadership in health care. This form of distributed leadership required a number of facilitating forces.

First, a clear and legitimate evidence-based episteme and associated targets appeared necessary to focus network stakeholders' minds on the need for activity and provide a 'burning platform' to drive forward service improvements. Otherwise networks could drift into being 'talking shops' rather than 'doing shops'. The networks we studied where there was a clear evidence-based episteme outlining standards and targets for care (the cancer and sexual health networks and the Metropolitan Older People's Network implementing end of life care guidance) appeared significantly more effective in terms of improving patient care than where they were absent (in the genetics networks and the Regional Older People's Network). Crucially, few people we interviewed contested the legitimacy of the evidence-based guidelines being implemented in terms of their positive impact on patient care.

Second, network leadership required individual network leaders who strongly identified with this evidence-based episteme and who were therefore able to provide the energy and passion to drive changes and engaged in what we describe as 'evidence-based identity work' to convince others locally to change too. We see evidence of effective network leaders being involved in and promoting the use of evidence-based guidelines and targets (for example the Clinical Director in the Metropolitan City Sexual Health Network) and deriving their sense of self from their network role and the evidence-based episteme (for example, the Network Management Team in the County Cancer Network). We also see these leaders actively involved in 'evidence-based identity work' which legitimates bringing local clinical practices in line with national guidelines in terms of what good clinicians should be doing to benefit patients, and highlighting and using 'peer pressure' to undermine the legitimacy of old practices that needed to change (see, for example, the County Cancer and Metropolitan City Sexual Health Network cases).

Thirdly, enhanced audits of local practices provided the visibility necessary to demonstrate that local practice was less than best practice. Leaders were actively involved in making local practices visible and engaged in identity work to legitimate doing as being in patients' interests. For example the County Cancer Network Management Team was actively involved in auditing local practices and the Metropolitan City Sexual Health Network conducted a network-wide review to expose one underperforming clinic.

Fourthly, local processes (techne) were necessary to bring episteme, identification, and visibility together in practical ways, so that local stakeholders were committed and signed up to achieving service improvements, as for example the 'processes' for deciding the reconfiguration of services in the cancer networks or the Metropolitan City Sexual Health Network's 'network-wide review'.

Others have seen the leadership wave in the NHS as focused on the implementation of government policy. They suggest that it may simply be a new form of managerialism or 'control' with a more socially (in particularly clinically) acceptable badge (O'Reilly and Reed, 2011), in which clinicians are caught up in a project of subjectification and seduced by an attractive self-narrative into pursuing a government agenda (Martin and Learmonth, 2010). Alvesson and Willmott (2002) describe how regulating identity can be a form of organizational control. Like Alvesson and Spicer (2012), we acknowledge the potential problems associated with recourse to leadership as a policy instrument, but unlike critical leadership scholars are also open to its emancipatory and positive aspects too.

Our interpretation of network leadership as the social construction of governmentality is essentially or at least potentially optimistic, at least based upon the network cases we examined. When it appeared to be most effective, network leadership was focused on improving evidence-based patient care and worked actively to overcome early resistance from some powerful medical professionals, who appeared originally to have put their own interests before those of patients. Network leaders were commonly (at least in part) driven by a passion to improve patient care, and often told personal anecdotes about experience of poor care in practice to explain what drove them. The opinion of change-resistant clinicians shifted through time with close engagement with local networks, as in the cancer cases. We suggest that the positive examples of network leadership as the social construction of govermentality can be seen, in Alvesson and Spicer's terms (2012), as an emancipatory form of leadership which positively benefited patients.

However, all the fieldwork took place before the financial crisis of 2008 onwards and in an NHS then oriented more towards quality improvement rather than the cost containment and increasing productivity agenda that we see as more dominant in the NHS as we write. Some warning signs were apparent in our cases. In the Metropolitan City Sexual Health Network case, we saw leaders disengaging from their network roles as a new and less cooperative policy context (payment by results and competition between hospitals) arose. We are aware of other cases from other studies where governmentality is socially constructed in ways that may damage patient care (McGivern and Fischer, 2012). Whether clinical leaders will identify with new policy episteme and socially construct governmentality in the same way if they personally experience it adversely affecting the quality of care for their patients is a major question for future research.

10

Inter-organizational learning in the networks: A disappointing pattern

We reviewed the broad New Public Management (NPM)/post-NPM debate in the public policy literature earlier in Chapter 2. Authors who have critiqued the NPM wave (Dunleavy, 1995; Newman, 2001; Sullivan and Skelcher, 2002; Osborne, 2006) often pointed to its 'fragmenting' effects and erosion of creative policymaking in favour of an excessive focus on operational efficiency. Its strengthening of vertical reporting weakened systemic capacity, particularly in the handling of 'wicked problems' that crossed agency boundaries. The NPM was also seen as weak on promoting innovation and policy learning, as opposed to its stress on financial control and performance measurement.

A frequent defence of 'flatter' organizational forms in the general organizational literature (e.g. Alvesson, 2004, on knowledge-intensive firms) is that they stimulate higher rates of organizational learning than alternative forms of markets or hierarchies. Public services networks might therefore be well placed to develop *inter*-organizational learning and joint problem solving across organizational boundaries: there is an important cognitive component to network working. Networks should promote such learning more than markets or hierarchies. Newman's (2001) articulation of the post-NPM Network Governance narrative moved these arguments into the public policy domain, arguing that 'modernized' policymaking would show a continuous learning style and capability.

So considering the development of inter-organizational networks in the public sector—we have to ask, what was the policy-led argument and driver? Rhodes (2000) and Rashman and Radnor (2005) suggest that New Labour's policy agenda supported the integration of public services through collaboration and encouraging inter-organizational networks, as a characteristic mechanism of governance. This development should produce 'joined-up' government and challenge the fragmented 'silo mentality' previously noted

(Newman et al, 2000). In local government, networked learning and improvement was driven by various schemes for improving capacity and sharing practice, including the Beacon Council Scheme (Boyne et al, 2002; Downe et al, 2004; Rashman and Radnor, 2005; Hartley and Benington, 2006). Whilst the specifics of how the Beacon Scheme operated have been explored, there has been a critique concerning whether these policies were based on a robust theoretical base (Newman et al, 2000; Hartley and Allison, 2002; Hartley and Benington, 2006).

How effective were these inter-organizational networks in stimulating inter-organizational learning? Research from the private sector quoted later argued that supporting conditions need to be in place and that, for example, the resources and capabilities of the donor and recipient firms are crucial. The critics of the New Labour policy argued that insufficient attention was paid to such capacity issues, a view supported by some evaluations (Rashman and Radnor, 2005; Hartley and Benington, 2006). In health care, the movement towards networks followed a slightly variant pathway. The policy framework was similar across the public sector, but as we have shown the Calman–Hine Report (1995) into cancer care proposed managed clinical networks of organizations and integrated care pathways for cancer care. So there was an early development of inter-organizational networks in some key sectors within health care. The Calman–Hine report saw Managed Cancer Networks as an opportunity to foster the flow of knowledge and clinical expertise across organizational and professional boundaries. Following the development of the cancer networks, inter-organizational networks were then proposed in other areas of health care. These ideas then became enshrined in National Service Frameworks (NSFs) (e.g. in sexual health and older people's services).

Yet empirical work suggests such policy-led ambitions to create learning networks have not always been realized in practice. Early work on NHS Managed Cancer Networks (Addicott et al, 2006) found that a relatively diffuse organizational learning agenda was in practice crowded out by a primary concern with top-down restructuring. So have obstacles to effective learning in public policy networks been underestimated? Pollitt (2009) even suggests that stable bureaucracies may display a better developed organizational memory—an important basis for effective learning—than the unstable post-bureaucratic and network-based forms favoured by these policies.

Inter-organizational learning: A literature review

Academic publications (Hamel, 1991; Child and Faulkner, 1998; Finger and Brand, 1999; Newell et al, 2002; Van Wijk et al, 2008), literature reviews of inter-organizational knowledge transfer (Easterby-Smith et al, 2008; Meier, 2011), and journal special issues (*Journal of Management Studies*: 45, p. 4) all evince the current level of interest in inter-organizational learning. As these publications demonstrate, much research focuses on the private sector. However, useful conceptual ideas and definitions can be drawn from this work. Deriving their framework from Szulanski (1996), Easterby-Smith et al (2008) offer a set of factors affecting the transfer of learning in dyadic networks. These are: the resources and capabilities of the donor and recipient firms; the nature of the knowledge being exchanged; and the inter-organizational dynamics. In considering the relevance of this framework to our own research, a number of observations may be made. The competitive nature of the underlying relationships between firms in the private sector is highlighted here, particularly in the debates concerning power asymmetry within the inter-organizational dynamics. The use of the terms 'donor' and 'recipient' appears to assume such asymmetry and to offer a perception of exchange as gain. This view is reinforced by the literature on 'learning races' (Hamel, 1991) which suggests that the firm which learns fastest dominates the relationship. These issues may therefore differ from those in public services networks where profit is not the core outcome. Meier's (2011) review of empirical evidence critiques the field as complex, fragmented, and incoherent, but nevertheless develops an empirically founded integrative framework with factors which mirror those of Easterby-Smith et al but with the addition of knowledge management systems.

Other authors highlighted competitive advantage as a driver of change (Pettigrew and Fenton, 2000) arguing that knowledge creation, collecting, and sharing are all critical for project and corporate success (p. 286). Hamel (1991) proposes that intent to learn is critical to inter-organizational learning.

Despite some recent growth, less research and academic writing focuses on inter-organizational learning between public sector organizations than private sector networks. So a recent systematic review by Rashman et al (2009) is highly pertinent. They make the point that public service organizations are subject to pressures for learning and innovation, similar to those in the private sector found by Pettigrew and Fenton (2000). In the public sector, these pressures do not derive primarily from market competition, but are catalysed by government policies, pressures for performance, and users' expectations. Indeed, in addition to governmental pressure, the health care sector is subject to many similar drivers as the private sector, for example, using new products, new drugs, and new delivery methods such as key hole surgery. And the authors argue that public organizations are critical to national competitiveness in creating the necessary infrastructure for private sector effectiveness.

Rashman et al (2009) provide a framework for understanding inter-organizational learning between public sector organizations. They outline various factors which empirically have been found to influence such processes. These factors include: the outer context; the policy and practice context, including the embeddedness of knowledge; the relationship characteristics; and recipient and source characteristics. Whilst such factors evidentially replicate many factors identified for private sector inter-organizational learning, there are illuminating differences, both of substance and emphasis: contextual influences are given greater priority; there is a firmer acknowledgement of the role of power; and knowledge intentions are influential. Rashman et al's (2009) argument is that public organizations face the same pressures to learn, but exist in a more complex context with conflicting tensions, such as those between the demands of political actors and citizens. Currie and Suhomlinova (2006) argue that regulatory and institutional pressures make it more difficult to freely share knowledge in the NHS. This literature suggests there are many distinctive and interacting aspects to inter-organizational knowledge sharing in the public sector.

This view is reinforced by other research which highlights further features differentiating the public health care sector. Health care is characterized as a highly professionalized domain with many different professions. Authors (Newell et al, 2002; Ferlie et al, 2005b; Oborn and Dawson, 2010) identify and analyse the difficulties of inter-professional and interdisciplinary learning. They point to epistemic boundaries which have to be breached for learning to occur, as well as organizational boundaries. Oborn and Dawson (2010) identify three practices which facilitate learning across communities of practice, namely, organizing discussions, acknowledging other perspectives, and challenging assumptions.

One influential element in bridging across epistemic boundaries lies in addressing the nature of knowledge itself. Tsoukas and Vladimirou (2001) argue for a definition of knowledge seen as the ability to draw distinctions and to exercise judgement, based on an appreciation of context. Thus understanding of context is intrinsic to the value and use of knowledge.

We are here interested in investigating the processes in the networks studied through which knowledge is shared and inter-organizational learning occurs. Mason and Leek (2008) identify the types of mechanisms which may influence practice—knowledge articulation, for example, through conferences; knowledge codification, for example, via documenting and review procedures. Mason and Leek (2008) focus on more mechanical aspects, but other factors, such as challenging assumptions (Oborn and Dawson, 2010) and management skill and capacity (Addicott et al, 2006) have also been identified as crucial. Surprisingly, there is very limited research in either the public or the private sectors directly addressing the attitudes to sharing and learning of the parties in a network. Hence the detailed analysis by Huxham and Hibbert (2008) is especially illuminating. Their research sets out to investigate appreciative aspects, namely attitudes towards the possibility of learning and the directional aspect, which is the acquisition or donation of knowledge. They present an initial conceptualization showing a spectrum of attitudes ranging across: selfish acquisition; sharing of knowledge in a controlled fashion via exchange; sharing of knowledge in a broad open manner, through exploring; and sidelining of learning thus excluding it from the collaborative agenda. Based on a substantial database, they empirically note variants from their initial conceptualization. These include 'protective' behaviour and an instrumental stance—'we give when it suits us'. In summary, they conceptualize the attitudes to learning manifested in networks as made up of complex combinations of varied stances, with frequently an asymmetry of attitudes. Rashman et al (2009) finish with an illuminating discussion of the paucity of outcome measures of organizational learning. Thus another key research gap is displayed. They discuss the time lags which occur between learning and implementing changes which make the empirical evaluation of learning very difficult. They argue that the 'improvement bias' in the literature tends to always assume that learning is a positive thing. Furthermore, there are few measures of the effectiveness of inter-organizational learning processes (a particularly difficult issue if one attempts to use an assessment of 'public value'). Of especial relevance to our work is the call from Meyer (2007) for research which incorporates contextual variables in study design and pursues more cross-context comparative research. Here we are attempting to respond to this call.

Comparing our cases, we are particularly interested to explore issues raised by these other authors. We focus on three broad themes:

- What differences in the attitudes of participants to learning do the cases display?

- How do we analyse the processes of inter-organizational learning revealed?

- What facilitates and what hinders inter-organizational learning?

Dimensions of inter-organizational learning: Empirical themes from the cases

To aid comparison, we present Table 10.1 which provides an overview of the type and quality of inter-organizational learning found across the cases.

193

Table 10.1. Organizational and inter-organizational learning in the networks

Extent of Learning	Network	Learning Pattern	Characteristics & Processes
Strong evidence of learning	County Cancer Network	Strong inter-organizational learning; reflecting on organizational processes; sharing information and expertise across boundaries; promoting learning in smaller groups.	Mainly single sector & professions with same epistemic base. Ability to reflect on past events and to change the process.
Strong evidence of learning	Urban Cancer Network	Strong inter-organizational learning; reflecting on organizational processes; sharing information and expertise across boundaries; promoting learning in smaller groups.	Mainly single sector & professions with same epistemic base. Ability to reflect on past events and to change the process; also develops a theory of how network adds value.
Strong/Medium evidence of learning	Metropolitan City Sexual Health Network	Reasonably strong inter-organizational learning; examples of cross-boundary sharing; large-scale Research Day.	Multi-sectoral; multi-professional with varied epistemic base. Develops mixed large-scale research arena as a learning space.
Medium evidence of learning	Cathedral City Sexual Health Network	Variable inter-organizational learning; some examples in the strategic group, but weak connection to the field or systemic learning.	Multi-sectoral; multi-professional with varied epistemic base.
Medium evidence of learning	Metropolitan Older People's Network	Variable inter-organizational learning; informal organizational learning internal to network sound; strong education and training emphasis; limited systematic forums and weak connection to the field.	Multi-sectoral; multi-professional with varied epistemic base. Processes focused internally, informal.
Limited evidence of learning	Regional Older People's Network	Limited learning in core management groups; limited inter-organizational forums; some wider learning through Older People's Champions.	Multi-sectoral; multi-professional with varied epistemic base. Enduring tensions between professions & agencies (health/ social care); 'cliques'; few systems for shared learning.

(continued)

Table 10.1. (*Continued*)

Extent of Learning	Network	Learning Pattern	Characteristics & Processes
Limited evidence of learning	Genetics Translation Network 2	Some internal learning, but weak inter-organizational learning; no joint intellectual fora; continuing epistemological differences.	Mainly single sector, a public health 'enclave' in a university setting! Few systems for shared learning, both epistemic and organizational boundaries; retreat into base academic disciplines.
Limited evidence of learning	Genetics Translation Network 1	Limited internal learning; weak inter-organizational learning; no joint intellectual fora; continuing epistemological differences.	Mainly single sector, university setting! Narrow focus on implementation; weak processes to discuss and resolve differences between groups; both epistemic and organizational boundaries.

Characterizing the complexity of knowledge sharing

To understand our subsequent discussion, the complexity and the dimensions of knowledge sharing and learning in inter-organizational networks first have to be clarified. As we previously argued, the nature of the knowledge to be 'learned' is a central issue. Much clinical knowledge is ambiguous and uncertain, whilst other aspects of clinical and scientific knowledge represent more codified forms of knowledge (Dopson and FitzGerald, 2005; the Cochrane Collaboration, 2012). The scale of the organizations and groups involved is evidentially of importance to inter-organizational learning, yet our empirical data also suggest that other characteristics are of relevance. As Rashman et al (2009) point out, we need to delineate the characteristics of the networks which influence inter-organizational learning.

Networks may include a range of stakeholders all drawn from the same sector, such as cancer networks; or include membership of organizations based in different sectors, such as sexual health networks. Similarly, the majority of individuals in a network across differing organizations may belong to the same profession, for example, the economic development group quoted by Huxham and Hibbert (2008), or include many professional groups, as in our networks in the care of older people.

Our evidence suggests one major source of 'complexity' in inter-organizational knowledge sharing arises from the diversity and range of sectors and partners in the network. Thus where a network includes members of a number of professions, knowledge sharing and learning will be more complex due to the epistemic, as well as organizational, boundaries involved (Ferlie et al, 2005b).

To illustrate these points, we offer examples of two networks. The County Cancer Network consisted of all the organizations involved in cancer care in the geographical area; this included three acute hospitals, four Primary Care Trusts (PCTs), a Community Health Trust, and seven, small independent hospices. The County Cancer Network was a large network which included organizations from health care and from the voluntary sector, but with the unifying dimension that many individual participants were from the medical or nursing professions. So whilst the member organizations had differing structures and incentives, there was a uniformity of purpose, namely improving cancer care. And equally importantly, there was a shared underlying knowledge base which most members were familiar with. On the other hand, The Cathedral City Sexual Health Network (Cathedral) included one Primary Care Trust; one acute hospital, one local authority, and several voluntary organizations focusing on HIV/AIDS, pregnancy, alcohol, and drugs advice, plus a Strategic Partnership Board. It was not the scale of Cathedral which was most relevant, but the wide diversity of the organizations *and* the individual participants. Here there was a central unifying focus, but a limited shared knowledge base. Cathedral did however have the advantage of a prior history of cooperation and some established relationships.

This latter point highlights another relevant dimension—the importance of local history. It takes time to build trust and to establish relationships (aided or impeded by the stability of membership). The Metropolitan City Sexual Health Network started from a well-established base of prior relationships to take decisions within a trusted group and commence activities rapidly. The Regional Network in Older People's Care (Regional), on the other hand, started life with a diverse range of stakeholders with no prior history of cooperation. So even at the individual level, the key participants had to learn about each other and work together.

If diversity and variability of background are core dimensions of complexity in inter-organizational learning, then the network's structures of governance and, in particular, the mechanisms of inclusiveness within a network are important facilitating features. In our study, we found a range of approaches to inclusiveness in the networks' activities. In Genetic Translation Network 1 (GTN1), no efforts were directed towards inclusiveness and there were limited attempts to establish cross-organizational or cross-professional fora. Indeed, there was little comprehension of the critical role of the PCT as commissioners of new services, until very late in the development process. This network differed dramatically from the approach adopted by the Regional

Older People's Network (Regional) where various 'exchange' fora were set up, with a recognition of the need to be inclusive, to work together, and to build trust:

> I suppose to enable multi-professional, multi-agency discussion. To come up with some sort of common agreed sort of themes for work around older people, that represent all of those different stakeholders' views and agreed ways of taking them forward, with the intention of actually achieving something as a group, as opposed to each organization attempting to do their own thing in an uncoordinated way. (Manager, Local Authority)

But the fora existed mainly at the top levels of the Network and experienced problems with membership and developing a clear action focus.

The processes of knowledge sharing and learning were also impacted by the resources available, largely human resources. As demonstrated previously, our two cancer networks were better resourced with a competent core of leaders and good quality central support, when compared with the two sexual health networks.

Manifested attitudes to knowledge sharing

It might be argued that open or 'willing' attitudes to sharing knowledge and learning from other organizations and individuals in a network form an essential precursor to joint activity and to positive outcomes. This proposition aligns with the data. Appendix 2's Table 1 on the comparative performance assessment of the networks suggests a potential link between such attitudes and network performance. Thus the research focus and analysis by Huxham and Hibbert (2008) is directly relevant to our research. As suggested by their prior research, different combinations of attitudes to knowledge sharing were evident in our cases.

Within the two cancer cases, we find evidence of reasonably open attitudes to sharing of knowledge and also explicit mechanisms for sharing and learning (discussed and illustrated in greater detail in the next section). In the County Cancer Network, these positive attitudes are particularly apparent at the leadership level, namely within the Network Management Team, who report they are all working together to a common end:

> We [the Network Management Team] are all essentially going in the same direction...[the Medical Director] will be looking at it from you know the doctor's point. I [Nurse Director] will be...looking at it from my perspective and [Network Director] looks at it from her perspective and [XXX] looks from hers. But it is the combination of all those collective expertise, I suppose which brings it together as a kind of, you know, a unified sort of collaborative. (Nurse Director)

It is apparent from this quote that the three members of the Network Management Team are sharing their expertise and respecting each others' contribution. These attitudes are confirmed by others, who acknowledge the collaboration:

> The three of them [Medical Director, Network Director, & Nurse Director] are on the whole very sympathetic and they have the interest of cancer patients at heart. (Patient Representative)

There is also fairly strong evidence that the County Cancer Network's leadership recognized the need to broach boundaries and facilitate sharing:

> My view of the purpose of the Network is to deliver high-quality cancer services that are equally accessible wherever you live within the Network boundaries and that deliver pathways irrespective of the organization and professional group that is responsible for those pathways. In other words it is breaking down all those boundaries. (Network Director)

The Network Director argued that a key part of her role was as a boundary-spanner, engaging various clinical groups in the Network. She stated her role was about:

> ...remaining quite grounded... being out and about... official... keeping tabs on what the reality is down in the ground, because you can get quite detached... [Being at] key meetings and have contributed to those key decisions... engaging with those clinical members of staff but then also delivery [rather than]... focusing on the key things I need to achieve and then kind of delivering on those.

The Network operated effectively within the clinical domain, engaging various clinical professions, but appeared less inclusive of other groups outside the clinical jurisdictions. Thus some groups in the Network felt it was less inclusive. Both patient representatives and a Hospice Director expressed doubts about their inclusion in key Board decisions:

> I think it is just somebody rings somebody and they have a meeting or a discussion beforehand so that by the time it comes to the Board the decision has been made. (Patient representative)

> ...I think some decisions are made there but it is quite clear other decisions are being made elsewhere... [and] I don't know who decides what goes on the agenda. (Hospice Director)

The cancer networks are interesting because they offer evidence of knowledge sharing occurring at several levels of activity. Thus in the County Cancer Network, we see much groundwork for organizational change and new care pathways are being performed by the specific tumour groups consisting of clinical staff at the local level. The attitudes within the tumour groups provide insights into some tensions between the various professions. The Urology Tumour Group Chair stated:

> I am signed up to the concept of centralization, less signed up to it now that I was, because in the long term I think it's probably less beneficial in terms of surgery than...chemotherapy.

In observing the discussions within this tumour group, we noted that the two most vocal urologists were sitting next to each other, seated adjacent to the Urology Tumour Group Chair (a surgeon) presenting a sense of 'them and us' between urologists and other professionals. Urologists appeared to be concerned about 'number crunchers who don't understand the patient pathway' misunderstanding their practice.

Whilst these tensions clearly existed, they were openly acknowledged and the Network Management Team and other key clinicians searched for appropriate ways of alleviating them and dealing with disagreements:

> Part of the process is about the Network really ironing out disagreements prior to signing off the plans and it would be again pretty problematic if the network sort of tried to sign off half-cooked plans without having gone through that sort of process. (Network Chair)

As a result of the positive attitudes of the leaders and their actions, including active management of conflict and processes of engagement, communication, and consultation to resolve issues, the outcomes of the reconfiguration of services were seen as positive:

> Urology has gone quite well. The clinicians very much led the process...There was very good communication and engagement with all the clinical teams...very extensive consultation with lots of people, patients, and everybody concerned. (Hospital Director)

Across the cases, there were often problems with disciplinary boundaries. One respondent in the Regional Network for Older People observed:

> if you have a positive experience of working with colleagues and you achieve your outcomes jointly, I don't think you're going to worry too much about what their professional background is. I think when there are difficulties, then such thoughts might start to occur as well. They're thinking like that because they are a doctor or whatever, yes and that's where barriers and obstacles can start to appear. (Manager, Local Authority)

Joint learning could be hampered by inter-organizational competition, either for service contracts at the provider level or for agency turf and jurisdictions:

> there are lots of times when it does feel like you're achieving something together, but also a lot of times where you feel, quite frankly, that you are competing with

the person sitting next to you. I think that's the nature of the voluntary sector in the city. I think it's the nature of the city council, I think it's the nature of the city council's relationship with the PCT. I think there is an awful lot of competition as well, rather than being open. (Manager, Specialist Charity)

An even more negative set of attitudes is displayed in the Genetics Translation Networks. In the GTN1 case, the various stakeholders forming the Network came together with a prior history. The academic researchers were perceived to have been at the forefront of research in human molecular genetics for many years. At the formation of the Network, they already held research grants from major funders. Two further stakeholder groups were an NHS genetics laboratory which offered a full regional service and an NHS clinical genetics department which provided a full range of clinical genetic services to patients. The research centre and the genetics laboratory were co-located. But the hospital genetics department was regarded as a 'backwater', with poor leadership historically. This contrasted with the notable success of genetics research in the university. Thus the inter-group attitudes of the key stakeholder groups contained tensions when they joined together in GTN1. The academic researchers who we refer to hereafter as *clinical researchers* perceived themselves as the 'elite' and were not motivated to learn from other groups. We deliberately distinguish the *clinical researchers* mainly trained in medicine from other *scientists* as we refer to them in the case, who were trained in scientific disciplines other than medicine. The clinical researchers conceived of the Network as a means of perpetuating and developing their own work:

It was a question of pulling a team together. But from our point of view, it was just using additional funds from government to add to the broad area of information about genetics out there. (Senior Cancer Professor)

There was no evidence that they were motivated to share or learn with and from others. They conceived of the bid for funds for the Network as a means to fulfil their own ends:

I mean it provided additional, terribly useful funds to do the work we wanted to do but it was maintaining the momentum we were building elsewhere. (Senior Cancer Specialist)

The clinical researchers dominated the activities of the Network and employed the only full-time Network manager, the Network Director. The main activities of the Network were originally organized around four separate work packages, all involving different teams. This division of labour, of itself, presents challenges for network learning. The Network Director was an able manager whose role predominantly appeared to have been to monitor progress, manage the budget, and act as a problem solver. But there was no evidence of the Network Director proposing or generating fora for cross-disciplinary learning.

Crucially, as a full-time member of staff, she had time to monitor progress in the science and assist with acquiring financial resources. So a considerable proportion of her activities were focused upwards in the hierarchy.

The Network Director performed a highly effective and useful boundary-spanning role by moving between the stakeholder groups. A second key successful negotiator across borders was the consultant geneticist working in the hospital and university who moved easily between the two domains. A third key negotiator and boundary spanner was the economist working within the social science institute. And the fourth important management figure was the NHS commissioner, who had a background in nursing, experience in managing specialist units, and an MBA. However, against a background of considerable fragmentation, there is a limit to what individual boundary spanners can achieve without further mechanisms for group learning. As a newly appointed consultant geneticist (NHS) reported:

> In this site there is a huge gap between academic and clinical genetics ... Professor X who is hugely well known to geneticists does not know who I am and walks past me.

This fragmentation not only existed between individuals, but also between the stakeholder groups:

> There are a huge number of people doing genetic type research and we are not at all interconnected. Just yesterday, I had an email which was from somebody in bio-chemistry saying 'Hey why don't we set up a regional molecular genetics laboratory?' So I e-mailed the lab manager and said 'can you believe this? They don't even know the lab exists, it's been here for fifteen years! (Clinical Geneticist)

So there was a knowledge gulf between groups who all had scientific backgrounds. These gulfs were enlarged if one considered the attitudes displayed towards those from social science backgrounds. So the sociologist in Project 1 was seen as one of:

> these weird sort of sociology people doing 'woolly' research. (NHS Lab Scientist)

Another scientist stated:

> Our world is very black and white so when a sociologist talks to me about barriers in networks it does not mean much to me. (Lab Scientist)

Overall, whilst some progress was made in one Project, eventually the fragile cooperation broke down. The GTN1 was collectively imprinted with the epistemology of the clinical researchers who founded it. Analysed from the perspective of the four attitudinal stances proposed by Huxham and Hibbert (2008), the GTN1 case might be described as displaying attitudes of 'sidelining' consideration of joint learning and excluding it from the collaborative agenda.

In reviewing our data, we observe a wide range of attitudes, from active leadership and facilitation of knowledge sharing, modelled by senior figures; through well intentioned attitudes, less effectually fulfilled; to less supportive attitudes and inactivity. These data suggest that positive attitudes need reinforcement by appropriate facilitation and leadership, which acknowledges the extent of the boundaries to be breached.

Formal and informal processes and knowledge sharing

The activities occurring within a network relate directly to the manifested attitudes as discussed in the previous section. Attitudes and practice can therefore be linked. One must acknowledge that inter-organizational learning is also situated in a wider context which influences the effectiveness of the learning processes adopted. One influential contextual characteristic is the nature and strength of the imperative (or otherwise) to develop new ways of working (Rashman et al, 2009; Oborn and Dawson, 2010). Throughout the networks studied, various formal and informal processes for facilitating learning can be detected. This section will now provide illustrations of these mechanisms.

As displayed in Table 10.1, these illustrations are set out in a continuum across the range, starting with positive examples and moving through to examples of negative inactivity. In considering these data one must bear in mind the differences of contextual complexity previously discussed. Our first positive illustrations focus on the cancer networks, but the reader is reminded that the organizations in cancer networks are all in the health care sector. On the other hand, the following examples drawn first from the Metropolitan and the Cathedral City Sexual Health Networks, and second from the Metropolitan and Regional Older People's Networks, have to contend with greater inter-sectoral as well as inter-organizational variety. Thus it is surprising to note the inactivity demonstrated in the two GTNs, situated as they were between universities and health care.

Both cancer networks in the study employed various formal and informal processes for shared learning. In the County Cancer Network, the cross-disciplinary learning was embodied in the person of the Medical Director and modelled by him. He was perceived as a 'hybrid' with both clinical and managerial expertise. As one respondent stated:

> [The Medical Director] has been absolutely fantastic from a clinical and a managerial point of view, because he does get on and do the clinical bits... chatting

behind the scene and getting clinicians to work together . . . if you don't have any discussions outside the meetings nothing would ever happen. So we are reliant on people going away and doing sort of guidelines, developing policies. (Network Director)

This quote provides a useful point of departure, since it illustrates several aspects of the learning processes. Firstly, it demonstrates how a credible clinical manager uses informal, one-to-one processes to influence and persuade others. Secondly, we see a range of individuals are engaged in actions, so this is not merely a top-down process. Thirdly, we observe that the County Cancer Network makes detailed change plans driven by the explicit standards from NICE, but also customized to the local context.

At a lower level in the network, small specialist tumour groups met regularly to decide on the recommendations for changes to care pathways and services for patients with a specific cancer. In these tumour groups, there was a strong emphasis on debating the clinical and scientific evidence.

You do need to enjoy the confidence of your colleagues, both from a personal and a clinical perspective . . . clinical skills, which are number one priority. Number two, yes, get on well with people and deal with conflict situations reasonably well . . . [by] dialogue, establishing facts, persuasion, firmness. (Urologist)

Very similar data were recorded from the Regional Cancer Network. Across all our cases, it was only in the two cancer networks that we observed reflection on and learning from experience and particularly past errors. In the County Cancer Network, there had historically been a difficult prior reconfiguration in Upper Gastrointestinal Cancer Services (Upper GI). As a result of their experiences with Upper GI, the Network Management Team learned the importance of process in facilitating the reconfiguration of cancer services, and making sure that all parties had agreed the process through which decisions were made. In Regional, a similar historical problem had occurred with the reconfiguration of gynaecological services, leading to the Network Management Team formally agreeing a conflict resolution process, which aided the effective re configuration of services thereafter.

A variant set of processes is apparent in the sexual health cases. Here the context is different, with greater complexity, more inter-sectoral stakeholders, and fewer resources. Moreover, the policy imperative to change, whilst present, is less pressing and the focus on what to change is less clear. So in both the Metropolitan and the Cathedral City Sexual Health cases, the networks generated their own focus. Metropolitan created the Metropolitan City Sexual Health Framework and generated benchmarking against targets, and then selected as its first priority achieving the 48-hour access target to see patients. The Clinical Director argued that the 48-hour target galvanized and focused the network, suggesting that targets were useful within networks and shaped their agenda:

> We shared ideas, innovations. We visited a unit, and we suggested improvements looking at their patient flow and how they ran their systems and clinics, and then suggest improvements, which they adopted, which all helped I think. (Clinical Consultant)

As with the County Cancer Network, the Network Coordinator embodied a range of relevant expertise and played a 'brokering' role:

> Credit must be given to [1st Network Coordinator]...a very effective manager...she has a very good rapport with people, that's through her background with being working for a drug firm as a rep., as patient coordinator, and patient education, all this. So she had a very good grasp with people and she's also very knowledgeable...in terms of HIV care. (Clinical Consultant)

In the Metropolitan Network, we saw a rare example of a large but regular forum meeting used to update relevant knowledge. It organized a '5th Wednesday' research day (held quarterly, every fifth Wednesday) which brought together professionals from different organizations within the Network to hear about the latest research and news happening within the Network. As well as being educational, the research day also facilitated informal networking between Network members, particularly between acute trusts and PCTs enabling them to share ideas and develop relationships. It was well attended, with over one-hundred people regularly present.

Metropolitan Network also facilitated the sharing of best practice (via workshops and ongoing support) about how to make changes, for example how to redesign sexual health clinics to enable walk-in appointments.

> we were ahead of the country for quite a long time because clinicians really did sign up to it and we had workshops and we invited all the great and the good to share best practice, and we developed a timetable for rolling out whatever this best practice was. (1st Vice-Chair)

Whilst this Network was effective in creating inter-organizational learning between clinical professional groups, as in the cancer networks, there was very limited evidence that they were effective in reaching out to voluntary groups or to those in local authorities who were also working in sexual health. Metropolitan also suffered from instability in the Network leadership which led to some fall off in momentum.

In the Cathedral City Sexual Health Network, there was a twelve-month process of consultation, which ensured everyone's views were included. They then produced a 'Framework for Delivery' detailing twenty-eight tasks, including timeframes and deliverables. Thus the network built focus and activity into their work. This Network was one of the few in the study who reached out to voluntary groups. An approach was made to a large national HIV/AIDS charity to merge with them to become one of their regional organizations. This was seen as a way of securing Cathedral City HIV Services in the future, particularly as anxieties about financial matters would be resolved. Another advantage of joining up with a big national organization was personal supervision for the manager.

In the networks in the Care of Older People, there were two varied contexts. As mentioned earlier, Regional was a complex network containing health care organizations, a large local authority, voluntary sector groups, and private home providers. The Metropolitan Older People's Network, on the other hand, was a smaller and more tightly knit network of public and private providers of hospice services and services for the dying. The Regional Older People's Network faced a similar problem to the sexual health networks—the lack of a clear focus for changes. But unlike the sexual health networks, it struggled to overcome this issue and define its own priorities. The Network clearly desired to be inclusive and set up two fora, the Executive Group and the Older People's Group, which met regularly, but infrequently. Due to the diffuse focus and the huge possible range of activities, but also the timeframe between meetings, progress was immensely slow. So the stakeholders began to lose interest and commitment.

I think that's more of a talking shop than it should be. (Manager, Specialist Charity)

The Metropolitan Older People's Network operated on an informal basis, with more understanding between the clinical stakeholders: the General Practitioners (GPs), the palliative care nurses, and the home managers (who mostly came from clinical backgrounds). As a result, a great deal was achieved through several key 'brokers', such as one of the Coordinators. The Lead Coordinator commented on sharing ideas and reflective practice:

I pinch ideas from everywhere... share information, that's a good thing and then you can develop it yourself... it's about building in reflective periods and actually trying to write down just very simply what went well, what didn't go so well, what could have been better.... It's a hard thing to measure I think. (Lead End of Life Care Coordinator)

Alongside face-to-face verbal communication, the care homes were implementing a mandatory Death and Dying form, which required the carers to talk to the residents and relatives on their wishes and implement written guidelines based on the end of life care Gold Standard, a nationally developed set of standards.

An unusual example of an informal approach to learning was an initiative in the Regional Older People's Network—a group called the Older People's Champions. The genesis of the idea for Older People's Champions was in the 'toolkit' for the NSF for Older People. The Older People's Champions were a loose grouping of interested parties, working in the broad field of older people. It was formed from 'volunteers' acting as advocates and champions for older people who were seen as an informal means of bringing about a widespread change of attitudes towards the treatment of older people in all spheres. The Champions had influence in their interactions within and between other groups. The Champions appeared influential in urging that services for older people should be delivered with dignity and respect, and they wielded their influence through their formal roles. Two aspects of this group were of particular interest. Firstly, this is a mass-movement group, with many committed members (Bate et al, 2004). Secondly, there is very little formal structure or indeed meetings. The Champions in Regional city met once per year for an information exchange conference.

In terms of processes, whether formal or informal, used to generate inter-organizational learning, the most inactive networks were the two GTNs. There was evidence of these Networks engaging in some self contained forms of work. In GTN1, this was mainly in the continuation of research now focused on the four work projects. In the GTN2, it was largely centred on the dissemination and publication of data and information felt to be useful to the public or professionals external to the Network. We found little attention paid to inter-organizational learning within the Networks themselves.

Starting to conceptualize inter-organizational learning processes and outcomes

In reviewing the evidence on inter-organizational learning, we draw attention again to the lack of robust, tested methods to assess learning outcomes in inter-organizational networks. Appendix 2 lays out our framework for assessing the performance of the networks overall. But limited attention has been given to assessing more specific outcomes anticipated from inter-organizational learning. In reviewing our data in the light of the available literature, we propose that the following criteria provide a useful starting point for developing such an assessment:

- Operational knowledge systems for accessing evidence-based knowledge and the extent and modes of inclusiveness within the network.

- The processes of learning in operation—the sharing of information and knowledge across locations as a key vehicle of change.
- The processes of learning in operation—sharing and learning taking place at multiple levels including local levels, in smaller groups and in multidisciplinary groups for individual benefit.
- Learning from past events.
- Evidence of changes in practices.

In order to assess inter-organizational learning in networks, one needs relevant supporting data. These data include evidence that network leaders were developing processes to access evidence-based knowledge. This was apparent in the two cancer networks, where both clinical updating and the analysis of local epidemiology were fed into the network system. However, few other practices of external data search, such as benchmarking or schemes like the Beacon Council Scheme, were detected (Downe et al, 2004; Rashman and Radnor, 2005; Hartley and Benington, 2006). In our cases, there is evidence of network managers working towards developing and improving inclusiveness, although with variable outcomes.

Considering evidence on the sharing of information and knowledge across locations as a key vehicle of change, one key indicator is the critical role played by individuals. We note that there were some senior figures who modelled behaviour, but also acted as effective 'bridges' in the cases, carrying ideas from one location to another as advocates.

In some cases, even if only partially, managers ensured that fora for learning existed and that the processes of learning were in operation. Within the networks, we noted a range of useful fora, large and small, most commonly those which engaged a multidisciplinary membership, such as the Multidisciplinary Teams (MDTs) developed in cancer, sexual health, and to a lesser extent older people's care. However, inter-sectoral engagement and debate was rarer and is a critical issue for the more complex networks. The networks were often poor at learning through reflection on past events. Only in the cancer networks did we perceive any systematic attempts to learn via reflection. This is illuminating as in many approaches to project management, this would be a 'standard' way of learning and it is a well-established mechanism for learning in professional communities of practice or professional enclaves. But it was rarely employed in the networks.

It might be argued that the ability to reach stated goals should be seen as a crucial outcome. Knight and Pye (2005) argue that one can see learning as an important influence on changing practices. Therefore in health care learning outcomes should in the long run be evident in changes to the way patients are cared for. The links between learning and overall service level outcomes are under-explored and we could not do this systematically in the current study.

Conclusion: A generally disappointing pattern

Overall, we found relatively low levels of inter-organizational learning in the cases. First, we observe that basic attitudes to sharing information and learning generate motivation to act and underpin all activity. Negative or careless attitudes to inter-organizational learning were detrimental. We note that some important aspects of inter-organizational learning were under-developed in most networks. These were: facilitating access to and sharing of evidence-based knowledge; reflecting on practice and projects; and developing regular, larger-scale forums for cross-fertilization of learning. The near absence of intersectoral forums for debate and learning is especially relevant to our analysis. It is clearly not easy to facilitate inter-organizational learning within managed networks across different sectors.

To draw out the reasons for these conclusions, we readdress the questions posed at the beginning of the chapter here:

- What differences in the attitudes of participants to learning do the cases display?
- How do we analyse the processes of inter-organizational learning revealed?
- What facilitates and what hinders inter-organizational learning?

In their analysis, Huxham and Hibbert (2008) offered four initial categories of attitudes: selfish acquisition; sharing of knowledge in a controlled fashion via exchange; sharing of knowledge in a broad open manner, through exploring; and the sidelining of any consideration of learning thus excluding it from the collaborative agenda. In our cases, there was only minimal evidence of selfish acquisition, but we observed evidence akin to the remaining three categories. Like Huxham and Hibbert, we observed a wider range of mixed attitudes, from active leadership and facilitation of knowledge sharing, modelled by senior figures; through well-intentioned attitudes, less effectually fulfilled; to less supportive attitudes and inactivity. From our data, a potentially significant association emerges between the attitudes manifested throughout the organizations in a network, their practices, and ultimately their performance outcomes (at least as we assessed them). This association is as yet tentative, but suggests an interesting focus for future research. Previous research (Addicott et al, 2006, 2007) has already highlighted the key role of network management teams in making cancer networks effective, at least as assessed against process outcomes.

We recall that Easterby-Smith et al (2008) presented four factors affecting the transfer of learning in dyadic networks: the resources and capabilities of the donor and recipient firms; the nature of the knowledge being exchanged; and inter-organizational dynamics. So to synthesise our analysis and to draw out some wider implications, we will explore these factors and the other factors emerging from these data. These observations illustrate some facilitators and inhibitors of inter-organizational learning.

As previous chapters demonstrated, the management capabilities of the organizations in a network play a key role in its effective functioning. This chapter illustrates that management capability also impacts the inter-organizational learning processes. We note here that in complex networks, senior management's ability was crucial in developing clarity of focus. To take effect, the processes of knowledge exchange needs to be converted into practices, and to achieve this, knowledge has to be focused on achieving a target or outcome. Thus the Cathedral City Sexual Health Network could transform useful knowledge into actions via their plan—'Framework for Delivery'. Targets which were well-understood (and driven by downward pressures from national policy), as in the cancer networks were useful.

We suggest that whilst the physical and financial resources of the network affect its ability to function, these may be less important to inter-organizational learning than human resources. Within these public sector and mixed public/private sector networks, there was minimal evidence of one dominant 'donor' organization, as in dyadic networks. There was however evidence of power differences between groups and individuals and a dominant episteme, as in the Regional Older People's Network and the GTNs.

There needs in our view to be a more active and progressive use of fora for sharing and joint activity, if major improvement in joint learning is to take place. Here the evidence suggests that networks which adopt a variety of mechanisms for knowledge sharing and debate, across organizational boundaries and across vertical and lateral organizational levels, fare best. It is probable that over-reliance on a single mechanism is insufficient to achieve inter-organizational learning in a complex network. As suggested, a clear, shared focus of activity which can generate shared practice is important. We noted that in large and complex networks, inter-organizational learning processes had to overcome both the physical and cultural boundaries between different organizations, as well as the occupational and epistemic boundaries between different professions and groups.

This leads to the observation, derived from our data, that the nature of the knowledge to be exchanged, as well as its relation to the participants in the exchanges is central. Confirming previous research (Ferlie et al, 2005b; Oborn and Dawson, 2010), the data suggest epistemic boundaries may be more difficult to negotiate than organizational boundaries or location. Informal and formal processes of sharing and learning within a network with a predominant and common disciplinary base, such as medicine, were more readily established. It was here easier to facilitate a process which fitted with the context. In networks which included cross-sectoral and cross-disciplinary membership, the timescales for developing an accepted and effective forum were longer and required careful facilitation. In the Metropolitan Older People's Network, informal knowledge sharing and bridging roles worked effectively in sharing learning across the organizations and across clinical professions. But in the Regional Older People's Network, the Executive Group struggled to establish inter-organizational learning processes across the social care professions, the clinical professions, the local authority managers, and the private and voluntary sector operators. These varied groups and individuals had a minimal knowledge base in common and it is difficult to judge whether time alone would have achieved greater progress. Oborn and Dawson (2010) maintain that challenging assumptions is one of the attributes which aids interdisciplinary learning, but there was limited evidence of such processes occurring in these cases. We observed that the nature of prior, historical working relationships also affected the rate of progress in developing learning mechanisms and processes.

In considering specific facilitators and inhibitors of inter-organizational learning, some additional factors emerge. The cases suggest the extent and nature of the complexity of the network has important consequences. To develop inter-organizational learning, an important prerequisite of appropriate actions is an ability to analyse and understand the context. This is crucial to the effective planning and resourcing of inter-organizational learning.

Based on our data and assessment of performance, networks seem particularly effective when there is a balanced team of people in core senior leadership roles. This suggests an extension to the concept of collective leadership, already noted as effective for the leadership of strategic change in health care (Denis et al, 2001). A collective leadership cadre facilitates the engagement of differing professions and disciplines. Team members from these differing professions may act as credible leaders, may model behaviour, and may inject knowledge from their own professional base and encourage sharing.

We also note the utility and the powerful and effective role played by some individual knowledge brokers. In all our higher-achieving cases, we observed key individuals often present at several levels within the network who played a bridging role and helped to breach both organizational and disciplinary boundaries. We have already illustrated the efficacy of modelling behaviour.

The main inhibitors of inter-organizational learning lie in the complexity of the networks themselves and the policy context. We have discussed the issues facing multi-sectoral and multidisciplinary networks in overcoming various boundaries. The policy context may be either supportive or inhibitive of learning. A learning focus may be usefully engendered by policy and quality frameworks which set standards. But inter-organizational learning may be inhibited by tight task-oriented policy targets, which allow little 'slack' for debate or learning. A further inhibitor noted is the embeddedness of knowledge within a discipline.

So will more effective inter-organizational learning in networks enable them to resolve the 'wicked problems' with which they are often confronted? Our case data and analysis offer some but (thus far) only limited hope. It is evident that inter-organizational learning may occur with considerable success within a large, unisectoral network. More limited evidence supports the tentative view that inter-organizational learning can develop in large, multi-sectoral networks. The core differences are not related to scale or even automatically to sectoral differences, but rather to the combined complexity of disciplinary, organizational, and sectoral differences. This research evidence also offers some clear indicators of what might be done to engender greater success. But it is further suggested that a more active and multi-faceted approach to inter-organizational learning would be required to support major improvement. This strategy may also require skilled mediation, following Waring and Currie's (2009) argument, and so far this has generally not been present.

11

Governmentality and health care networks

In this chapter, we return to our earlier theoretical framing around governmentality introduced in Chapter 3 to explore its significance for interpreting our case study material now introduced. Broadly speaking, our cases suggest a form of health care governance which is changing its shape from the old model of large vertically integrated public bureaucracies and is now incorporating a greater range of actors (notably elite clinical and academic segments) in novel arenas and using more indirect steering technologies. However, the centre (notably government departments and agencies such as the Department of Health (DoH) and National Institute of Health and Clinical Excellence (NICE)) does not disappear: rather it takes on a different shape but still tries to survey and steer the wider health care field as suggested in the Anglo governmentality perspective (Miller and Rose, 2008). We return to the four broad Foucauldian themes introduced earlier to pursue this line of argument further.

Theme 1: A power knowledge nexus—The national apparatus of Evidence-Based Medicine

As noted earlier, Harrison et al (2002) see Evidence-Based Medicine (EBM) as a distinct mode of 'scientific bureaucratic' medicine which seeks to steer clinical fields through the production of standardized clinical guidelines (Timmermans and Berg, 2003). Over the last decade, EBM has been institutionalized through the work of NICE (created in 1999) which has developed as an influential specialized national advisory agency. Informed by NICE, various National Service Frameworks (NSFs) have produced evidence-based guidance and standards for the health care field in various key sectors. So much EBM production is located at the national level, although informing activity in the local networks. We will now examine four EBM foundational texts which strongly relate to the four network settings studied.

Cancer Services: The cancer arena represents a particularly well-developed example of a power/knowledge nexus, as it is strongly connected to the heartland of biomedical research and scientific knowledge production with a large number of Randomized Control Trials (RCTs). The evidence and standards-based policy framework in the cancer field develops strongly and consistently (DoH, 1995, 2000b, 2007; NHSE, 2001), leading to various substantial Improved Outcome Guidance (IOG) documents (of which our tracer of Urology Improved Outcome Guidance is but one example). There is an advisory ensemble which includes senior academic clinicians as well as senior civil servants. More cancer patients are being enrolled in trials, including the major £30m (Protect) trial for prostate cancer (DoH, 2007) in urology, so the underpinning biomedical knowledge base is of substantial and increasing scale. Our two cases indicated that the Urology IOG over the long-term substantially steered the local clinical fields, producing important shifts in clinical working practices.

Who has helped construct the Urology Improved Outcome Guidance as an influential text? The methodological appendix 2 (NICE, 2002) states it is based on: 'systematic reviews of the best available evidence on diagnosis, treatment and service delivery. The evidence is assessed by experts and the recommendations are the product of extensive discussion with leading clinical specialists'. The methods underpinning the systematic review of best evidence are discussed in more detail under Theme 3, but here we comment on who is centrally involved in such a review. Clearly the possession of high levels of clinical and research expertise is important in becoming a member of the inner core. The National Cancer Guidance Steering Group's membership (appendix 3.1) mixes senior clinical academics (from research-intensive universities), clinicians, and health services researchers with a senior health policy grouping. The National Service Director for cancer is an eminent clinical academic and is Vice-Chair of this group. Another eminent clinical academic is the Chair. It is stated that the urology standards were developed in consultation with leading clinicians, so reflect informed clinical opinion as well as formal evidence. By contrast, there are few National Health Service (NHS) general managers, non-executives from a business background, or expert patients in this group. There is also a large cohort of expert reviewers of evidence, which is seen as less clear in this area than with some other cancers.

While it appears that the core of the advisory apparatus has been largely colonized by high-level scientific, clinical, research, and policy groupings, this is not the whole picture. There is also a large initial and creative proposal-generating event which mixes many health care professionals with some direct patient representation. The forward by the Chairman is open and forward-looking in tone: it is remarked that increasingly active patient groups have helped draw attention to service deficiencies within what had been a rather backward sector. It is also stated that there needed to be more multi-disciplinary teamwork with a bigger role for nursing than hitherto, diluting traditional uniprofessional domination. The document opens the way to a major and broadly based change management and service improvement effort.

Sexual Health Services: The national Sexual Health Strategy (DoH, 2001a) shares similar features with the cancer services field, but more softly expressed. There are some differences in tone. It starts by asserting: 'this strategy has been developed by involving service users, members of target groups and professionals in the field'. The text includes an epidemiological assessment of changing sexual infection caseloads, calling for: 'the development of nationally agreed guidelines on HIV treatment and care, together with locally agreed operational guidelines in the form of care pathways' (para 4/61). Epidemiological forms of knowledge are well developed in this text. However, an increasing number of trials for antiretroviral drugs to treat HIV were strengthening an underpinning biomedical research base. While it is acknowledged in the text that the evidence base for preventive work was imperfect, the ambition was: 'ensuring that there is a sound evidence base for effective prevention of HIV and other sexually transmitted infections'. Interestingly, and at least in the Metropolitan area, the Network was seeking to implement sets of guidelines developed by clinical/professional groups more than a government agency (although they were reinforced by many of the principles in the National Sexual Health Strategy).

Its Steering Committee again mixed leading clinical academics, clinicians, health services researchers, and civil servants. The Chair was a senior clinical academic from a research intensive university and the Vice-Chair a senior medical civil servant. However, there is substantially more representation from CEOs of voluntary sector organizations so that this policy arena appears somewhat more pluralist than the cancer field.

Older People's Services: The National Service Framework for Older People (DoH, 2001b) can be seen as broader and softer in nature than the two other texts. This text has a strong multi-agency perspective referring extensively to the role of the social care sector and to voluntary organizations as well as to health care. Given the complex interactions between physical, mental, and social factors, a stated ambition was to ensure the provision of seamless services which crossed agency boundaries effectively.

It developed standards for services which (p. 9) should be: 'evidence based where possible, or if not, to be based on the consensus of best clinical practice'. A conventional hierarchy of evidence model was used (p. 11) which ranked (for example) systematic reviews of RCTs as A1 and case studies as C2. Professional, user, and carer opinion are included as low-grade sources of evidence at the bottom of the table. The relationship between this table and decisions about the standards actually set is opaque. For example, the first standard is 'rooting out age discrimination' which relates to behavioural changes rather than clinical evidence. Older People's Champions were to be designated to help achieve this objective. The second standard is organizationally focused, namely provision of 'person-centred care' where a single cross-agency assessment process and integrated commissioning were to have a key role.

However, standard sources of evidence fed into the text including the Cochrane database of systematic reviews and relevant systematic reviews conducted by the NHS Centre for Reviews and Dissemination (e.g. on stroke rehabilitation). The recently inaugurated NICE was already conducting appraisals in relevant areas, such as on new drugs for Alzheimer's. In 2001, the new Social Care Institute for Excellence was set up to spearhead a similar research effort in the social care sector.

The External Reference Group was (unusually) co-chaired by a clinical professor and a senior manager from social services. There were also carer and user groups set up to provide advice. Its membership was broader than the other reference groups considered here, including senior managers, namely two Directors of Social Services and a Health Authority CEO. It also set up taskforces with a wide range of representation.

Genetics Translation Networks: Department of Health (2003) is the key policy text which paved the way for national funding of the GTNs. It notes the fundamental scientific advances now apparent, arguing that 'the human genome project will pave the way for a revolution in health care'. However, the production of such scientific knowledge was still at an early stage and it was difficult to predict how it would evolve. The emphasis of the text is therefore on investment to create new high-quality capacity and on mainstreaming specialist genetic services within NHS services. In the future, it might be possible to codify this new scientific knowledge: 'as evidence emerges, genetic knowledge and technologies will need to inform the development of National Service Frameworks' (DoH, 2003, p. 52). 'As the evidence base develops' (p. 52), the Department would feed developments in genetics into NICE's work programmes. In the meantime (p. 53) 'authoritative and credible advice from recognised experts in the field can be useful in sharing best practice'. So the scientific knowledge base was still too undeveloped and indeed unpredictable to turn into evidence-based guidelines for the field.

The composition of its Advisory Group again demonstrates a core of senior clinical academics from major research-intensive universities (including its chair), leavened with a sprinkling of other representatives such as a nurse/counsellor and a CEO of a voluntary organization. The inclusion of a senior academic philosopher was an interesting development, signalling a strong concern for a consideration of ethical implications of new genetics science.

In summary, the concept of a power/knowledge nexus helpfully drew our attention to novel national-level policy arenas which all display extensive technical advisory apparatuses. They advise on the production of national texts which set agendas and have at least some (although variable) influence in the local networks studied. On the one hand, we suggest that the composition of these advisory groups shows some pluralism with participation of expert patients and other stakeholders. NICE emerges as a key agency in producing legitimate knowledge influential with the clinical field across a variety of fields. Davies et al (2006) well describe NICE's broader efforts to foster citizen participation in deliberative decision-making. On the other hand, a closer examination of composition suggests that the advisory apparatuses examined here retain a research-intensive core of senior clinical academics. These are of course advisory rather than executive bodies but their advice is seen as legitimate and difficult to reject. This analysis also reveals the presence of important and novel knowledge producers, notably national and international groups of health services researchers. We acknowledge that this formal data on advisory group composition is not as powerful as qualitative data on behaviours, and future research could well investigate decision-making processes in these groups in more depth and consider whose voices appear to be most influential.

Theme 2: Subjectification, the technology of the self and networks' clinical managerial hybrids

Some cases (especially the two cancer cases and the Metropolitan City Sexual Health case) suggest a transition at an individual level from clinical to managerial, or rather clinical-managerial hybrid, selves. A key and interesting sub-group of clinicians has been drawn into the core of these networks as governing agents: they are responsible for leading the implementation of national policy agendas in their localities and are accountable upwards for so doing.

Foucauldian notions of subjectification and the technology of the self helpfully suggest how these long-term career trajectories and identity shifts unfold through self-discipline, the pursuit of long-term goals, and even self-realization (Starkey and McKinlay, 1998) rather than through exploitation or the mere internalization of surveillance. Clinical-managerial hybrids were originally from clinical backgrounds but were then progressively drawn into management roles over extended periods of time: for instance, moving from nursing, through service improvement or clinical audit work, to network management. Their hybrid role was therefore 'strategic' rather than 'incidental' (e.g. County Network Director; Urban Medical Director), developing new roles, tasks and skills (McGivern et al, 2012). They actively pursued a hybrid clinical/management agenda, based on a belief in service and quality improvement (Newman, 2005) as guiding values.

The management style found was often based on small mixed teams with good interpersonal relations. Such teams displayed an entrepreneurial, change orientated, and value-led (patient-centric) style (e.g. County Managed Cancer Network Director), distinct from the neutral affect and routine maintenance management seen as characteristic of public bureaucrats (Newman, 2005; O'Reilly and Reed, 2010). We note in the County Managed Cancer Network case consistent comments about 'hard work', 'passion', 'inspiration', and 'life and soul' with their ethical overtones, contrasting with descriptions of the instrumental behaviour of the urologists. We here suggest that the Network Director was recreating herself as the kind of value-led manager and agent for positive change she wanted to be. As she commented: 'my identity is being all things to all people in the Network'.

As discussed in the chapter on network leadership, key hybrid clinicians leading networks (for example, in the Cancer Networks, and the Metropolitan Sexual Health and Older People's Networks) strongly identified with their roles, which were in turn framed by evidence-based guidelines, rather than the managerialist governmentality framing hybrid clinical roles as discussed by Doolin (2002). As the Nurse Director in the County Cancer Network noted:

> What I do is pluck out the nursing and patient implications of those guidelines...who I am [is]...delivering all the stuff that I should be delivering around nursing and patient-focused improvements, that is what I should be about and should be doing.

Similarly, the Clinical Director leading the Metropolitan City Sexual Health Network had been involved in writing national standards for sexual health care and passionately argued that:

> We should all be working to...[national sexual health] standards, each [hospital] Trust should be doing that and they should be monitoring that. We can, as a network, help pull that together and I think we need to do more of that...[create] peer pressure and support to help them [clinicians] improve quality.

The palliative care nurse leading the end of life care project in the Metropolitan Older People's Network, saw no difference between complying with end of life care guidelines and providing the good palliative care she passionately believed in.

Drawing on the concept of 'identity work' (Alvesson and Willmott, 2002; Sveningsson and Alvesson, 2003), these actors can be seen as engaging in 'evidence-based identity work', constructing their own identities and the way others conceive professionals, professional sub-specialties, and professional roles, in relation to evidence-based knowledge/power regimes. Future work should investigate the relationship between subjectification, the technology of the self, and hybrids' values and identity shifts further.

Theme 3: The transparency of novel but clinically related grey sciences

In recent core methodological guidance for the production of the NICE clinical guidelines as a generic research output (NICE, 2009), three developing 'grey sciences' can be discerned (Ferlie and McGivern, 2011): information science, systematic reviewing, and health economics. Interestingly, they are not directly related to accountancy or financial audit-based forms of knowledge or techniques, although health economics has a similar concern with transparent resource use. Information science mixes established librarian-based knowledges, new Information and Communication Technologies (ICTs) and searchable electronic databases. Systematic reviewing brings in new analytic techniques from the Health Services Research Community such as: cost-effectiveness analysis, Quality Adjusted Life Years (QUALYs), and the Incremental Cost Effectiveness Ratio (ICER). There is a strong concern with measuring clinical outcomes as well as resource use in cost-effectiveness judgements, preferably based on meta-analyses of RCTs. So clinical research knowledge has not been entirely displaced by resource-based knowledge in these three 'grey sciences': rather the two form a novel hybrid. As the production of NICE guidelines appears highly standardized, these analytic techniques are diffusing widely (given the high volume of appraisals).

Perhaps the text which best exemplifies these wider logics and analytic techniques is the Urology Improved Outcomes Guidance (NICE, 2002, appendices 1 and 2). Specialist university-based research units were commissioned to produce costs estimates (from a health economics perspective) of recommendations for service changes and also a systematic review of the best available evidence of clinical outcomes and how they might vary in relation to service configuration. While a conventional hierarchy of evidence model is employed in this text, it is also noted that there are few RCT-based studies of service delivery and organization-related questions to draw on so that other methods may have to be used.

A similar hybrid logic underpins the development of clinical (rather than financial) audit systems observed as important locally in a number of our sites. Clinical audit activity has expanded since the 1990s, enabling the collection of structured information about the nature of clinical services. While clinical audit data are often collected by a health care professional (for example, a research nurse) rather than an accountant, they provide more explicit and comparative information about service delivery patterns which may have developed idiosyncratically over time and may act as a lever for external questioning of clinical activity patterns and contribute to service change. Clinical managerial hybrids are here involved in making local clinical practices visible and hence potentially reformable in the light of explicit national targets and standards.

Theme 4: The Panopticon: Electronic surveillance and self surveillance?

Was the development of an electronic Panopticon apparent in the cases and if so, did it generate behavioural effects? What was the relationship between the possibility of constant electronic surveillance and self surveillance by clinical managerial hybrids and clinicians?

GTN1 provided interesting material. As in all the GTNs, the DoH belatedly introduced a periodic (three monthly) performance assessment template which was electronically based. This was rejected as too frequent by the scientists, who took the view that the pace of genetics science research moved more slowly. It appeared not to influence the behaviours of the key academics in the site substantially: they did not internalize the metrics suggested by the template or become 'obedient' subjects. Rather they mostly continued with their previous core mission of academic research and with unchanged identities as academic scientists. The filling in of the templates was delegated to the Network Director who acted as a buffer protecting the academic core from reporting demands. The reporting seemed ritualistic and not to be used by the centre: there were even complaints from the site that there was never any feedback. So this case suggests a failed governmentality project with successful resistance from elite scientists.

We suggest that Cancer Networks were more affected by surveillance regimes. However here the effects of the electronic Panopticon were less related to the Networks reporting data upwards and the all-seeing centre than intervening in cases of poor performance. They were more to do with clinicians internalizing the visibilities associated with legitimate evidence-based guidelines. Accordingly, they changed their practices in order to avoid being seen as poor clinicians in these legitimated terms. So surveillance in the Cancer Network cases was related to technologies of the self and identity work, particularly with Network leaders making local practices visible by audits and engaging in local identity work further legitimating evidence-based practice.

In the Sexual Health Networks, while Network Management Teams were electronically reporting data upwards around the 48-hour access target, the impact of doing so was more powerful in terms of its effects on professional identities. The Metropolitan City Sexual Health Network, for example, reorganized the way it provided sexual health services to a 'walk in' basis to meet the 48-hour target and their success in doing so bolstered the identities of those involved (making it impossible to wait for more than 48 hours for an appointment). Leaders of the Metropolitan Sexual Health Network conducted a Network-wide review, which made the practices of poorly performing clinicians visible, and then orchestrated the application of professional 'peer pressure' to get one key clinician to change. So again the surveillance of practices made visible against evidence-based guidelines was closely related to issues of professional identity and identity work.

In the Regional Older People's Network case, the lack of clear guidelines and targets that were considered serious undermined the impact of electronic surveillance here. In the Metropolitan Older People's Network case, electronic surveillance of General Practitioners' (GPs') Quality Outcomes Framework data relating to the development of end of life care registers was helpful in enrolling GPs in making changes to bring care in line with national guidelines. However, the impact of surveillance here was also limited.

Overall, *direct* control systems seem not to have had a major impact across the cases. In the case with most material (GTN1), they appear to have acted in a ritualistic fashion, with the Network Director absorbing the reporting requirements and hence buffering the academic core from contact as a form of 'tick box' compliance as we (McGivern and Ferlie, 2007) have found elsewhere in the NHS. While data were reported upwards, they appear not have been used by the centre to intervene in the sites and there were complaints about the lack of feedback.

However, we do see *Panopticon* control systems as having an indirect impact on the identity work and associated behaviours of actors in the Cancer Networks and Metropolitan City Sexual Health Network. Here clinicians changed their practices when they were made visible against evidence-based standards of best practice. The threat of potentially being seen to be clinically sub-standard led several clinicians to change their practices, where they had previously resisted doing so. So surveillance can here be seen as an ingredient in the construction of wider governmentality.

How do our empirical findings address the wider clinical resistance (Timmons, 2003; Doolin, 2002, 2004) or enrolment in governmentality (Waring, 2007) debate? We suggest that the cases demonstrate a mix of surveillance and self-surveillance. Both the cancer plan and the national sexual health strategy elaborated national targets for the localities, but the latter had discretion about local implementation (for example, the choice of evidence base in the Cancer Networks). Expert clinical advisory committees informed these national strategies, so that they reflected elite professional opinion as well as formal evidence.

These 'managed' networks face demanding national targets and are performance-monitored by the centre, but are given substantial local discretion about implementation. A novel and differentiated control regime mixes top-down and bottom-up modes of change and surveillance with self-surveillance. High-performing networks are given 'earned autonomy'; but low-performing networks face monitoring, support, and intervention from central agencies. The networks secured high levels of clinical enrolment at both national and local levels so there is strong professional support.

Locally, clinically dominated sub-groups (e.g. Urology Tumour Groups) were involved in devising and implementing local strategies. The two Cancer Networks did not impose decisions on the Urology Tumour Groups but rather collaborated with them in redesigned processes to produce decisions both within national guidelines and which generated clinical acceptance and even enthusiasm locally. The urologists were progressively drawn into the policy/management domain. They started by questioning the legitimacy of guidelines and audit, but prolonged debate, exposure to data, and dialogue with peers within the Tumour Groups shifted their position from resistance towards enrolment. There was a similar process in the Metropolitan City Sexual Health Network. Overall, there was developing clinical enthusiasm for service reconfiguration across the County Cancer Network and in one sector in the Urban Network, with a more nuanced picture in the other sector.

A set of strategically placed clinical-managerial hybrids actively shifted historic clinical practices. We suggest prolonged exposure of clinicians to novel practices and knowledge in such groups help enact governmentality in practice (e.g. Tumour Groups, HIV sub-group) and foster self-directed changes to clinical working practices. So overall (and with negative examples such as GTN1) we found neither enduring clinical resistance to a governmentality project, nor simple acceptance, but rather gradual enrolment over time with an important persuasion role being played by 'reformed' clinical managerial hybrids.

Concluding discussion: The added theoretical value of a governmentality perspective

We conclude that a governmentality perspective enabled us to see and analyse important developments in the UK health policy domain which would have remained invisible within conventional professional dominance or New Public Management (NPM) prisms.

In Chapter 3, we specified four themes from the governmentality literature to apply to our cases. Broadly speaking, there appeared firstly to be a strong power/knowledge nexus apparent in our cases (most notably cancer) operating at national level as an elaborate advisory apparatus. These apparatuses produce texts, notably evidence-based policy frameworks, which were widely legitimate with clinicians at field level, based on logics and particular techniques of analysis which have now diffused widely across the health care field. NICE emerges as a key knowledge-producing agency at national level. While NICE has constructed sophisticated consultation mechanisms which include patient representatives (Davies et al, 2006), we suggest that at the core lie groupings of senior clinical academics and (and this is novel) health services researchers, operating within a distinct approach to knowledge production. NICE is an 'arm's length' agency with operational independence but also engaging with many different stakeholders (clinical academics, health care professionals, other relevant professionals, health services researchers, patient representatives) as co producers of (strong) recommendations to the DoH. It thus engages a broader range of actors in making difficult recommendations jointly about effective ways of allocating scarce resources in visible health care arenas.

Secondly, the technology of the self perspective helpfully highlighted the long-term development of a set of clinical managerial hybrids (rather than general managers) who moved into the core of managed networks, representing important links between the managerial, policy, and clinical domains. It suggests that their careers may be gradually unfolding, aided by hard work, commitment, and acquiring new skills. They often were in roles for long periods of time. They adopted an energised and committed style of management, aided by the service improvement based agenda dominant during this time period. We suggest that these hybrids may be engaging in 'evidence-based identity work', constructing senses of self, professions, and professional roles in relation to evidence-based guidelines.

Thirdly, the concept of 'grey sciences' initially pointed towards the possible growth of financial and audit-like techniques of calculation and recording. However, we found more clinically orientated 'grey sciences' emerging from within the EBM movement and its recently created institutions (e.g. NICE) that covered the clinical field as the number of clinical guidelines increased. Grey sciences such as health economics mix a concern for cost-effectiveness with a focus on clinical outcomes.

Finally, we found that the electronic Panopticon and electronic surveillance regimes were generally weakly developed and lacking the force of those apparent in patient safety arenas (Waring, 2007; Currie et al, 2008). Even where they existed (e.g. GTN1) they were not internalized by the objects of surveillance (elite academic scientists) who viewed themselves in different academic terms and successfully insulated themselves from the operation of these reporting systems. However in other cases, for example the Cancer Networks and Metropolitan City Sexual Health Network, we see evidence of clinicians and hybrids internalizing evidence-based practices, and actively making local practices visible and mobilizing peer pressure to change how clinicians practice.

We conclude that the governmentality perspective represents a useful theoretical perspective with which to analyse the governance and operation of the managed networks studied. We consider where further governmentality-related research in health care organizations could be developed in the final chapter.

12

New Labour and UK health care: Managed networks, wicked problems, and post-NPM organizing

In this final substantive chapter, we return to the public policy orientated arguments introduced in Chapter 2 and draw out implications of our analysis for health care policymakers and managers. We first of all seek to characterize New Labour's impact on UK health care organizing, reflecting on the implications of our case material. We argue that its reform strategy contained an important strand of network-based policies as well as the New Public Management (NPM) (Bevan and Hood, 2006a) and market-orientated models examined so far by other authors (Mays et al, 2011). Managed networks are, in our view, an emblematic network governance reform under New Labour, although our cases suggest it is one as yet with partial results. We then apply the 'wicked problems' framework reviewed in Chapter 2 to our cases, suggesting that such conditions appear pervasive and hence should be persuasive in the design of health policy. We reflect on the wider implications of this conclusion for choice of governance mode in health care. We finally explore the implications of the limited degree of organizational change found for the wider NPM/post-NPM debate introduced in Chapter 2.

Characterizing the impact of New Labour on UK health care organizing

In Chapter 2, we argued UK health care management was subjected to a major wave of NPM-style reforms in the 1980s and 1990s, notably the introduction of general management, private sector style corporate governance regimes, quasi markets, and transparent performance management. The substantial period of New Labour governments (1997–2010), which were operating with large parliamentary majorities and in financially buoyant times, represented a potential to take stock of NPM reforms and to rebalance their underly-ing trajectory. A broad set of academic ideas around 'network governance' (Newman, 2001), 'the hollowed out state' (Rhodes, 1997a, 2007) and 'New Public Governance' (Osborne, 2006; 2010) was available to inform redesign of policy and initially appeared to have some impact in Cabinet Office thinking (Cm 4310, 1999) about the machinery of government. Flagship government-wide policies such as 'joined-up government' accepted the need to unpick some fragmenting effects of NPM reforms. There was also a 'deagentification' or reduction of the number of executive agencies across various public serv-ices (e.g. a merger between the Prisons and Probation Executive Agencies in criminal justice) to promote a whole care pathway and integrated case man-agement perspective. The new stress on evidence-based policy had early and strong impact in the health care sector.

So what do we see from our cases about the impact of New Labour reforms on health care organizing? The chameleon-like character of New Labour pol-icy makes such assessment complex as different and even competing policy streams were apparent, waxing and waning over sub-periods of time. What indeed was the core content of New Labour reforms in health care? Different authors advance alternative interpretations. Bevan and Hood (2006a) stress the continuation of NPM instruments such as strong targets and the replacement of 'non-performing' senior management teams. By contrast, Mays et al (2011) discuss New Labour's health policy reforms in terms of reliance on market-led reforms, notably provider diversity and choice, which became more apparent after the mid-2000s. They do not discuss the earlier period of network-based reforms or the Cabinet Office's (1999) '*Modernising Government*' document in any depth: the dominance of a market-led approach is assumed.

Both these NPM and quasi market-based accounts are, in our view, partial and badly need rebalancing to take account of network governance-based policies. We here presented case examples of managed networks from four contrasting but major health care sectors, all set up in the early 2000s. Other important examples of managed networks could have been included in the study, such as heart disease (see McGivern et al, 2009; Sheaff et al, 2010), diabetes (Greene et al, 2009), or mental health (Sheaff et al, 2010) which all exhibited a similar combination of an evidence-based National Service Framework (NSF) and local managed networks as a supposed delivery mech-anism. So the managed network phenomenon appeared to have consider-able breadth across different and important health care settings. While the Genetics Translation Networks (GTNs) were wound up after five years, the Cancer and Sexual Health Networks engaged in longer-term service redesign and exhibited considerable longevity. Indeed, the new coalition government has now confirmed that managed Cancer Networks will continue even after its policy shift back to principles of competition and choice in other areas of health care. So some managed networks set up in about 2000 achieved considerable longevity and staying power.

Moreover, managed networks were a practical and achievable reform to public policy consistent with basic academic work on the perceived dysfunctional effects of earlier NPM reforms (Sullivan and Skelcher, 2002; Dunleavy et al, 2006), notably inter-agency fragmentation, silo working, poor organizational learning, slow diffusion of innovations across fields, and loss of lateral and systemic capacity. They also reflect in practice the major themes of joined-up government and evidence-based policy (at least in those sectors covered by NSFs) developed in New Labour's important initial review of the machinery of government (Cm 4310, 1999). So they are an emblematic network governance-based reform which puts important ideas about public management reform into practice and which should not be forgotten.

Our initial and admittedly partial assessment of their effectiveness (see Table 1 contained in Appendix 2 for details) is decidedly mixed. Both GTNs achieved in our view very limited impacts in terms of bringing together the core academic and clinical constituencies and were closed after five years (although interestingly, *after* one of the GTNs closed former members were able to translate a genetics test into practice as an NHS service). The Regional Older People's Network made little progress in what was admittedly a complex and perhaps intractable policy arena. The Cathedral City Sexual Health Network went through periods in which it appeared overloaded and to be making little substantive progress. A major weakness of poorly functioning networks is that they can degenerate into 'talking shops' with high time and transaction costs. Their functioning can also be blighted by the long-run impact of successive reorganizations, as in both Cathedral City and the Regional Older People's Network. The Cancer Networks remained hospital dominated with limited influence from primary care or hospices. The networks tended to concentrate on visible targets of access and service redesign rather than more indirect and diffuse behaviour change objectives (as in the Metropolitan City Sexual Health case), despite the presumed advantage of network forms in securing participation and engagement from user groups.

However, our three 'high performing' networks (the two Cancer Networks and the Metropolitan Sexual Health Network) displayed some of the claimed advantages of network forms. Both Cancer Networks managed to achieve a complex and evidence-based reorganization of urology services across large geographical patches (although it took five years), while retaining strong levels of clinical leadership and engagement. There was some broadening of multidisciplinary teamwork and of user influence on what had been a highly consultant-dominated arena. There was a growth of the collection of local evidence and examples of organizational learning by the Network teams. The Urban Cancer Network managed to move service planning to a more population-based mode, challenging the traditional hegemony of the elite teaching hospital. The Metropolitan City Sexual Health Network showed examples of effective diffusion of service redesign within the Network and a knowledge orientation in its well-attended Research Away Days. These networks appeared to balance top-down pressures to implement priorities with local engagement successfully, against the argument that formalization and top-down direction would drive out their organic and bottom-up character (Rhodes, 2007).

We have argued that a radical transition to network-based working would be dependent on underpinning movement within three supporting domains: the lateral movement of information and knowledge using Information and Communication Technologies (ICTs); inter-organizational learning within the network; and a shift from vertical management to broader leadership (as explored in Chapters 8 to 10). Substantively, we concluded that there was indeed a substantial shift to broader leadership, but much more contained movement within the other two domains. We explore the broader implications of this empirical conclusion of limits to radical transition later.

The 'wicked problems' rationale—pervasive and persuasive

In Chapter 2, we reviewed the 'wicked problems' (Clarke and Stewart, 1997; Sullivan and Skelcher, 2002) argument for network forms and defined possible indicators by which to explore whether or not such 'wicked problems' were apparent. Did the case studies suggest this rationale was pervasive in practice—and hence should be persuasive in policy design—or is the argument no more than a chimera?

Table 12.1 indicates that conditions consistent with 'wicked problems' were found in most of our cases. The networks often worked on cross-cutting objectives across agencies and professions only realistically achievable over the long term (for example, both Cancer Networks reconfigured urology services but over a five-year period). Secondly, the wide range of actors found in the networks included not only various functions from within the National Health Service (NHS) (both commissioning and providing arms; hospitals and primary care) but also local government, universities, and voluntary and private sector agencies. These are indeed fragmented and multi-sectoral arenas where cooperation cannot be guaranteed: for example, the 'hard' boundary in the GTNs between the NHS and the university sector proved resistant to networking.

Thirdly, there were challenging behaviour change objectives within network activity, for example in the Sexual Health Networks (reducing new infections of HIV and high teenage pregnancy levels). In the Older People's Networks, such objectives involved not only working with service users but

Table 12.1. The Networks and wicked problems

Network	Cross-Cutting Outputs	Range of Stakeholders	Networks' Behaviour Change Objectives	Co-production with Citizens
GTN1	From academic to translational science.	2 Ministries, NHS providers and commissioners, NHS labs, university, social science.	Academic behaviour.	Some (slight) interest in wider ethical and social issues; weakly present in practice.
GTN2	As above.	As above, plus public health.	As above.	As above.
Urban Cancer	Improved health outcomes; system redesign on a population basis; high-quality patient pathways.	NHS: Commissioners and providers; palliative care; cancer research; service improvement partnership; Various voluntary organizations including hospices.	Earlier patient presentation; broadening of provider perspectives and behaviours.	Expanding role of user reps.
County Cancer	As above.	NHS hospitals and commissioners; voluntary organizations including hospices.	As above.	Slight influence from user reps.
Metropolitan City Sexual Health	Fewer HIV/AIDS infections; systemic service redesign.	NHS hospitals and commissioners; public health; health promotion; city HIV consortium; voluntary organizations, including a major provider.	Healthy sexual behaviours.	Disappointing.
Cathedral City Sexual Health	Fewer HIV/AIDS infections; lower teenage pregnancy; systemic service perspective.	City council; NHS commissioners and providers; family planning; schools; community nursing; social services; voluntary organizations.	As above.	As above.
Metropolitan Older People	Improvement in end of life care across a local care system.	NHS: Primary care; hospitals; NHS supervisory tier; hospice; family doctors; nurses; social services; independent sector care homes.	Addressing social taboos; changing provider, societal and family behaviours.	Some—greater control over how to die.

(continued)

Table 12.1. (Continued)

Network	Cross-Cutting Outputs	Range of Stakeholders	Networks' Behaviour Change Objectives	Co-production with Citizens
Regional Older People	Cross-city integrated strategy and service redesign. Legacy of national policy failure.	City council; Social Services: NHS hospitals, primary care, commissioners, various voluntary organizations including a major provider; large independent care home sector.	Changing societal and provider attitudes to elderly people.	Designation of city-wide 'Champions' for older people; social movement-based approach.

also fundamental attitudinal change amongst service providers (for example, treating older people with respect), family (improving engagement in care for a loved one who was dying), and society as a whole (making older people more visible, breaking the silence about death as a taboo subject). The GTNs' efforts to shift genetics academics from basic academic to translational research appeared to have very modest success.

Fourthly, we found some—although only slight—evidence of increased co-production and influence from users and citizens. For example, the Older People's Champions were designated as a collective source of social change in the Regional Older People's case, although they did not have a decisive impact. User representatives had a higher profile than before in the Board of one Cancer Network. However, there was less change than in the other indicators. The Sexual Health Networks were limited in terms of their engagement with local voluntary organizations and affected communities (for example, while representatives of local sexual health charities sat on the Metropolitan City Sexual Health Network Board, members of the local HIV positive African community barely knew of the Network's existence). The Metropolitan City Sexual Health Network highlighted tangible objectives of service redesign and meeting access waiting times rather than diffuse work with voluntary groups around behaviour change in hard-to-reach communities. The sociological research in one GTN had very limited internal impact. There was little use of new ICTs to promote public participation or indeed enhanced surveillance of deviant sub-groups of citizens.

We conclude that the 'wicked problems problem' is not a chimera but remains of pervasive importance in our cases. It should therefore be persuasive in designing health care governance modes. We believe that this is an important conclusion. Looking to the future, the continuing growth of the very elderly population will surely increase the importance of achieving effective collaboration in their care further, yet it remains fraught with problems (as the chapter on Older People's Networks indicated). The growth of chronic, complex, and behaviourally related conditions such as obesity and type 2 diabetes represents another important health policy arena with many characteristics associated with 'wicked problems'. So these arguments may be even more important in the future.

We suggest that this growing range of 'wicked problems' is more compatible with networks rather than hierarchies or markets as a governance mode because they more readily foster the development of systemic capacity with strong lateral linkages between many different stakeholders that is needed. The patients and affected families become more than customers in this perspective, they are active co-producers in care and in the management of chronic conditions (such as diabetes), which should be of increasing importance in the design of UK health policy. Well-functioning network forms should also be able to diffuse knowledge, learning, and desired service change more readily across the network. At the most ambitious level (beyond those changes observed in our study), this would involve networks helping to promote important behavioural changes across society in a 'healthy' direction (e.g. smoking, alcohol, diet).

From NPM to network governance: A partial transition and a hybrid state?

We previously argued that the NPM paradigm (Ferlie and FitzGerald, 2002) is well embedded in UK health care and speculated that the later network governance paradigm would be too partial and limited a counter-model to dislodge it, in part because of its own ideological incoherence. A challenging coherent ideology is theoretically seen as fundamental in any archetype transition so its lack may prove fateful. The competing but plausible interpretations of the content of New Labour's reform agenda in health care—NPM, markets, or networks—suggest that this early argument may have proved correct. The implication is that transition to a post-NPM form may prove difficult and challenging as the NPM forms are resilient (Osborne, 2010) and difficult to dislodge.

Reviewing our cases, what evidence do we find about the survival or removal of key NPM reforms? There are clearly some important signs of a transition to post-NPM forms. First of all, there is little sign of the empowered Chief Executive Officers (CEOs) or non-executive directors often seen as characteristic of NPM: empowered general management has given way to softer and broader forms of leadership, often undertaken by clinical managerial hybrids. Nor are there developing markets or quasi markets in the sites with few private sector actors (apart from the private residential care sector in the Regional Older People's case). This finding draws limits to market-led interpretations of the New Labour period. Actors within the networks remain overwhelmingly drawn from public sector agencies and professions. The networks seek to rebuild systemic capacity by bringing commissioners and providers in closer communication, in essence unpicking key NPM reforms. Contrary to the post-Fordist model, public expenditure on health care increased markedly in the New Labour period with little further privatization. The strong stress on evidence-based policies and guidelines is an important network governance reform which is widely evident. So there are some important signs of aspects of the network governance model being enacted in practice.

Yet aspects of the NPM narrative remain strongly embedded. Performance measurement and management continues strongly, with frequent reporting up to the centre. Sometimes reporting appears ritualistic (as in the GTNs); in other cases, it has sharp reputational consequences (as in the Cathedral City Sexual Health Network being 'on the naughty list' for teenage pregnancy). The centre sets many standards and targets for the localities, as in the National Service Frameworks (albeit with some local discretion). It retains control over the allocation of jurisdictions over services, as in the periodic externally driven accreditation of cancer centres. Overall, the cases suggest an uneasy hybrid as argued by Clegg et al (2011), with competing logics and modes of organizing and no radical transition to post-NPM forms. The suggestion that important aspects of the NPM remain embedded is potentially important. We now return to two other post-NPM models reviewed in Chapter 2 and comment on their apparent validity in our case study data.

Post-Fordism and the State

Jessop's (1994) post-Fordist model of the State sees the fiscal crisis of the Keynesian Welfare State as resolved by assertive New Right regimes which seek to reduce social costs and increase productivity. This 'hollowed out Schumpeterian workfare State' (Jessop, 1994) acts to promote process and market innovation in open economies, stressing competitiveness, labour market flexibility, human capital formation, and lower social costs. It is 'hollowed' out by the loss of functions by the national State to supranational regimes, strong regions, and local governance.

However, many of Jessop's examples are drawn from the labour market and welfare programmes and he does not really consider health care, with its specific features including strong professions and a well-developed science base. The presumption that the post-Fordist state would act to contain social costs and adopt more productivist policies can be questioned. Far from squeezing public expenditure on health or subordinating it to the demands of the labour market, New Labour substantially increased health care spend on a universalist basis, moving it up significantly towards the EU average as a percentage of GDP (DoH, 2007). We found little marketization and weak deregulation of professionalized labour markets with continuing barriers to entry and exit. The private sector remained largely absent from the cases (except the Older People's cases): for example, the venture capitalists we expected to appear in the GTNs did not materialize. Elite professionals (e.g. the urologists in the Cancer Networks) remained influential and were not deskilled. The 'clannishness' of the health care sector proved resilient and immune from market forces (at least in this time period).

There was little transfer of health policy competences upwards to the EU or downwards to strong regions (although all our networks are English; devolution to Scotland and Wales has had important effects in those jurisdictions). The metropolitan tier had a slight influence in one Sexual Health Network but this subnational influence was an exception. So we conclude that the post-Fordist model of the State was not supported descriptively in our cases.

The post-bureaucratic organization: Weakly present

Our review of the literature on the post-bureaucratic organization in Chapter 2 drew attention to Reed's (2011) two archetypes of the rational bureaucratic organization and the post-bureaucratic organization. Reflecting on these archetypes, we suggest a few post-bureaucratic organization features were present in our cases; but most were absent. There was strong evidence of an enthusiastic and value-based management style from the 'disciplined selves' (as explored in the leadership chapter) of clinical managerial hybrids, as opposed to bureaucratic neutral affect. There was a broadening of Multidisciplinary Teams (MDTs). There was operational decentralization and an ability to customize policies locally, but also the (attempted) retention of strategic control through such policy instruments as: NSF, NICE guidelines, performance management, and frequent upwards reporting.

However, many key post-bureaucratic organization features were only weakly present. There was little evidence of project-based working; rather, networks engaged in strategic change exercises over a number of years (five-years in the Urology IOG). Attempts at process integration were evident at times but had weak impact. There was little evidence of portfolio careers where more managers would be brought in from outside on a part-time or project basis. The knowledge base was, if anything, moving from a tacit to a more explicit form, with the rise of NICE and of its evidence-based guidelines as a legitimate underpinning for network activity. Above all, public sector institutions (e.g. NICE) and the health care professions remained strongly present, with associated power to structure the health care field. So the post-bureaucratic organization archetype had only weak descriptive validity in the cases, apart from some self-surveillance and internalization by clinicians of Evidence-Based Medicine (EBM) guidelines.

Characterizing the managed network form: Suggesting an ideal type

So if the post-bureaucratic organizational form does not characterize our cases what might? We here sketch an ideal type of a managed network form. While the use of ideal types has been criticized, they remain useful in clarifying underlying organizational configurations, especially novel or emergent ones (Reed, 2011). This analysis draws on features emerging in our empirical cases but moves beyond these 'concretely existing' hybrids to explore what a 'pure' form might resemble. We also move here from a descriptive to a more normative style of argumentation.

We suggest that managed networks should be constructed in health policy arenas characterized by 'wicked problems' conditions and are not suitable for simpler arenas (such as in elective surgery) where more market-led solutions may well be appropriate. So managed networks will normally be operating in conditions of high organizational and social complexity including such features as: extensive co-production with users and families; attempted attitudinal, behavioural, and societal changes; the bringing together of different professional and epistemic cultures and the brokering of large-scale and complex reorganizations.

They should seek to secure substantial professional ownership (from a range of different professions) and legitimacy. To achieve this, they will work closely with the professions and gain their support whilst still seeking to encourage reforms. A synthesized evidence base (now sets of quality standards) produced by NICE or other agencies should support their legitimacy in the eyes of the professions. A collaborative and team-based leadership style would also foster such ownership, exercised jointly by well-respected clinical-managerial hybrids and general managers (but including social care or other non-health care managers in cases of inter-sectoral working). The management style is likely to be energetic, value-driven, and 'hands on' rather than greyly bureaucratic. Dominant network values relate to service and quality improvement exercises (more so than financial control which may prove a challenge in the current period). They will need adequate financial and staff resourcing (as well as time) for undertaking these complex tasks.

Data, information, and knowledge need to flow through the network laterally to connect the knowledge bases of the various parties, to a much greater extent than in our cases. There should be the extensive use of educational and training interventions to augment and broaden existing uniprofessional knowledge bases. The network should consider these issues explicitly through a knowledge mobilization strategy.

The network should promote inter-organizational learning and joint problem solving actively, again to a greater extent than in our cases. In order to engage with such inter-organizational learning, individual agencies have to migrate to becoming 'learning organisations' first before then building inter-organizational learning spaces. The network should protect space for local reflection and experiment from the demands of short-term actions and upwards reporting.

They should remain managed network forms and not slip back into tacit professionalized networks. So there should be appropriate continuing arrangements for upwards reporting and accountability against national objectives. However, these reporting requirements should not be so excessive and micro-based as to drive out the organic and bottom-up form of networking: the two principles need to be held in balance (as some of our networks were able to do). Accountability might take the form of periodic judgements of overall performance (such as annual performance statements against key outcome measures) or even periodic contests for jurisdictions through designation and accreditation exercises. A poorly performing network should face assessment and, if need be, challenged for its jurisdiction. Even the prospect of such accountability exercises could promote active internal monitoring and progress chasing to combat the danger of drifting into a 'talking shop' mode.

Finally, these networks need to promote effective user involvement and co-production. We did find examples of increasing user involvement in some cases (e.g. the Urban Cancer Network) but more work is needed. The use of a social-movement-based approach (Older People's Champions) in one case is potentially interesting. In their study of decision-making in NICE, Davies et al (2006) describe the innovative attempt to design new deliberate processes which involve citizen representatives in formulating NICE guidelines. Some obvious questions emerge. To what extent are such individual users really 'representative' of their communities? What is the power balance between professionals and users in such deliberative arenas and of the deliberative process? Do social-movement-based approaches produce desired collective attitudinal changes in practice?

Concluding discussion

We here revisited the discussion on public and health policy reforming in the New Labour period (1997–2010), first outlined in Chapter 2. We first of all suggested that network-based reforms are a major, enduring, and indeed emblematic strand of New Labour's reforms to health care, alongside the continuing use of managerial instruments (Bevan and Hood, 2006a) and choice/market-based reforms (Mays et al, 2011) that other authors have emphasized. New Labour's policy stress on managed networks as a key example of network governance reforms should not be forgotten and we place it back centre stage in this account. Broadly speaking, we found an NPM/network governance hybrid evident in practice: the resilience and embeddedness of some NPM reforms was noteworthy.

Examining our eight case studies, we found a subset of three of them where the advantages claimed for networking appeared to be strongly evident in practice; the rest were as yet more disappointing. Going back to the 'wicked problems' argument for moving to network-based governance, we concluded that the wicked problems conditions specified in Chapter 2 are pervasive in practice and hence should be persuasive in policy design. The emblematic example is the chapter on services for older people with the complexity of the arena particularly evident in the important Regional case. If anything, such wicked problems conditions will grow further in the future (along with the size of the very elderly population). We argued that network-based governance is in these sectors a promising reform which still needs more time to embed itself in practice (Ferlie et al, 2011a) and that reversion to principles of hierarchy or quasi markets would only make already difficult wicked problems even more intractable.

In Chapter 2, we also reviewed three possible post-NPM models: the post-Fordist State; the post-bureaucratic organization, and network governance. We found little evidence to support the productivist assumptions of the post-Fordist state in the NHS which remained a buoyantly and publicly funded service with only modest marketization, at least within the networks we studied. The resilience of NHS 'clannishness' was noteworthy. There were also only weak signs of a move to a post-bureaucratic organization archetype (Reed, 2011) in what remain highly professionalized and institutionalized settings. There were more signs of a transition to core network governance principles such as the use of managed networks itself was important; also the stress on clinical leadership and principles of evidence-based policy—although these co existed with some enduring NPM principles (Clegg et al, 2011) including performance measurement and management—within a hybrid form. We finally sketched an ideal type of a managed clinical network form which attempted to elucidate a core set of principles for positive forms of future working.

This is of course only our distinctive interpretation of health care reforming in what is now a historically bounded period (1997–2010) of New Labour governments which has come to an end with the election of the Coalition government. We explore the relevance of this analysis for present health policy and management in the final chapter.

13

Concluding discussion—overall contribution and forward look

Health policy, pervasive wicked problems, and managed networks—a qualified defence

Two overall themes have been developed throughout this book. Our first and more substantive contribution is to an emerging body of public policy literature assessing New Labour's reforms in health policy during its 1997–2010 period in office. The time is now ripe for such an *ex post* assessment as we have moved into a new political and financial period with a new government. Different authors have advanced a variety of accounts of the New Labour period in health policy: Bevan and Hood (2006a) stressed the continuation of New Public Management (NPM)-style policy instruments of top-down 'targets and terror'. Mays et al (2011) recently examined the impact of New Labour's cycle of market-led reforms; but they do not discuss its prior cycle of network-based reforms at all. It is in our view limited to construe New Labour's health care reforms solely in terms of its later stress on choice and competition: its earlier network-based reforms were important and continued. Neither do Mays et al (2001) present extensive primary data on the local implementation processes of New Labour's health care reforms. We seek to provide in-depth comparative case studies of a set of 'real life' health networks all set up around 2000, thereby adding to the literature on the implementation of network governance reforms.

We suggest that managed networks are an emblematic network governance-based reform within health care which need to be remembered in accounts of the period. On the basis of this empirically informed study, what are their main strengths and weaknesses in the field? In terms of disadvantages, they could be highly time consuming, containing a strong emergent and local element not always consistent with short-term and top-down policy priorities, and have high transaction costs (as in the Regional Older People's case).

237

Our analysis suggests they were making generally slow progress in terms of stimulating inter-organizational learning and using cross-organizational Information and Communication Technologies (ICTs) to move information and knowledge around the network. They needed sufficient local and skilled management time and support to function, otherwise they could degenerate into 'talking shops' (as in the Cathedral City Sexual Health case). Strong and enduring boundaries between the different players could block effective cooperation (as in one Genetics case). Although they operated in domains consistent with 'wicked problems' conditions, they sometimes concentrated on amenable service redesign issues rather than engage with local community groups around more complex behaviour change objectives (as in the Metropolitan City Sexual Health case).

Nevertheless, we conclude with a qualified defence of network forms, at least in those sectors characterized by 'wicked problems' conditions. This concept well-describes complex, resistant, and systemic policy arenas which we suggest were apparent in many of the networks studied (for example, Older People's Care): so we found the wicked problems concept to be both pervasive in practice and persuasive in terms of policy design. The pace of network-led service change was often slow (e.g. the reconfiguration of urology services in the Cancer Networks took five years). But it is unclear how hierarchical or market-based approaches could have reconfigured urology cancer services across large geographical areas in a way that the two managed Cancer Networks eventually and legitimately did. The Metropolitan City Sexual Health case showed examples of tackling poor clinical practice effectively by the Network in a way which stand-alone organizations in that area had been unable to do. The networks developed strong clinical engagement, legitimacy, and active clinical leadership, especially where evidence-based guidelines or National Service Frameworks (NSFs) underpinned their activity. The development of the National Institute of Health and Clinical Excellence (NICE) and its clinical guidelines helped support and legitimate these managed networks' activities. We therefore offer a qualified defence of managed networks as the 'least bad' governance mode in respect of those many health policy arenas which fit the conditions of 'wicked problems' and suggest our empirical cases caution against an over-radical shift to quasi markets in these sectors.

Our findings compared to other recent studies

How do our findings compare with other recent studies of UK managed health care networks? There is a developing body of literature against which our findings can be compared. One way of assessing the external generalizability of case study-based work is to benchmark it against related studies to see if similar empirical findings are emerging.

Sheaff et al's (2010) analysis of four English health care networks (two in mental health, two in heart disease) took a distinctive angle in charting their adaptation to continuing health system reorganization (the reemergence of a separate commissioning function). The embedded network 'macro cultures'—specifically a strong base in the health professions—were resilient and slow to change, beyond ready production of the new managerial artefacts required by the new commissioning system. Their focus appears somewhat different from the one adopted here.

Martin et al's (2009) examination of leadership processes in case studies of two UK cancer genetic networks confirms some of our findings. They concluded that the 'higher performing' site exhibited distributed or small-team-based leadership appealing to the multiple professions necessarily involved in service change. The style represented a hard/soft mix. A key leadership task was to provide collective vision across the site through the 'making of meaning' for affected health care professionals, aligning national models and local contexts (which the higher performing site was more able to do).

Currie et al (2011) examined leadership processes in case studies of two UK local government-based (rather than health care-based) networks, where similar New Labour-style network governance reform ideas were apparent. They found that continuing demands of strong performance management and upwards reporting meant that leadership was exercised by a powerful few and remained fragmented by agency rather than showing a fully dispersed and concertive fashion. Both these articles' findings appear consistent with our findings, specifically in the domain of leadership.

Greene et al's (2009) single case study of a diabetes network in Scotland takes a quality and process-related approach to changing patterns of service delivery. They asked: was there evidence that this managed clinical network improved the quality of diabetes care? Many themes elaborated here are confirmed in their study, which also had the advantage of measuring service changes directly through well-elaborated intermediate indicators of clinical quality (e.g. measurement of blood pressure, recording of smoking status) more than we could. Type 2 diabetes was a growing health care problem but required services to be delivered across organizational and professional boundaries. The well-developed evidence base suggested a strong case for uncomplicated cases to be treated more in primary care. This desired service shift then required the redesign of the whole care pathway. After the network had been set up, there was rapid improvement in simpler processes of care, with slower improvements in complex indicators that required system redesign (e.g. assessment of foot vascular status). New information systems played an important supporting role, as did various educational interventions. There was active engagement by many local clinicians with enthusiastic, visionary, and collaborative leadership by clinicians at the centre of the network. Greene et al (2009) did not report data from a comparator site of a diabetes care system operating without a network, so it is difficult to make strong inferences, but many of their themes are consistent with our analysis.

This literature review suggests that similar findings are apparent across a cluster of recent UK studies so that our findings do not look deviant or of a 'one off' nature. We also argue that 'wicked problems conditions' (as in the care of older people and obesity/type 2 diabetes) will become even more important over the next decade and should rightly influence the design of health policy.

A governmentality-based theoretical perspective

Our second contribution is more theoretical. We took a (relatively conservative) Anglo governmentality-based perspective (using Miller and Rose, 2008) which draws on a Foucauldian framing to complement standard NPM and network governance accounts of UK health management reforms. How useful was this governmentality perspective in helping reconceptualize the managed network form?

The first observation is networks often displayed hybrid forms in practice with a coexistence of different modes (e.g. the introduction of payment by results and Foundation Trust status were important continuing NPM-based reforms which could erode network-based working). In addition, governmentality-based principles were patchily expressed: strongest in the cancer cases and one sexual health case and weaker elsewhere. Unsurprisingly, a partial change in the governance mix rather than a radical paradigm shift was evident.

Despite these reservations, we found that the governmentality perspective helpfully enabled us to see important developments in the health care organizational field not evident within different theoretical prisms. At the core of a governmentality project in this health care field lies a broadening of government action from its historic institutional core to a successful incorporation of more successfully enrolled actors and using indirect steering technologies rather than simple command. What specifically did we see in relation to these high-level themes in our cases?

Key governmentality-related developments included the emergence of an energised and value-driven cadre of clinical managerial hybrids as local governing agents and leaders (and the somewhat marginal role of general managers) within a number of the managed networks. We here analyse local governing agents rather than governed populations, the latter being a more common focus in Foucauldian analysis. We bring in other Foucauldian concepts to analyse this shift, seeing these hybrids as being long-term tracks to 'new selves', consistent with a subjectification and technology of the self perspective (McKinlay and Starkey, 1998), and highlighting the importance of 'identity work' (Alvesson and Willmott, 2002; Svenningson and Alvesson, 2003). We describe 'evidence-based identity work' in which key actors in health care networks constructed and legitimated their personal identities, as well as those of professional colleagues (including delegitimating practices at odds with guidelines), in governmentality-related terms which went on to change the nature of legitimated clinical practices.

Secondly, we see a well-developed 'power knowledge nexus' at a national level, specifically in scientific- and expert-based advisory groups set up by NICE, which emerges as a key 'hands off' agency. There is also a flurry of national health policy initiatives, such as various NSFs, which absorb such knowledge. We subjected core texts to analysis (e.g. NICE, 2002) from a Foucauldian perspective. We argue that while such arenas contain a degree of pluralism and co-production (Davies et al, 2006), traditional (academic clinicians) and novel knowledge (health services researchers) elites still lie at their core and prescribe dominant methods and techniques of analysis. The texts produced by such groups legitimately guide local action and influence local clinicians; enrolling them in forms of governmentality reinforced by the involvement of clinical and academic elites.

Thirdly, we see the pursuit of transparent priority-setting through expanding the new 'grey sciences' of Evidence-Based Medicine (EBM) (notably health economics, systematic reviewing, and information science) as well as local clinical audit. These 'grey' sciences are clinically related as well as resource focused and form a 'hybrid knowledge' which fuses these two elements. As such, they differ significantly from the pure 'accountization' analysis elaborated elsewhere (Miller and Rose, 2008). What is noteworthy is their high degree of methodological standardization (NICE, 2009) and their rapid proliferation, given the large scale of guideline production that NICE undertakes.

Fourthly, we took ideas in relation to the electronic Panopticon (Zuboff, 1984), surveillance, and self-surveillance to explore the behavioural effects of developing electronic templates and reporting regimes. Overall, they were found not to be powerful enough to lead to strong identity shifts and enrolment in governmentality (e.g. Genetics Translation Network 1 (GTN1)). They may be more fruitful in other health policy arenas, as preliminary analysis of an infection control system suggests (Murray, 2012). We now move from

considering the overall conclusions from the current study to consider implications for future health policy and organizational research within health
care organizations.

Forward look: Will managed networks endure?

So are managed networks a New Labour policy that has now fallen out of
favour after the change of government (2010)? Are they now only yesterday's
reform, succeeded in their turn by new (or revived) policy principles that
value choice, competition, and provider diversity?

The picture appears to be more complex: current English health policy is
such that some managed clinical networks will continue, including managed
cancer networks. At the time of writing, it is not clear whether a wider set of
'strategic clinical networks' will be set up, although this question surfaced
during the Futures Forum listening exercise (2011) which canvassed clinical
and other stakeholder opinion in relation to the new government's initial
proposals for health care reform.

A recent consultation document (NHSCB, 2012) in the public domain
produced initial proposals for discussion. It states that the NHS Futures
Forum had recommended clinical networks should have a role in supporting commissioners and providers to support outcomes for patients
and that in response the government had confirmed that (strategic) clinical networks should be retained and strengthened. However, only a small
number of strategic clinical networks will be prescribed to allow for local
determination and innovation. We comment that their proliferation may
well be controversial and resisted by General Practitioners (GPs) in Clinical
Commissioning Groups who might see their own role being eroded. NHS
Commissioning Board (2012) argues that selection of such managed clinical
networks needs to be informed by coherent principles, such as a clear link
to national outcome ambitions; the presence of a large-scale change programme or complex care pathways and major quality improvement issues.
As NHS Commissioning Board (2012) clearly suggests that only a limited
number of major strategic clinical networks will survive the present reorganization, so it is important to extract as much learning as possible from
their previous iteration.

Here we make three general observations about possible future trends in
UK health policy and their effects on managed networks. Clearly, the major
differences in the circumstances of UK health care policy in 2012 when compared to 2002 need to be recognized.

Firstly, the sharp deterioration in UK public finances from 2009 onwards,
given the banking crisis, has ended the financial buoyancy that the NHS—and

indeed public services as a whole—enjoyed for almost a decade. So the old agenda of quality and service improvement apparent in our case studies has subsequently been retilted towards an agenda focussing to a greater extent on rapid and radical productivity and efficiency gains (all which might predict a revival of NPM values and policy instruments), while hopefully not reducing quality. This shift may make it more difficult to secure the continuing engagement of clinical-managerial hybrids who emerged as a key leadership and linking group in our study. Will the clinical-managerial hybrids found to be so important quietly move out of fraught managerial roles and migrate back to the less controversial domain of clinical practice?

Secondly, our cases suggested that the EBM movement and associated national institutions (especially NICE) provided a legitimate knowledge base underpinning local network activity. So what will happen to the influence of these ideas and institutions over the next decade? The evidence-based policy ideas influential in the American Great Society programmes of the late 1960s (Oakley, 2000) lost policy traction in the 1970s and 1980s, associated with a transfer of political control from Democratic to more sceptical Republican administrations. So history suggests the EBM issue can move down as well as up public policy agendas.

However, proposals (Cm 7881, 2010) from the new government envisage a continuing and important role for NICE in developing sets of evidence-based quality standards and there has certainly been no threat to its continued existence. Given NICE's role in providing evidence-based guidelines with wide legitimacy in the clinical field and which underpinned much of our networks' large-scale change management activity, this continuity is welcome.

What might the effects of a longer-term shift to market logics in health policy to received notions of EBM be? Some influential market-orientated reformers in health care (Porter and Olmsted Teisberg, 2006, p. 7) appear sceptical of the process and guideline orientation of the EBM movement which does not place enough emphasis on creating leading-edge outcomes for patients: 'the whole process orientated approach is misguided. Standardised process guidelines belie the complexity of individual patient circumstances and freeze care delivery processes rather than foster innovation. What is needed is competition on results, not standardised care. What is needed is competition on results, not just evidence based medicine'. This sentence is admittedly complex. It appears not to reject EBM thinking entirely but to complement what the authors see as more dynamic and flexible market-orientated thinking. It signals the possibility that a market-based approach will move on from current EBM approaches. So will any policy turn to market-based approaches, erode the production and authority of evidence-based clinical guidelines (e.g. the Urology IOG) and texts which provided a legitimate platform for much network activity, and replace them with stronger competitive forces, albeit focused on patient value? Or might evidence-based standards still be an important element in market-based approaches to health care, with service providers competing on cost to deliver services that comply with such (minimum) standards of care?

Thirdly, will the 'wicked problems' conditions consistent with network governance-based working endure or even expand further? We see this scenario as highly likely given the rise of the 'chronic disease paradigm' in an ageing society. Such a perspective should therefore increasingly complement the traditional health policy focus on the acute sector and elective conditions (e.g. elective surgery). Older people's services represent a classic case where needs (and the number of people affected) are both complex and increasing: imagine an 85-year-man living on his own with slowly developing prostate cancer, mild dementia, backache, growing mobility problems, and an increasing tendency to fall (as in the personal experience of one of the authors in recently dealing with the care of an ageing parent). A case management-based approach which pulls together a timely package of different services as and when needed across different agencies and professions is surely the best way to approach the organization of such complex care.

Possible future research into networks in health care

As previously discussed, it appears that some strategic clinical networks will endure. So in which areas might further research into managed networks in health care best be concentrated? Let us start with a possible health policy agenda. An important example of an emergent 'wicked problem' is the rising level of obesity and type 2 diabetes (Greene et al, 2009) where there are integral economic/business and lifestyle issues to consider as well as clinical and scientific ones. Buchanan and FitzGerald (2011, p. 70) refer to an organogram of agencies presently involved in the National Childhood Obesity Strategy first produced by *The Times* showing strategy was currently being delivered by 'five government departments, dozens of quangos and hundreds of local agencies'. They suggest that the child protection arena shares similar features. The riddle of the effective organization and financing of older people's care currently remains unresolved with the recent Dilnot Commission (2010) report's recommendations on the funding of adult social care still to be responded to by government (at the time of writing). Given the large-scale resource flows involved and the size of the population affected, this is a very major area. These arenas seem ripe for the development of network-based approaches and for continuing organizational research on their nature and impact.

A second important area lies in translational research. Our cases of the GTNs proved disappointing in terms of their ability to bring together traditionally separate clinical and academic worlds within a functioning knowledge mobilization-orientated network. Yet a continuing translational research agenda (Cooksey, 2006) still seeks to bring together clinical, academic, and scientific worlds within novel organizational forms, notably in the five recently created UK Academic Health Sciences Centres. Of course, realistic timescales for significant 'bench to bedside' research flows are very long term. Future research should investigate the linking mechanisms involved in these knowledge mobilization efforts further (Ferlie et al, 2010; Ferlie et al, 2012b). How does scientific knowledge flow across organizational and professional boundaries and move towards the realm of clinical practice? What organizational and governance arrangements can help support such field-level processes (if any)? Greenhalgh and Wieringa (2011) suggest that the 'knowledge translator' metaphor is unhelpful in explaining the process of knowledge mobilization because it conceptually misrepresents the nature of generating, sharing, and applying knowledge. So theoretically, what sort of conceptual framing helps researchers observe and analyse such processes?

A third area lies in large-scale service reconfigurations. If the current productivity-orientated agenda eventually produces a major and perhaps contested reorganization of acute services, such merger processes may well be brokered by large-scale managed networks which have the scale to operate across large geographical areas (as in the prior reconfiguration of cancer services, Addicott and Ferlie, 2007). It would be interesting and important to track such reconfiguration processes and the role that managed networks play within them.

Fourthly, it would be interesting to explore the extent and implications of greater diversity in managed networks. Most networks studied in this study were still largely dominated by public sector-based agencies and occupations and might be regarded as somewhat 'clannish'. There were no venture capitalists, for instance, found in the GTNs and even the University Technology Transfer Office found in GTN1 had a minor role in practice. Perhaps the most important exception was the large grouping of private sector residential and nursing homes in the Regional Older People's Network (although they felt themselves to be somewhat secondary actors). If there is greater diversity on the provider side, then more private and not-for-profit actors may populate these networks. We would need to explore the effects of any such growth of non-public sector personnel on the way in which these networks function. Evolving health care markets may well not be neoclassical or rely on spot contracts in frictionless markets. Given the importance of trust and quality (critically important but difficult to observe), softer forms of markets may be indicated. If markets gather strength in the health care sector, will they still be highly relational in nature, retaining important elements of the network form?

Developing governmentality as a theoretical framing in health care organizations

We argue that that UK health care management research needs to connect with a social science base and secure broader theoretical emplacement as well as relate to the world of public policy. In particular, we wish to explore whether new theoretical prisms which go beyond the well-established professional dominance vs NPM debate help reconceptualize important empirically evident developments in new and creative ways.

The governmentality perspective adopted in this study helpfully connected health care management research with important Foucauldian ideas already highly influential in a cluster of related social science fields, thereby expanding the repertoire of theoretical constructs available. This theoretical perspective has already been used by various authors to analyse a cluster of novel health policy arenas including: clinical governance systems (Flynn, 2004); patient quality and safety regimes (Waring, 2007; Currie et al, 2009); clinical reaction to electronic information systems and surveillance (Doolin, 2004); medical leadership (Doolin 2002); and the production of national research policy texts (Shaw and Greenhalgh, 2008).

It would be interesting to examine in further depth two governmentality-related themes. The first is the nature and operation of what we have termed the 'power/knowledge nexus' within EBM policy arenas. Are we correct to claim there is a senior clinical academic/health services researcher core to such networks or are they more plural and distributed in nature than this assertion suggests? This may require more observational work of (for example) NICE Guideline Development Groups to examine patterns of influence, building on Davies et al (2006). Such work should include more extensive analysis of the nature of the knowledge and texts produced in these domains, considering how such knowledge is produced and by whom. Another field of interest is mapping the precise techniques of analysis employed in guideline production, seen in governmentality terms as pervasive yet mundane control technologies. While there is a Foucauldian-based stream of work emerging on EBM arenas, these areas (perhaps surprisingly) do not appear to have been explored in any depth.

A second promising governmentality-related theme for future work is to take the 'technologies of the self' perspective to investigate the (self) construction of local governing agents further. We are specifically interested in exploring the nature of what we describe as 'evidence-based identity work' undertaken by the cadre of clinical managerial hybrids. As noted above, these actors did not internalize evidence-based practice because they were being watched and could be punished for not doing so. Rather they identified with them as ways of improving patient care, fitting with their own conceptions of what it meant to be a good clinician.

Key questions include: how energized and committed are they to evidence-based guidelines? Have they internalized national policy objectives as legitimate? If so, what are the mechanisms and processes at work? Are they on long-term career tracks which realize their personal ambitions? How is evidence-based identity work affected if national policy moves from emphasizing improving the quality of patient care to providing more cost-effective care? We were not able to explore questions of identity work and identity shifts here in any detail but hope to do so in the future.

A further intriguing question to explore is: what are the limits to a governmentality perspective in health care organizations? Where does it fail as an explanatory framework and why? Any erosion of a tight power/knowledge nexus in favour of a socially distributed and dialogically based form of organizing in NICE groups, for example, would not be readily consistent with a governmentality perspective and would require reconceptualization. The emergence of strong markets which allocate resources with a lesser role for change management activity by energized clinical managerial hybrids would be another development which could tell against a governmentality perspective.

So the argument that managed networks are an emblematic network governance reform to health policy introduced in the New Labour period rebalances other current interpretations which stress either surviving NPM-style managerialism or a market-like tilt to competition, choice, and diversity. Current indications are that some managed networks have survived the change of political control in 2010, along with key underpinning agencies such as NICE, so they are more than yesterday's reform.

Throughout the text, we have therefore followed two main analytic threads across the set of empirical cases and tried to make two overall contributions. The first has been to use the concept of a 'wicked problem' where network-based modes of organization appear better suited than recourse either to markets or hierarchies. Comparing our cases against 'wicked problems' conditions, we concluded that such conditions were pervasive in practice and should be persuasive in policy design. Looking to the future, the importance of 'wicked problems' could well increase still further, given (for example) the growth of the population of very old people with multiple needs and also the important obesity/type 2 diabetes issue.

The second thread was more theoretical: using a governmentality perspective to reconceptualize modes of organizing in these managed networks. They are not market driven, nor are they strongly hierarchical, nor are they a traditional tacit professional network. They fit none of the conventional professional dominance, NPM, or market-driven paradigms often used in the analysis of health care organizations. Specifically, the combination of energized clinical managerial hybrids acting as local governors at the core of these networks, a national evidence-based policy framework produced through the advice of a widely legitimate power/knowledge nexus, and the rise of new 'grey sciences' of EBM to support such policy documents help enact governmentality in these health care settings.

We conclude that managed networks in health care were an important network governance reform under New Labour and that they respond well to 'wicked problems' conditions. They should not now be forgotten—and indeed some have survived—and we suggest that more empirical and theoretically informed work is needed to track their evolution in this new period.

Study design and methods

Our study used comparative and case study methods to explore decision-making processes over a period of time (that is, taking a processual and longitudinal approach) within a set of health care managed networks, specifically studying four pairs of managed networks purposefully selected from different health care arenas. This Appendix considers why we adopted this research design and the operational methods used. It explores some methodological issues which arose and how we responded to them. It finally outlines how we made a performance judgement in relation to the networks studied.

Study design and methods

As the objectives of our study related to 'how' and 'why' questions rather than 'how many' or measurement-based questions, we selected a qualitative methodology (Yin, 1994) based on comparative case studies. Such a design can explore processes in organizations over time and the meaning that organizational actors attach to their actions. Such qualitative designs contain some induction as well as deduction, so that findings and concepts can rightfully emerge during the study as well as being identified and tested from the start, as in deductive or hypothesis-based studies. Some qualitative studies are purely inductive as in grounded theory (Glaser and Strauss, 1967), but others (such as our study) mix deductive and inductive elements in an iterative way. A key objective was to review academic streams of literature early on in the study so that the research team was sensitized to possible theories before fieldwork. The theoretical implications of field data can then be more easily induced.

Our fundamental unit of analysis was the nature and impact of the network as an organizational entity (rather than a cohort of individuals or a small group). We undertook comparative case studies of a set of purposefully selected health care networks. Multiple case study designs (Yin, 1994, 1999) have been commended for increasing external generalizability beyond a single case study, especially with purposeful selection of cases. Multiple case study designs balance strong internal validity with a degree of external validity, also providing the opportunity for structured comparison between cases (Stake, 2000) which can reveal trends and regularities. Both Eisenhardt (1989) and Langley (1999) argue that with sets of 8–10 cases, it is possible to generate low-level patterns with a degree of generalizabilty, without sacrificing internal validity.

The focus of analysis in the case studies (Yin, 1994) is the nature, behaviour, and impact of the network studied and specifically decision making in relation to selected 'tracer issues' over time. The focus on concrete tracers enabled us to make an initial assessment of network impact, using intermediate process indicators. Tracers represented important local policy priorities which were also nationally mandated and so might vary from one locality to another.

Study methods

We operated a strategy of 'triangulation' through multiple data sources (Stake, 2000) to ensure internal validity. We started each case study with a collection of written policy documents and national policy-level interviews to build up background knowledge of the health policy issue concerned. We carried out twenty policy interviews for the clinical Genetics Networks; seven for the Cancer Networks; eleven for the Sexual Health Networks; and twenty-three for the Older People's Networks, making a total of sixty-one policy interviews in all. We then wrote up a summary of policy developments for each health policy issue. We also identified possible fieldwork sites in these interviews. We hoped initially to use these interviews to identify higher and lower performing sites but this proved problematic and we revised our approach to performance assessment (see below).

Once ethical approval and access had been secured, fieldwork started in each site with observation at key meetings and collection of local documents (such as minutes of key committees, local policy, and strategy documents) to get a 'sense' of the site. This early work also helped suggest respondents for later interviews. This was followed by about twenty semi-structured interviews of about one hour each, combining a common core with some questions customized to the issue and the site. Our sampling strategy was a combination of respondents suggested to us by initial contacts and documentation, and 'snowball' sampling. We wanted to interview respondents in various roles: managers, nurses, and doctors, as well as non-National Health Service (NHS) respondents (e.g. leaders of voluntary organizations) where their names cropped up. We also observed meetings to get a sense of group dynamics. There were no major access difficulties, but particular gaps in two cases (General Practitioners (GPs) in the Metropolitan City Sexual Health case; social services management in the Metropolitan Older People's Case) were apparent.

We carried out thrity-one interviews in the clinical Genetics Networks, forty-nine in the Managed Cancer Networks, forty-nine in the Sexual Health Networks, and thirty-eight in the Older People's Network. So we undertook a total of 228 interviews (167 case study interviews and sixty-one policy interviews). In addition, a team member had already been researching one of the clinical Genetics Network before this study, undertaking fifty-four earlier additional interviews and observing twenty-five meetings (2002–2007). These data have been included in the case study as a 'free good'.

Case study selection

We recruited eight cases to the study, consisting four pairs of different managed networks. The intention was to sample broadly across different types of health care networks so as to generate comparative analysis (Goodwin et al, 2004). But which networks should we study and why? Our initial selection of network type was influenced by the following dimensions:

- The differential content of the work of the network: we initially distinguished between four subtypes of networks organized around the delivery of a clinical service in the NHS, a broader client-group network involving a range of different agencies, a network involving basic science rather than care delivery, and a network relating to public health and a population perspective.

- The form of the network: professionally dominated 'enclave' (vs) more hierarchically managed (vs) locally emergent networks.

- Organizational form: organic/emergent (vs) mandated/imposed network forms.

- Membership of the network: public (vs) private providers, professional/managerial balance, overall size of the network.

For each case study, we wrote an analytic description and history of the network as a whole, and then examined in greater depth a significant stream of network activity (so-called tracer issues) in relation to objectives that the network had set for itself to assess progress and observe patterns of interaction and decision making (e.g. 48-hour access targets in the Metropolitan City Sexual Health case).

Drawing on these four criteria, we selected a pair of cases from the following health network forms, having also taken advice from the project Advisory Steering Committee.

Clinical Genetics Networks: are science-based networks which are seeking to advance a translational form of science. They included academic scientists as a major stakeholder group. We initially hoped that there would be novel non-NHS actors, such as venture capitalists, but this did not prove to be the case. The tracer issue was the fate of various translational projects devised by the networks.

Managed Cancer Networks: relate to a major NHS clinical service with concern about historically poor clinical outcomes. These are managed networks designed to implement the targets in the NHS Cancer Plan (DoH, 2000b). We had done some prior work on cancer networks (Addicott et al, 2006) which we built on in this study. Our tracer issue was the implementation of Improved Outcome Guidance (IOG) (NICE, 2002) for urology.

Sexual Health Networks: were selected as population-based networks of interest to public health. They have implications for the health of the nation and for health promotion. We were interested in the role of public health in these networks (less than originally anticipated) and the way these networks outreached to local community groups. Our tracer issues were the development of HIV/AIDS services for ethnic minority groups, together with 48-hour access targets to sexual health clinics in one site and the reduction of teenage pregnancies in the other.

Older People's Networks: were selected as client-group networks. They involve a large number of different agencies (social care as well as health care) and professions. They are seen as highly multidisciplinary. This policy arena involves a large private sector in residential and nursing care. Given the stress on communicating information across agency boundaries, we thought that the role of Information and Communication Technologies (ICTs) would be interesting to follow. The initial tracer issue was the Single Assessment Process (SAP) on discharge from hospital care, although this proved difficult to operationalize. We finally selected the development of intermediate care and end of life policy as tracers, although in one site we concentrated on end of life policy.

Case sites were selected in the two regions involved in the study, with a rough geographical balance. The interview pro forma was informed by early literature reviews of academic work on networks from political science and organizational studies perspectives so was informed by theory. This literature review was refined and extended in our final project report (Ferlie et al, 2009b), for example developing early thoughts on governmentality as a candidate conceptual framework.

We initially wrote up early case study work (clinical genetics) on a single case basis. In team discussion, we agreed to a refined case study template to cover all eight cases. We then produced four sets of pairs of case studies, organized to the same template. They form the basis for some of the chapters here. Case writers were asked to discuss which candidate theories identified in the literature review were apparent in their cases. We wanted the final report to include thematic discussion as well as case studies so we held long team meetings at the end of the project to identify themes and explore how they related to case study data. The early thematic chapters in the report (Ferlie et al, 2009b) informed the more developed and analytic chapters here. This analytical phase at the end of the project was helpful. We also held an end of project workshop to which representatives of the sites were invited to discuss the findings.

Developing a performance assessment framework

An original objective of our study was a performance assessment of the networks selected with subsequent identification of key success factors that distinguished between higher and lower performers. Other organizational process studies conducted by some of the present authors (Pettigrew et al, 1992) have also contained a performance-related dimension. Originally we hoped to select *ex ante* comparative pairs of higher and lower performers as rated by peers in national policy interviews but this design proved difficult to operationalize. We relaxed the criteria for case study selection to secure access pragmatically to enough sites and then moved to *ex post* performance assessment of the sample.

So how did we approach such an *ex post* performance assessment? Through our own academic networks, we found the work of Turrini et al (2010) who conducted a structured review of international journal publications on the effectiveness of public services networks and proposed an assessment framework which we applied and developed. In turn, Turrini et al (2010) built on the work of Provan and Millward (1995) and Provan and Sebastian (1998) who studied the effectiveness of mental health care networks in American cities. They defined 'network effectiveness' as a combination of the improvement of the clients' health status and well-being as perceived by two key stakeholders—the clients' families and therapists. The Turrini et al (2010) model proposes five key dimensions of network effectiveness:

1. Client-level effectiveness.
2. Overall community-level effectiveness.
3. Ability to reach stated goals.
4. Capacity for innovation and change.
5. Sustainability and viability.

We interpreted these dimensions as follows.

Client-level effectiveness (including the quality of service delivery): this dimension focuses on the aggregate outcomes for network clients and is not easy to operationalize. In our study, we found it impossible to gather clinical outcome data (e.g. shifts in five-year survival rates in the case of Cancer Networks; before and after self-reports from patients and carers). Even if it had been possible to gather such data, it would have been difficult to attribute causation to the effects of networks as opposed to other forces (e.g. increased spending; new drugs and treatments). Where networks were mandated, there were no localities without them so an experimental/control design was impossible. Nor was 'service quality' easy to define as we had so little direct data on quality. We therefore used proxy or intermediate measures, notably the implementation of policies or guidelines seen as 'evidence based' (e.g. the urology Improved Outcome Guidance (IOG)). Such proxy indicators are strong where there is a well-developed evidence base. We used intermediate proxies of service process (e.g. 48-hour waiting time target in the Sexual Health Networks) where they could be seen clearly to relate to service improvements.

Overall community-level effectiveness: this dimension broadens the initial focus on client-level outcomes to include wider community-level outcomes such as greater distributional effectiveness; more equitable provision; improved community access or enhanced participation; and activation of the community in decision making. We developed some similar community-level concepts in this study. As Turrini et al (2010) argue, as well as these two dimensions of external impact, a network needs to develop internal capacity in such fields as sustainability, legitimacy, and maintenance if it is to survive. They suggest three key internally facing dimensions:

The network's ability to reach stated goals: the network is more likely to survive if it can achieve the key tasks it has been set or set itself.

The network's capacity for innovation and change: networks able to introduce significant service changes and innovations may be more valued and survive. We refined this dimension to include a particular interest in service improvement activity.

The network's sustainability and viability: this refers to the ability of the network to survive over a long time-frame and to move from one policy cycle or agenda to another.

So we adopted the Turrini et al (2010) framework for *ex post* performance assessment, but developed it by adding three further dimensions:

6. Inclusiveness and engagement of stakeholders.

7. Shared learning.

8. Unintended outcomes (both perverse and serendipitous).

Inclusiveness and engagement of stakeholders: this proxy indicator for an effective organizational process assesses the extent to which the network mobilized its key stakeholders in concrete and real activity as opposed to being a 'paper' network.

Shared learning: this dimension addresses the argument that network-based organizations are effective at processes of inter-organizational learning, leading to more effective problem solving, and joint organizational change.

Unintended outcomes (both perverse and serendipitous): we need to be alert to the unintended as well as the intended effects of networks and avoid narrow or linear thinking in assessment. Unintended effects may be positive or indeed negative.

We summarize the application of this assessment framework against the eight cases in Table 1. These overall ratings were made in team discussions towards the end of the project, with all team members having read the cases. These discussions were

Table 1. Performance assessment of the eight networks studied

Network	Scoring	Comments
Genetics Translation Network 1	Low/moderate	2002–2007: mixed results; sudden cardiac death test successfully translates but other projects show less movement; difficult to move from academic to translational science; some internal tensions and clashes; generous financial resource base.
Genetics Translation Network 2	Low	2002–2007: enclave; tries to form a new discipline but sees itself and is seen as 'maverick' and isolated from key stakeholders; generous financial resource base.
County Cancer Network	High	Long history: met key policy targets; organizational learning; simpler setting; skilled management team; high resource base.
Urban Cancer Network	Very high	Long history: met key policy targets; organizational learning; highly complex setting; more inclusive process; skilled management team; high resource base.
Metropolitan City Sexual Health Network	Moderate/high	Complex setting: strong on target setting, redesign, and learning; weaker on public health and voluntary sector involvement.
Cathedral City Sexual Health Network	Moderate	Smaller-scale setting: coping well given low resource base and continuing reorganizations which distract from service development.
Metropolitan Older People's Network	Moderate	Small-scale setting: 'win-win situation'; PCT funding; clear focus; good relations between the health care professions; not sustained over the long run; weaker links with other groups.
Regional Older People's Network	Low	Relatively recent creation: large scale and complex setting; diffuse focus; multi-sectoral working; very thinly resourced and overloaded; limited progress but still in start up phase?

informed by the performance assessment model developed here. We concluded that the three 'highest performers' were the two Cancer Networks and the Metropolitan City Sexual Health Network.

Bibliography

Abbott, A. (1988) *The System of the Professions*, London: University of Chicago Press.

Ackroyd, S. (1996) 'Organization Contra Organizations: Professions and Organizational Change in the United Kingdom', *Organization Studies*, 17: 599–623.

Addicott, R. and Ferlie, E. (2007) 'Understanding Power Relationships in Health Care Networks', *Journal of Health Organisation and Management*, 21(4/5): 393–405.

Addicott, R., McGivern, G., and Ferlie, E. (2006) 'Networks, Organizational Learning and Knowledge Management', *Public Money and Management*, 26(2): 87–94.

Addicott, R., McGivern, G., and Ferlie, E. (2007) 'The Distortion of a Managerial Technique? The Case of Clinical Networks in UK Health Care', *British Journal of Management*, 18(1): 93–105.

Adler M. W. (1980) 'The Terrible Peril: A Historical Perspective on the Venereal Diseases', *British Medical Journal*, 19 July 1980, vol. 281: 206–11.

Age U.K. (2012) 'Care in Crisis Report', London: Age U.K.

Age U.K./Joseph Rowntree Foundation (2011) 'Future of Care Homes', Presentation by J.Meyer and T. Owen. Also at www.ageuk.org.uk/documents/en-gb/for-professionals/research/futureofcarehomesmyhomelifepresentation(november2011) .pdf?dtrk=true. Accessed 27 October 2012.

Alvesson, M. (2004) *Knowledge Work and Knowledge Intensive Firms*, Oxford: Oxford University Press.

Alvesson, M. and Deetz, S. (2006) 'Critical Theory and Postmodern Approaches to Organization Studies' in (eds) Clegg, S., Hardy, C., Lawrence, T., and Nord, W., *Sage Handbook of Organization Studies*, Thousand Oaks: Sage, pp: 191–217.

Alvesson. M. and Spicer, A. (2012) 'Critical Leadership Studies: The Case for Critical Performativity', *Human Relations*, 65(3): 367–90.

Alvesson, M. and Sveningsson, S. (2003) 'The Great Disappearing Act: Difficulties in Doing "Leadership"', *Leadership Quarterly*, 14: 359–81.

Alvesson, M. and Wilmott, H, (2002) 'Identity Regulation as Organizational Control: Producing the Appropriate Individual', *Journal of Management Studies*, 39: 619–44.

Amin, A. (ed.) (1994) *Post Fordism—A Reader*, Oxford: Basil Blackwell.

Armstrong, P. (1994) 'The Influence of Michel Foucault on Accounting Research', *Critical Perspectives on Accounting*, 5: 25–55.

Ashworth, R., Boyne, G., and Entwistle, T. (eds) (2010) *Public Services Improvement—Theories and Evidence*, Oxford: Oxford University Press.

Barker, J. R. (1993). 'Tightening the Iron Cage: Coercive Controlling Self-Managing Teams', *Administrative Science Quarterly*, 38: 408–37.

Bate, P., Bevan, H., and Robert, G. (2004) 'Towards a Million Change Agents, A Review of the Social Movements Literature: Implications for Large Scale Change in the NHS', NHS Modernization Agency.

BBC News (2011) Shares in Southern Cross Suspended, 11 July.

Beck, U. (1994) 'The Reinvention of Politics towards the Theory of Reflexive Modernization' in (eds) Beck, U., Giddens, A., and Lash, S., *Reflexive Modernization: Politics, Traditions and Aesthetics in the Modern Social Order*, Cambridge: Polity Press, pp. 1–55.

Bennett C (1992) 'Working across boundaries' in (ed.) Peter Jones, *HIV Prevention: A Working Guide for Professionals*, London: Health Education Authority, pp. 99–112.

Bennett C. and Ferlie E. (1994) *Managing Crisis and Change in Healthcare: The Organizational Response to HIV/AIDS*, Buckingham: Open University Press.

Benning, A., Dixon-Woods, M., Ghaleb, M., Suokas, A., Dawson, J., Barber, N., et al. (2011a) 'Large Scale Organisational Intervention to Improve Patient Safety in Four UK Hospitals: Mixed Method Evaluation'. *British Medical Journal*, 342: d195.

Benning, A., Dixon-Woods, M., Nwulu, U., Ghaleb, M., Dawson, J., Barber, N., et al. (2011b) 'Multiple Component Patient Safety Intervention in English Hospitals: Controlled Evaluation of Second Phase'. *British Medical Journal*, 342: d199.

Berridge V. (1996) *AIDS in the UK: The Making of Policy 1981–1994*, Oxford: Oxford University Press.

Berridge V. and Strong P. (1993) *AIDS and Contemporary History*, Cambridge: Cambridge University Press.

Bevan, G. and Hood, C. (2006a) 'Have Targets Improved Performance in the English NHS?', *British Medical Journal*, 332: 419–22.

Bevan, G. and Hood, C. (2006b) 'What's Measured is What Matters: Targets and Gaming in the English Public Health Care System', *Public Administration*, 84(3): 517–38.

Bevir, M. and Rhodes, R. A. W. (2003) *Interpreting British Governance*, London: Routledge.

Bevir, M. and Rhodes, R. A. W. (2010) *The State as Cultural Practice*, Oxford: Oxford University Press.

Bolden, R. (2011) 'Distributed Leadership in Organizations: A Review of Theory and Research', *International Journal of Management Reviews*, 13: 251–69.

Bolden, R., Hawkins, B., Gosling, J., and Taylor, S. (2011) *Exploring Leadership: Individual, Organizational and Societal Perspectives*, Oxford: Oxford University Press.

Boltanski, L. and Chiapello, E. (2005) *The New Spirit of Capitalism*, London: Verso.

Boyle, G. (2003) 'What is Public Service Improvement?', *Public Administration*, 81(2): 211–27.

Boyne, G. A., Gould-Williams, J. S., Law, J., and Walker, R. (2002) 'Best Value—Total Quality Management for Local Government?' *Public Money & Management*, 22, 3: 9–16.

Braithwaite J., Runciman W. B., and Merry, A. F. (2009) 'Towards Safer, Better Healthcare: Harnessing the Natural Properties of Complex Sociotechnical Systems', *Quality and Safety in Health Care*, 18: 37–41.

Brivot, M. and Gendron, Y. (2011) 'Beyond Panopticonism: On the Ramifications of Surveillance in a Contemporary Professional Setting', *Accounting, Organisations and Society*, 36(3): 135–55.

Brooks, S. and Grint, K. (eds) (2010) *The New Public Leadership Challenge*, Basingstoke: Palgrave Macmillan.

Buchanan, D., Addicott, R., FitzGerald, L., Ferlie, E., and Baeza, J. (2007a) 'No One in Charge: Distributed Change Leadership in Health Care', *Human Relations*, 60(7): 1065–90.

Buchanan, D., FitzGerald, L., and Ketley, D. (eds) (2007b) *The Sustainability and Spread of Organisational Change*, London: Routledge.

Buchanan, D. and FitzGerald, L. (2011) 'New Lock, New Stock, New Barrel, Same Gun: The Accessorized Bureaucracy of Health Care' in (eds) Clegg, S., Harris, M., and Hopfl, H., *Managing Modernity: Beyond Bureaucracy?* Oxford: Oxford University Press, pp. 56–80.

Burchell, G., Gordon, C., and Miller, P. (1991) *The Foucault Effect—Studies in Governmentality*, Chicago: University of Chicago Press.

Cadbury, A. (1992) (Chairman) *Financial Aspects of Corporate Governance*, London: Gee.

Castel, R. (1991) 'From Dangerousness to Risk' in (eds) Burchell, G., Gordon, C., and Miller, P., *The Foucault Effect—Studies in Governmentality*, Chicago: University of Chicago Press, pp. 281–98.

Castells, M. (1996) *The Network Society*, Oxford: Basil Blackwell.

Ceci, C. (2004) 'Nursing, Knowledge and Power: A Case Analysis', *Social Science and Medicine*, 59: 1879–89.

Challis D., Darton R., Johnson L., Stone M., and Traske K. (1991) 'An Evaluation of an Alternative to Long-stay Hospital Care for Frail Elderly Patients. The Model of Care', *Age and Ageing*, 20: 236–44.

Chan, A. (2000) 'Redirecting Critique in Post Modern Organization Studies: The Perspective of Foucault', *Organization Studies*, 21: 1059–75.

Child, J. and Faulkner, D. (1998) *Strategies of Co-operation: Managing Alliances, Networks and Joint Ventures*, Oxford: Oxford University Press.

Clarke, M. and Stewart, J. (1997) *Handling the Wicked Issues—A Challenge for Government*, University of Birmingham: School of Public Policy Discussion Paper.

Clarke, J., Newman, J., Smith, N., Vidler, E., and Westmarland, L. (2007) *Creating Citizen-Consumers*, London: Sage

Clegg, S. (1998) 'Foucault, Power and Organizations' in (eds) McKinlay, A. and Starkey, K., *Foucault, Management and Organization Theory*, London: Sage, pp. 29–48.

Clegg, S., Courpasson, D., and Phillips, N. (2006) *Power and Organizations*, London: Sage.

Clegg, S., Harris, M., and Hopfl, H. (2011) *Managing Modernity: Beyond Bureaucracy?* Oxford: Oxford University Press.

Clegg, S., Pitsis, T., Rura-Polley, T., and Marcosszeky, M. (2002) 'Governmentality Matters: Designing an Alliance Culture of Inter-organizational Collaboration for Managing Projects', *Organization Studies*, 23: 317–38.

Cm 4011 (1998) *Modern Public Services for Britain: Investing for Reform*, London: HMSO.

Cm 4192 (1999) *With Respect to Old Age: Long Term Rights and Responsibilities*, Royal Commission on Long Term Care, London: HMSO.

Cm 4310 (1999) *Modernising Government*, London: HMSO.

Cm 4818 (2000) *The NHS Plan*, London: HMSO.

Cm 6499 (2005) *Independence, Well-being and Choice*, London: HMSO.

Cm 6737 (2006) *Our Health, Our care, Our say: A New Direction for Community Services*, London: HMSO.

Cm 7881 (2010) *Equity and Excellence—Liberating the NHS*, London: HMSO.

Cm 8062 (2011) *A Child-centred System the Munro Review of Child Protection: Final Report*, May 2011, Department of Education TSO (The Stationery Office).

Cochrane Collaboration (2012) *The Cochrane Collaboration for Systematic Reviews*, See: www.cochrane.org/cochrane-reviews. Accessed 8 August 2012.

Cohen, L. and Musson, G. (2000) 'Entrepreneurial Identities: Reflections from Two Case Studies', *Organization*, 7: 31–48.

Cooksey Report (2006) *Review of UK Health Research Funding*, London: HM Treasury.

Cooper, Z., Gibbons, S., Jones, S., and McGuire. A. (2010) *Does Hospital Competition Increase Efficiency? An Analysis of the Recent Market Based Reforms in the English NHS*, London School of Economics: Centre for Economic Performance Working Paper 988.

Coopey, J. and Burgoyne, J. (2000) 'Politics and Organizational Learning', *Journal of Management Studies*, 37(6): 869–86.

Courpasson, D. (2000) 'Managerial Strategies of Domination: Power in Soft Bureaucracies', *Organization Studies*, 12: 141–61.

Courpasson, D. and Dany, F. (2003) 'Indifference or Obedience? Business Firms as Democratic Hybrids', *Organization Studies*, 24(8): 1231–60.

Crilly, T. and Le Grand, J. (2004) 'The Motivations and Behaviours of Hospital Trusts', *Social Science and Medicine*, 58(10): 1809–23.

Cross, M. (2006) 'Will Connecting for Health Deliver its Promises?', *British Medical Journal*, March 11, 332(7541): 599–601.

Currie, G. and Suhomlinova, O. (2006) 'The Impact of Institutional Forces upon Knowledge Sharing in the UK NHS: The Triumph of Professional Power and the Inconsistency of Policy', *Public Administration*, 84(1): 1–30.

Currie, G., Boyett, I., and Suhomlinova, O. (2005) 'Transformational Leadership within Secondary Schools in England—A Panacea for Organizational Ills?', *Public Administration*, 83(2): 265–96.

Currie, G., Humphreys, M., Uchasaran, D., and McManus, S. (2008) 'Entrepreneurship Leadership in the English Public Sector—Paradox or Possibility?', *Public Administration*, 86(4): 987–1008.

Currie, G., Waring, J., and Finn, R. (2008) 'The Limits of Knowledge Management for UK Public Services Modernisation: The Case of Patient Safety and Service Quality', *Public Administration*, 86(2): 363–85.

Currie, G., Lockett, A., and Suhomlinova, O. (2009a) 'The Institutionalization of Distributed Leadership: A "Catch 22" in English Public Services', *Human Relations*, 62: 1735–62.

Currie, G., Lockett, A., and Suhomlinova, O. (2009b) 'Leadership and Institutional Change in the Public Sector: The Case of Secondary Schools in England', *Leadership Quarterly*, 20: 604–16.

Currie, G. and Lockett, A. (2011) 'Distributed Leadership in Health and Social Care: Concertive, Conjoint or Collective?', *International Journal of Management Reviews*, 13: 286–300.

Currie, G., Grubnic, S., and Hodges, R. (2011) 'Leadership in Public Services Networks', *Public Administration*, 89(2): 242–64.

Davies, B. and Ferlie, E. (1984) 'Patterns of Efficiency Improving Innovations: Social Care and the Elderly', *Policy and Politics*, 12 (July), 281–95.

Davies, C., Wetherell, M., and Barnett, E. (2006) *Citizens at the Centre—Deliberative Participation in Health Care Decisions*, Bristol: Policy Press.

Dean, M. (1999) *Governmentality: Power and Rule in Modern Society*, London: Sage.

Denham, J. (2000) *Announcement of Establishment of First 13 Primary Care Trusts in April 2000*, press release Department of Health, 7 January.

Denis, J-L., Lamothe, L., and Langley, A. (2001) 'The Dynamics of Collective Leadership and Strategic Change in Pluralistic Organizations', *Academy of Management Journal*, 44: 809–37.

Denis, J-L., Langley, A., and Cazale, P. L. (1996) 'Leadership and Strategic Change under Ambiguity', *Organization Studies*, 17(4): 673–99.

Denis, J-L., Langley, A., and Rouleau, L. (2005) 'Rethinking Leadership in Public Organizations' in (eds) Ferlie, E., Lynn, L., and Pollitt, C., *The Oxford Handbook of Public Management*, Oxford: Oxford University Press, pp. 446–67.

Denis, J-L., Langley, A., and Rouleau, L. (2007) 'Rethinking Leadership in Public Organizations' in (eds) Ferlie, E., Lynn, L., and Pollitt, C., *The Oxford Handbook of Public Management*, Oxford: Oxford University Press, pp. 446–67.

Department of Health (1992) *The Health of the Nation: A Strategy for Health in England*, London HMSO.

Department of Health and Welsh Office (1995) 'A Policy Framework for Commissioning Cancer Services: A Report by the Expert Advisory Group on Cancer to the Chief Medical Officers of England and Wales' (The Calman Hine Report) London: Department of Health.

Department of Health (1997) *The New NHS: Modern, Dependable*, Cm 3807, London: HMSO.

Department of Health (1998a) *Information for Health: An Information Strategy for the Modern NHS 1998--2005*, NHS Executive September 1998.

Department of Health (1998b) *A First Class Service—Quality in the new NHS*, London: Department of Health.

Department of Health (1999) *Saving Lives: Our Healthier Nation*, London: HMSO.

Department of Health (2000a) *NHS Plan—A Plan for Investment; A Plan for Reform*, London: Department of Health.

Department of Health (2000b) *NHS Cancer Plan*, London: Department of Health.

Department of Health (2000c) *Consultants' Contracts: Annual Appraisal for Consultants*, Advance Letter (MD) 6/00, London: Department of Health.

Department of Health (2001a) *Better Prevention, Better Services, Better Sexual Health—The National Strategy for Sexual Health and HIV*, London: HMSO.

Department of Health (2001b) *National Service Framework for Older People*, London: HMSO.

Department of Health (2002) *Shifting the Balance of Power: The Next Steps*, London: HMSO.

Department of Health (2003) *Our Inheritance, Our Future—Realising the Potential of Genetics in the NHS*, London: HMSO, Cm 5791–II.

Department of Health (2004a) *Choosing Health, Making Healthy Choices*, London: HMSO, Cm 6374.

Department of Health (2004b) *National Standards, Local Action: Health and Social Care Standards and Planning Framework 2005/06–2007/08*, London: HMSO.

Department of Health (2004c) *A Toolkit for Older PEOPLE'S champions: A Resource for Non-executive Directors, Councillors and Older People Acting as Older People's Champions*, London: Department of Health.

Department of Health (2005) *Health Care Reforms in England*, London: Department of Health.

Department of Health (2007) *Cancer Reform Strategy*, London: Department of Health.

Department of Health (2008) *End of Life Care Strategy*, London: Department of Health.

Department of Health (2009) *Living with Dementia: A National Dementia Strategy*, London: Department of Health.

Dilnot Commission (2010) 'Fairer Funding for All', *Report of the Commission on the Funding of Care*, London: Department of Health.

Doolin, B. (2002) 'Enterprise Discourse: Professional Identity and the Organisational Control of Hospital Clinicians', *Organization Studies*, 23, 369–90.

Doolin, B. (2004) 'Power and Resistance in the Implementation of a Medical Management Information System', *Information Systems Journal*, 14: 343–63.

Dopson, S. and FitzGerald, L. (eds) (2005) *Knowledge To Action? Evidence Based Health Care in Context*, Oxford: Oxford University Press.

Downe, J., Hartley, J., and Rashman, L. (2004) 'Evaluating the Extent of Inter-organisational Learning and Change in Local Authorities through the English Beacon Council Scheme', *Public Management Review*, 6(4): 531–54.

Du Gay, P. (ed.) (2005) *The Values of Bureaucracy*, Oxford: Oxford University Press.

Dunleavy, P. (1995) 'Policy Disasters: Explaining the UK's record', *Public Policy and Administration*, 10(2): 52–70.

Dunleavy, P., Margetts, H., Barstow, S., and Tinkler, J. (2006) *Digital Era Governance*, Oxford: Oxford University Press.

Easterby-Smith, M., Lyles, M. A., and Tsang, E. W. K. (2008) 'Inter-organizational Knowledge Transfer: Current Themes and Future Prospects', *Journal of Management Studies*, 45(4): 677–90.

Eisenhardt, K. (1989) 'Building Theories from Case Study Research', *Academy of Management Review*, 14(4): 532–50.

Emirbayer, M. and Mische, A. (1998) 'What is Agency?', *American Journal of Sociology*, 103(4): 962–1023.

Entwistle, T. (2010) 'Collaboration' in (eds) Ashworth, R., Boyne, G., and Entwistle, T., *Public Services Improvement—Theories and Evidence*, Oxford: Oxford University Press, pp. 162–183.

Fairhurst, G. T. (2009) 'Considering Context in Discursive Leadership Research', *Human Relations*, 62: 1607–34.

Ferlie, E. and FitzGerald, L. (2002) 'The Sustainability of the New Public Management in the UK' in (eds) McLaughlin, K., Osborne, S., and Ferlie, E., *New Public Management—Current Trends and Future Prospects*, London: Routledge, pp. 341–53.

Ferlie, E. and Pettigrew, A. (1996) 'Managing through Networks—Some Issues and Implications for the NHS', *British Journal of Management*, 7(S): S81–99.

Ferlie, E., Ashburner, L., FitzGerald, L., and Pettigrew, A. (1996) *The New Public Management in Action*, Oxford: Oxford University Press.

Ferlie, E., Lynn, L., and Pollitt, C. (eds) (2005a) *The Oxford Handbook of Public Management*, Oxford: Oxford University Press.

Ferlie, E., FitzGerald, L., Wood, M., and Hawkins, C. (2005b) 'The Non Spread of Innovations: The Mediating Role of Professionals', *Academy of Management Journal*, 48(1): 117–34.

Ferlie, E., Musselin, C., and Andresani, G. (2009a) 'The Governance of Higher Education Systems—A Public Management Perspective' in (eds) Paradeise, C., Reale, E., Bleiklie, I., and Ferlie, E., *University Governance—Western European Comparative Perspectives*, Dordrecht, Netherlands: Springer, pp. 1–20.

Ferlie, E., FitzGerald, L., Addicott, R., McGivern, G., Dopson, S., and Exworthy, M. (2009b) *Networks in Health Care: A Comparative Study of their Management, Impact and Performance*, Final Report to NIHR SDO, London: Department of Management, King's College London, also see: http://www.netscc.ac.uk/hsdr/projdetails.php?ref=08-1518-102. Accessed 8 August 2012.

Ferlie, E., Jashapara, A., Crilly, T., and Peckham, A. (2010) 'Research Utilisation and Knowledge Mobilisation—A Scoping Review', Final Report to NIHR SDO. See: http://www.netscc.ac.uk/hsdr/projdetails.php?ref=08-1801-220. Accessed 8 August 2012.

Ferlie, E. and McGivern, G. (2011) *The New Public Management, the New Public Governance or Governmentality? The Case of Clinical Guidelines in UK Health Care*, Paper for British Academy of Management Conference, Aston University, UK, September 2011, King's College London: Department of Management.

Ferlie, E., FitzGerald, L., McGivern, G., Dopson, S., and Bennett, C. (2011a) 'Public Policy Networks and "Wicked Problems": A Nascent Solution?', *Public Administration*, 89(2): 307–24.

Ferlie, E., McGivern, G., and FitzGerald, L. (2011b) *From Cage to Gaze? Foucauldian Organizing in English Health Care*, Working Paper, Department of Management, King's College London.

Ferlie, E. (2012) *A Preliminary Review of Recent Critical Papers on Knowledge Management in Knowledge Intensive Organisations*, Kings College London: Department of Management, Internal working paper.

Ferlie, E., McGivern, G., and FitzGerald, L. (2012a) 'A New Mode of Organizing in Health Care? Governmentality and Managed Networks in Cancer Services in England', *Social Science and Medicine*, 74: 340–47.

Ferlie, E., Crilly, A., Jashapara, A., and Peckham, A. (2012b) 'Knowledge Management in Health Care—A Critical Review of the Generic Management and Health Care Literatures', *Social Science and Medicine*, 74(8): 1297–304.

Finger, M. and Brand, S. (1999) 'The Learning Organization in the Public Sector' in (eds) Easterby-Smith, M., Burgoyne, J., and Araujo, L., *Organizational Learning and the Learning Organization: Developments in Theory and Practice*, London: Sage Publications, pp. 130–56.

Bibliography

Fischer, M. and Ferlie, E. (2012) *Conflicting Modes of Clinical Risk Management: Explaining Escalating Contradictions and Organisational Crisis*, King's College London: Department of Management, Internal working paper.

FitzGerald, L., and Ferlie, E. (2000) 'Professionals: Back to the Future?', *Human Relations*, 53: 713–39.

Flynn, R. (2002) 'Clinical Governance and Governmentality', *Health, Risk & Society*, 4(2): 155–73.

Flynn, R. (2004) 'Soft Bureaucracy, Governmentality and Clinical Governance: Theoretical Approaches to Emergent Policy' in (eds) Gray, A. and Harrison, S., *Governing Medicine—Theory and Practice*, Buckingham: Open University Press, pp. 11–26.

Fotaki, M., Boyd, A., Smith, L., McDonald, R., Roland, R., Sheaff, R., Edwards, A., Elwyn, G. (2005) 'Patient Choice and the Organisation and Delivery of Health Services: Scoping Review', Report for National Coordinating Centre for NHS Service Delivery and Organisation (NCCSDO), Manchester: Centre for Public Policy and Management.

Fotaki, M. (2007) 'Patient Choice in Health Care in England and Sweden: From Quasi Markets and Back to Market? A Comparative Analysis of Failure in Unlearning', *Public Administration*, 85(4), 1059–75.

Foucault, M. (1973) *Madness and Civilisation*, London: Random House.

Foucault, M. (1974) *The Birth of the Clinic*, London: Random House.

Foucault, M. (1977) *Discipline and Punish*, London: Penguin.

Foucault, M. (1986) *A History of Sexuality, Vol 2: The Uses of Pleasure*, Harmondsworth: Viking.

Foucault, M. (1991) 'Governmentality' in (eds) Burchell, G., Gordon, C., and Miller, P., *The Foucault Effect: Studies in Governmentality*, Chicago: University of Chicago Press, pp. 87–104.

Foucault, M. (2007) *Security, Territory, Population—Lectures at the College of France, 1977–78*, New York: Picador.

Freidson, E. (1970) *Professional Dominance*, New York: Atherton Press.

French, J. and Raven, B. (1968) 'The Bases of Social Power' in (eds) Cartwright, D. and Zander, A., *Group Dynamics*, New York: Harper and Rowe, pp. 259–69.

Giddens A. (1997) *The Third Way: The Renewal of Social Democracy*, Cambridge: Polity Press.

Glaser, R. and Strauss, A. (1967) *The Discovery of Grounded Theory*, Chicago: Aldine.

Goleman, D. (2006) *Social Intelligence: The New Science of Human Relationships*. New York: Bantam Books.

Greene, A., Pagliari, C., Cunningham, S., Donnan, P., Evans, J., Eurlie-Smith, A., Morris, A., and Guthrie, B. (2009) 'Do Managed Clinical Networks Improve Quality of Diabetes Care? Evidence from a Retrospective Mixed Methods Evaluation', *Quality and Safety in Health Care*, 18(4): 456–561.

Greenhalgh, T. and Wieringa, S. (2011) 'Is it Time to Drop the "Knowledge Translation" Metaphor? A Critical Literature Review', *Journal of the Royal Society of Medicine*, 104(12): 501–9.

Greenhalgh, T., Stramer, K., Bratan, T., Byrne, E., Russell, J., and Potts, H. W. W. (2010) 'Adoption and Non-adoption of a Shared Electronic Summary Record in England: A Mixed-method Case Study', *British Medical Journal*, 16 June, 340: c3111.

Grey, C. (1994). 'Career as a Project of the Self and Labour Process Discipline', *Sociology* 28(2): 479–97.

Grey, A. (2004) 'Governing Medicine: An Introduction' in (eds) Gray, A. and Harrison, S., *Governing Medicine: Theory and Practice*, Buckingham: Open University Press, pp. 1–8.

Goodwin, N. (2008) 'Are Networks the Answer to Achieving Integrated Care'? *Journal of Health Services Research and Policy,* 13(2) April 2008: 59–60.

Goodwin, N., Perri 6, Peck, E., Freeman, T., and Posaner, R. (2004) *Managing Across Diverse Networks—Lessons from Other Sectors*, London School of Hygiene and Tropical Medicine: NCC SDO.

Gordon, C. (1991) 'Governmental Rationality: An Introduction' in (eds) Burchell, G., Gordon, C., and Miller, P., *The Foucault Effect—Studies in Governmentality*, Chicago: University of Chicago Press, pp. 1–52.

Grint, K. (2005) 'Problems, Problems, Problems: The Social Construction of Leadership', *Human Relations*, 58: 1467–94.

Gronn, P. (2002) 'Distributed Leadership as a Unit of Analysis', *Leadership Quarterly*, 13: 423–51.

Hamel, G. (1991) 'Competition for Competence and Inter-partner Learning within International Strategic Alliances', *Strategic Management Journal*, 12, Summer Special Issue: 83–103.

Harris, M. (2011) 'Network Governance and the Politics of Organisational Resistance in UK Health Care: The National Programme for Information Technology' in (eds) Clegg, S., Harris, M., and Hopfl, H., *Managing Modernity: Beyond Bureaucracy?* Oxford: Oxford University Press, Chapter 5, pp. 105–29.

Harris, M., Clegg, S., and Hopfl, H. (2011) 'Introduction: Managing Modernity—Beyond Bureaucracy?' in (eds) Clegg, S., Harris, M., and Hopfl, H., *Managing Modernity: Beyond Bureaucracy?* Oxford: Oxford University Press, pp. 1–9.

Harrison. S., Moran, M., and Wood, B. (2002) 'Policy Emergence and Policy Convergence: The Case of "Scientific Bureaucratic Medicine" in the United States and the United Kingdom', *British Journal of Politics and International Relations*, 4: 1–24.

Hartley, J. and Allison, M. (2002) 'Good, Better, Best? Inter-organizational Learning in a Network of Local Authorities', *Public Management Review*, 4: 101–18.

Hartley, J. and Benington, J. (2006) 'Copy and Paste, or Graft and Transplant? Knowledge Sharing Through Inter-organizational Networks', *Public Money & Management*, 26(2): 101–8.

Hartley, J., and Benington, J. (2010) *Leadership in Health Care*. Bristol: Policy Press.

Hartley, J., and Skelcher, C. (2008) 'The Agenda for Public Services Improvement' in (eds)

Hartley, J., Donaldson, C., Skelcher, C., and Wallace, M., *Managing to Improve Public Services*, Cambridge: Cambridge University Press, pp. 3–24.

Hasselbladh, H. and Bejerot, E. (2007) 'Webs of Knowledge and Circuits of Communication: Constructing Rationalised Agency in Swedish Health Care', *Organization*, 14(2): 175–200.

Heifetz, R. A. (1994) *Leadership without Easy Answers*, Cambridge, MA: Harvard University Press.

Henwood, M. (2006) *NHS Continuing Care in England: Issues and Developments*, London: King's Fund.

Hogg, M. A. (2001) 'A Social Identity Theory of Leadership', *Personality and Social Psychology Review*, 5(3): 184–200.

Hood, C. (1991) 'A Public Management for all Seasons?', *Public Administration*, 69 (Spring): 3–19.

Hood, C., Rothstein H., and Baldwin, R. (2001, 2004) *The Government of Risk: Understanding Risk Regulation Regimes*, Oxford: Oxford University Press.

Hopper, T. and MacIntosh, N. (1998) 'Management Accounting Numbers: Freedom or Prison—Geneen versus Foucault' in (eds) McKinlay, A. and Starkey, K., *Foucault, Management and Organisation Theory*, London: Sage, pp. 126–50.

Hultberg, E., Glendinning, C., Allebeck, P., and Lonnroth, K. (2005) 'Using Pooled Budgets to Integrate Health and Welfare Services: A Comparison of Experiments in England and Sweden', *Health and Social Care in the Community*, 13(6): 531–41.

Huxham, C. and Hibbert, P. (2008) 'Manifested Attitudes: Intricacies of Inter-partner Learning in Organisations,' *Journal of Management Studies*, 45(3): 502–29.

Huxham, C. and Vangen, S. (2000) 'Leadership in the Shaping and Implementation of Collaboration Agendas: How Things Happen in a (Not Quite) Joined Up World', *Academy of Management Journal*, 43: 1159–76.

Iedema, R., Degeling, P., Braithwaite, J., and White, L. (2004) '"It's an Interesting Conversation I'm Hearing": The Doctor as Manager', *Organization Studies*, 26: 15–33.

Iedema, R., Flabouris, A., Grant, S., and Jorn, C. (2006) 'Narrativising Errors of Care: Critical Incident Reporting in Clinical Practice', *Social Science and Medicine*, 62: 134–44.

Iedema, R. and Rhodes, C. (2010) 'The Undecided Space of Ethics in Organisational Surveillance', *Organizational Studies*, 31(2): 199–217.

Jamous, H. and Peloille, B. (1970) 'Changes in the French University Hospital System' in (ed.) Jackson, I., *Professions and Professionalisation*, Cambridge: Cambridge University Press, pp. 119–52.

Jessop, B. (1994) 'Post Fordism and the State' in (ed.) *Post Fordism—A Reader*, Oxford: Basil Blackwell, pp. 251–79.

Jessop, B. (2000) 'Governance Failure' in (ed.) Stoker, G., *The New Politics of British Local Governance*, Basingstoke: Macmillan, pp. 11–32.

Jessop, E. G. (2002) 'Leading and Managing Public Health Networks', *Journal of Public Health Medicine*, 24: 1.

Johnson, T. (1995) 'Governmentality and the Institutionalisation of Expertise' in (eds) Johnson, T., Larkin, G., and Saks, M., *Health Professions and the State in Europe*, London: Routledge, pp. 7–24.

Karreman, D. and Alvesson, M. (2009) 'Resisting Resistance: Counter Resistance, Consent and Compliance in a Consulting Firm', *Human Relations*, 62(8): 1115–44.

Ketley, D. and Bevan, H. (2007) 'Changing by Numbers' in (eds) Buchanan, D., FitzGerald, L., and Ketley, D., *The Sustainability and Spread of Organizational Change*, London: Routledge, pp. 3–21.

Kilo, C. M. (1998) 'A Framework for Collaborative Improvement—Lessons from the Institute of Healthcare Improvement's Breakthrough Series', *Quality Management in Health Care*, 6(4):1–13.

Klijn, E. H. (2005) 'Networks and Inter-organization Management' in (eds) Ferlie, E., Lynn, L., and Pollitt, C., *The Oxford Handbook of Public Management*, Oxford: Oxford University Press, pp. 257–81.

Knight, L. and Pye, A. (2005) 'Network Learning: An Empirically-derived Model of Learning by Groups of Organizations', *Human Relations*, 58(3): 369–92.

Knights, D. and Willmott, H. (1989) 'Power and Subjectivity at Work: From Degradation to Subjugation in Social Relations', *Sociology*, 23(4): 535–58.

Knorr-Cetina, K. (1999) *Epistemic Cultures: How the Sciences Make Knowledge*, Cambridge, MA: Harvard University Press.

Kurunmaki, L. (2004) 'A Hybrid Profession: The Acquisition of Management Accounting Expertise by Medical Professionals', *Accounting, Organizations and Society*, 29: 327–47.

Lane, P. J., Koka, B. R., and Pathak, S. (2006) 'The Reification of Absorptive Capacity: A Critical Review and Rejuvenation of the Construct', *Academy of Management Review*, 31(4): 833–63.

Langley, A. (1999) 'Strategies for Theorising from Case Study Data', *Academy of Management Review,* 24(4): 692–710.

Le Grand, J. (2003) *Motivation, Agency and Public Policy*, Oxford: Oxford University Press.

Leigh-Star, S. and Griesemer, J. (1989) 'Institutional Ecology, "Translations", and Boundary Objects: Amateurs and Professionals in Berkeley's Museum of Vertebrate Zoology, 1907–1939', *Social Studies of Science*, 19(3): 387–420.

Leaning, M. S. (1993) 'The New Information Management and Technology Strategy of the NHS', *British Medical Journal,* 307: 217.

Levay, C. and Waks, C. (2009) 'Professions and the Pursuit of Transparency in Health Care: Two Cases of Soft Autonomy', *Organization Studies*, 30(5): 509–27.

Lewis, P. A., Dunn, R. B., and Vetter, N. J. (1994) 'NHS and Community Care Act 1990 and Discharges from Hospital to Private Residential and Nursing Homes', *British Medical Journal*, 309: 28.

Llewellyn, S. (2001) 'Two Way Windows: Clinicians as Medical Managers', *Organization Studies*, 22(4): 593–623.

Margetts, H. (2005) 'Virtual Organizations' in (eds) Ferlie, E., Lynn, L., and Pollitt, C., *The Oxford Handbook of Public Management*, Oxford: Oxford University Press, pp. 305–25.

Martin, G. and Learmonth, M. (2010) 'A Critical Account of the Rise and Spread of "Leadership": The Case of Health Care', *Social Science and Medicine*, 74: 281–8.

Martin, G. P., Currie, G., and Finn, R. (2009) 'Leadership, Service Reform and Public Services Networks—The Case of Cancer Genetics Pilots in the English NHS', *Journal of Public Administration Research and Theory*, 19(4): 769–94.

Mason, K. and Leek, S. (2008) 'Learning to Build a Supply Network: An Exploration of Dynamic Business Models', *Journal of Management Studies*, 45: 759–84.

Mays, N., Dixon, A., and Jones, L. (2011) *Understanding New Labour's Market Reforms in the English NHS*, London: King's Fund.

McGivern, G. and Dopson, S. (2010) 'Inter Epistemic Power and Transforming Knowledge Objects in a Biomedical Network', *Organization Studies*, 31(12): 1667–86.

McGivern, G. and Ferlie, E. (2007) 'Playing Tick Box Games: Interrelating Defences in Professional Appraisal', *Human Relations*, 60(9): 1361–85.

McGivern, G. and Fischer, M. (2010) 'Medical Regulation, Spectacular Transparency and the Blame Business', *Journal of Health Organization and Management*, 24(6): 597–610.

McGivern, G. and Fischer. M. (2012) 'Reactivity and Reactions to Regulatory Transparency in Medicine, Psychotherapy and Counselling', *Social Science and Medicine*, 74(3): 289–96.

McGivern, G., Lambrianou, A., Ferlie, E., and Cowie, M. (2009) 'Enacting Evidence into Clinical Practice: The Case of Coronary Heart Disease', *Public Money and Management*, 29(5): 307–12.

McGivern, G., Currie, G., Ferlie, E., and FitzGerald, L. (2012) *Professional Identity Work and Institutional Maintenance: The Cases of Incidental and Strategic Hybrid Medical Managers*, Working Paper, King's College London: Dept of Management.

McKinlay, A. and Starkey, K. (1998) *Foucault, Management and Organisation Theory*, London: Sage.

McNulty, T. and Ferlie, E. (2002) *Reengineering Health Care*, Oxford: Oxford University Press.

Medical Foundation for AIDS and Sexual Health (2008) *Progress and Priorities— Working Together for High Quality Sexual Health: Review of the National Strategy for Sexual Health and HIV*, London: MedFASH.

Meier, M. (2011) 'Knowledge Management in Strategic Alliances: A Review of Empirical Evidence', *International Journal of Management Reviews*, 13(1): 1–23.

Meyer, K. E. (2007) 'Contextualising Organizational Learning: Lyles and Salk in the Context of their Research', *Journal of International Business Studies*, 38: 27–37.

Miller, P. and Rose. N. (1990) 'Governing Economic Life, *Economy and Society*, 19(1): 1–31.

Miller, P. and Rose, N. (2008) *Governing the Present*, Cambridge: Polity Press.

Mintzberg, H. (1983) *Structure in Fives—Designing Effective Organisations*, Englewood Cliffs, NJ: Prentice Hall.

Mitchell, T. (1991) 'The Limits of The State—Beyond Statist Approaches and their Critics', *American Political Science Review*, 85(1): 77–96.

Montgomery, K. (2001) 'Physician Executives: The Evolution and Impact of Hybrid Professionals' in (eds) Blair, J., Fottler, M., and Savage, G., *Advances in Health Care Management*, Amsterdam: JAI/Elsevier Press, pp. 215–41.

Moran, M. (2003) *The British Regulatory State—High Modernism and Hyper Innovation*, Oxford: Oxford University Press.

Murray, E. (2012) 'The Recruitment of ICT to Design a Web Based (Foucauldian) Surveillance Mechanism: Disciplinary Accountability or Democratic Transparency?', London: Imperial College Medical School Working Paper presented at the European Group of Organizational Studies Conference, Helsinki, July 2012.

National Care Home R&D Forum (2007) *My Home Life: A Review of the Literature*, Help the Aged/Age U.K.

Newell, S., Robertson, M., Scarborough, H., and Swan, J. (2002) *Managing Knowledge Work*, London: Prentice Hall.

Newman, J. (2001) *Modernizing Governance*, London: Sage.

Newman, J. (2005) 'Enter the Transformational Leader: Network Governance and the Micro Politics of Modernization', *Sociology*, 39(4): 717–34.

Newman, J. and Clarke, J. (2009) *Publics, Politics and Power*, London: Sage.

Newman, J., Raine, J., and Skelcher, C. (2000) *Innovation and Best Practice in Local Government*, London: DETR.

NHS Executive (NHSE) (1999) *Guidance on Commissioning Cancer Services: Improving Outcomes in Gynaecological Cancers*, London: NHSE.

NHS Executive (NHSE) (2000) *Manual of Cancer Services Standards*. London: NHS Executive.

NHS Executive (NHSE) (2001) *Manual of Cancer Services Standards*, London: NHSE.

NHS Commissioning Board (2012) *Proposals for Clinical Networks in the Modernised NHS*, London: NHS CB.

NICE (2002) *Improving Outcomes in Urological Cancers—The Manual*, London: NICE.

NICE (2009) *Guidelines Manual*, London: NICE.

NICE (2011) *End of Life Care for Adults Quality Standard*, London: NICE.

Niskanen, W. A. (1994) *Bureaucracy and Public Economics*, Cheltenham: Edward Elgar.

Nye, J. (2008) *The Powers to Lead*, Oxford: Oxford University Press.

Oakley, A. (2000) *Experiments in Knowing*, Cambridge: Polity Press.

Oborn, E. and Dawson, S. (2010) 'Learning across Communities of Practice: An Examination of Multi-disciplinary Work', *British Journal of Management*, 21(4): 843–58.

Office of National Statistics (2007) *Mid Year Population Estimates 2007*, London: HMSO.

O'Reilly, D. and Reed, M. (2010) '"Leaderism": An Evolution of Managerialism in UK Public Services Reform', *Public Administration*, 88: 960–78.

O'Reilly, D. and Reed, M. (2011) 'The Grit in the Oyster: Professionalism, Managerialism and Leaderism as Discourses of UK Public Services Modernisation', *Organization Studies*, 23: 1079–101.

Osborne, S. (2006) 'The New Public Governance', *Public Management Review*, 8(3): 377–87.

Osborne, S. (2010) 'The (New) Public Governance: A Suitable Case for Treatment?' in (ed.) Osborne, S. *The New Public Governance*, London: Routledge, Chapter 1, pp. 1–16.

Patterson, M., Nolan, M., Rick, J., Brown, J., Adams, R., and Musson, G. (2011) *From Metrics to Meaning: Culture Change and Quality of Acute Hospital Care for Older People*, Final Report to NIHR SDO, project 08/1501/93. Also at http://nihr.sdo.ac.uk.

Pawson, R., and Tilley, N. (1997) *Realistic Evaluation*, London: Sage.

Pettigrew, A. M. and Fenton, E. (eds) (2000) *The Innovating Organization*, London, Sage.

Pettigrew, A. M., Ferlie, E. and McKee, L. (1992) *Shaping Strategic Change*, London: Sage.

Pfeffer, J. and Salancik, G. R. (1978) *The External Control of Organizations: A Resource Dependence Perspective*, New York: Harper and Row.

Philp, I. (2004) *Better Health in Old Age—Report*, London: produced by COI Communications for the Department of Health.

Pickard, S. (2009) 'The Professionalization of General Practitioners with a Special Interest: Rationalization, Restratification and Governmentality', *Sociology*, 48: 250–67.

Pickard, S. (2010) 'The Role of Governmentality in the Establishment, Maintenance and Demise of Professional Jurisdictions: The Case of Geriatric Medicine', *Sociology of Health and Illness*, 32: 1072–86.

Pisano, G. (2006) 'Can Science Be a Business?: Lessons From Biotech', *Harvard Business Review*, October: 104–25.

Pollitt, C. (2009) 'Bureaucracies Remember; Post Bureaucratic Organizations Forget?', *Public Administration*, 87(2): 198–218.

Pollitt, C., Talbot, C., Caulfield, J., and Smullen, A. (2004) *Agencies: How Governments Do Things through Semi Autonomous Organizations*, Basingstoke: Palgrave Macmillan.

Porter L. and McLaughlin, G. (2006) 'Leadership and the Organizational Context: Like the Weather?', *Leadership Quarterly*, 17: 559–76.

Porter, M. and Olmsted Teisberg, E. (2006) *Redefining Health Care: Creating Value Based Competition on Results*, Boston, MA: Harvard Business School Press.

Power, M. (1997) *The Audit Society*, Oxford: Oxford University Press.

Power, M. (2011) 'Foucault and Sociology', *Annual Review of Sociology*, 37: 35–56.

Priore, M. and Sabel, C. (1984) *The Second Industrial Divide*, New York: Basic Books.

Pronovost, P. J., Berenholtz, S. M., and Morlock, L. L. (2011) 'Is Quality of Care Improving in the UK'? *British Medical Journal*, 342: c6646.

Propper, C., Sutton, M., Whitnall, C., and Windmeijer, F. (2007) 'Did "Targets and Terror" Reduce English Waiting Times for Elective Hospital Care?', University of Bristol: CMPO Working Paper 07/179.

Provan, K. and Millward, H. B. (1995) 'A Preliminary Theory of Interorganizational Network Effectiveness: A Comparative Study of Four Community Mental Health Teams', *Administrative Science Quarterly*, 40: 1–33.

Provan, K. and Sebastian, J. (1998) 'Network within Networks: Service Link Overlap, Organizational Cliques and Network Effectiveness', *Academy of Management Journal*, 41(4): 453–63.

Pye, A. (2005) 'Leadership and Organizing: Sensemaking in Action', *Leadership*, 1: 31–50.

Radnor, Z. J., Holweg, H., and Waring, J. (2011) 'Lean in Healthcare: The Unfilled Promise?', *Social Science and Medicine*, 74(3): 364–71.

Rashman, L. and Hartley, J. (2002) 'Leading and Learning? Knowledge Transfer in the Beacon Council Scheme', *Public Administration*, 80(3): 523–42.

Rashman, L. and Radnor, Z. (2005): 'Learning to Improve: Approaches to Improving Local Government Services', *Public Money & Management*, 25(1): 19–26.

Rashman, L., Withers, E., and Hartley, J. (2009) 'Organizational Learning and Knowledge in Public Service Organization: A Systematic Review of the Literature', *International Journal of Management Reviews*, 11(4): 463–94.

Raven, B. H., Schwartzwald, J., and Koslowsky, M. (1998) 'Conceptualizing and Measuring a Power/Interaction Model of Interpersonal Influence', *Journal of Applied Social Psychology*, 28(4): 307–32.

Raymond E. (2012) *The Cathedral and the Bazaar* (open source publication). http://catb.org/~esr/writings/cathedral-bazaar/.

Reed, M. (1999) 'From the "Cage" to the "Gaze"? The Dynamics of Organizational Control in Later Modernity' in (eds) Morgan, G. and Engwall, L. *Regulation and Organizations*, London: Routledge, pp. 17–49.

Reed, M. (2005) 'Beyond the Iron Cage? Bureaucracy and Democracy in the Knowledge Economy and Society' in (ed.) Du Gay, P. *The Virtues of Democracy*, Oxford: Oxford University Press, 115–40.

Reed, M. (2011) 'The Post Bureaucratic Organisation and the Control Revolution' in (eds) Clegg, S., Harris, M., and Hopfl, H., *Managing Modernity: Beyond Bureaucracy?* Oxford: Oxford University Press, pp. 230–56.

Rhodes, R. A. W. (1997a) *Understanding Governance*, Buckingham: Open University Press.

Rhodes, R. A. W. (1997b) 'From Marketisation to Diplomacy: It's the Mix that Matters', *Australian Journal of Public Administration*, 56(2): 40–53.

Rhodes, R. A. W. (2000) 'The Governance Narrative: Key Findings and Lessons from the ESRC's Whitehall Programme', *Public Administration*, 78(2): 345–63.

Rhodes, R. A. W. (2007) 'Understanding Governance: Ten Years On', *Organization Studies*, 28(08): 1243–64.

Rittel, H. and Webber, M. (1973) 'Dilemmas in a General Theory of Planning', *Policy Sciences*, 4: 155–69, Amsterdam: Elsevier.

Rose, N., O'Malley, P., and Valverde, M. (2006) 'Governmentality', *Annual Review of Law and Social Science*, 2: 83–106.

Royal College of Nursing, the British Geriatric Society and the Royal College of Psychiatrists (1987) *Improving Care of Elderly Patients in Hospital*, London, RCN.

Salaman, G. (2005) 'Bureaucracy and Beyond: Managers and Leaders in the "Post Bureaucratic" Organization' in (ed.) Du Gay, P., *The Values of Bureaucracy*, Oxford: Oxford University Press, pp. 141–64.

Sanders, T. and Harrison, S. (2008) 'Professional Legitimacy Claims in the Multidisciplinary Workplace: The Case of Heart Failure Care', *Sociology of Health and Illness* 30(2): 289–308.

Scally, G. and Donaldson, L. (1998) 'Clinical Governance and the Drive for Quality Improvement in the New NHS in England', *British Medical Journal*, 317: 61–5.

Schwalbe, M. and Mason-Schrock, D. (1996) 'Identity Work as Group Process', *Advances in Group Processes*, 13: 113–47.

Sewell, W. (1992) 'A Theory of Structure: Duality, Agency and Transformation', *American Journal of Sociology*, 98(1): 1–29.

Shaw, S. and Greenhalgh, T. (2008) 'Best Research—for What? Best Health—for Whom? A Critical Exploration of Primary Care Research Using Discourse Analysis', *Social Science and Medicine*, 66(12): 2506–19.

Sheaff, R., Marshall, M., Rogers, A., Roland, M., Sibbald, B., and Pickard, S. (2004) 'Governmentality by Network in English Primary Health Care', *Social Policy and Administration*, 38(1): 89–103.

Sheaff, R., Benson, L., Farbus, L., Schofield, J., Mannion, R., and Reeves, D. (2010) 'Network Resilience in the Face of Health Systems Reform', *Social Science and Medicine*, (70): 779–86.

Shilts, R. (1987) *And the Band Played On,* London: Penguin.

Simonin, B. L. (1999) 'Ambiguity and the Process of Knowledge Transfer in Strategic Alliances', *Strategic Management Journal*, 20: 595–623.

Smart, B. (1982) 'Foucault, Sociology and the Problem of Human Agency', *Theory and Society*, 11: 121–41.

Smircich, L. and Morgan G. (1982) 'Leadership: The Management of Meaning', *Journal of Applied Behavioral Science*, 18(3): 257–73.

Smith, C., Valsecchi, R., Mueller, F., and Gabe, J. (2008) 'Knowledge and the Discourse of Labour Process Transformation: Nurses and the Case of NHS Direct for England', *Work, Employment and Society*, 22: 581–99.

Snellen, I. (2005) 'E Government—A Challenge for Public Management' in (eds) Ferlie, E., Lynn, L., and Pollitt, C., *The Oxford Handbook of Public Management*, Oxford: Oxford University Press, pp. 398–421.

Social Exclusion Unit (1999) 'Teenage Pregnancy' Report (Cm 4342), London: HMSO

Social Services Select Committee (1987) *Problems Associated with AIDS*, Session 1986–87, 3rd Report HCP, 182, London: House of Commons.

Speed, E. (2011) 'Applying Soft Bureaucracy to Rhetorics of Choice: The UK NHS, 1983–2007' in (eds) Clegg, S., Harris, M., and Hopfl, H., *Managing Modernity: Beyond Bureaucracy?* Oxford: Oxford University Press, Chapter 4, pp. 81–104.

Spillane, J. (2006) *Distributed Leadership*, San Francisco, CA: Jossey Bass.

Spurgeon, P., Clark, J., and Ham. C. (2011) *Medical Leadership: From the Dark Side to Centre Stage*, Oxford: Radcliffe.

Stake, R. (2000) 'Case Studies' in (eds) Denzin, N. and Lincoln, Y., *Handbook of Qualitative Research*, London: Sage, pp. 435–54.

Starkey, K. and McKinlay, A. (1998) 'Afterword: Deconstructing Organization— Discipline and Desire' in (eds) McKinlay, A. and Starkey, K., *Foucault, Management and Organisation Theory*, London: Sage, pp. 230–41.

Stjernberg, T. and Phillips, A. (1993) 'Organizational Innovations in a Long Term Perspective: Legitimacy and Souls of Fire as Critical Factors of Change and Viability', *Human Relations*, 46: 1193–219.

Stoker, G. (2004) *Transforming Local Governance*, Basingstoke: Palgrave Macmillan.

Strathern, M. (2011) 'An Experiment in Interdisciplinarity: Proposals and Promises' in (eds) Camic, C., Gross, N., and Lamont, M., *Social Knowledge in the Making*, Chicago: Chicago University Press, pp. 257–84.

Sullivan, H. and Skelcher, C. (eds) (2002) *Working across Boundaries: Collaboration in Public Services*, Basingstoke: Palgrave Macmillan.

Sveningsson, S. and Alvesson, M. (2003) 'Managing Managerial Identities: Organizational Fragmentation, Discourse and Identity Struggle', *Human Relations*, 56: 1163–94.

Sveningsson, S. and Larson, L. (2006) 'Fantasies of Leadership: Identity Work', *Leadership*, 2(2): 203–24.

Swan, J., Bresnen, M., Newell, S., and Robertson, M. (2007) 'The Object of Knowledge: The Roles of Objects in Biomedical Innovation', *Human Relations*, 60: 1089–838.

Szulanski, G. (1996) 'Exploring Internal Stickiness: Impediments to the Transfer of Best Practice within the Firm', *Strategic Management Journal*, 17, Winter Special Issue: 27–43.

Teelken, C., Dent, M., and Ferlie, E. (eds) (2012) *Leadership in the Public Services: Promise and Pitfalls*, London: Routledge.

Timmermans, S. and Berg, M. (2003) *The Gold Standard*, Philadelphia: Temple University Press.

Timmons, S. (2003) 'Failed Panopticon: Surveillance of Nursing Practice through New Technology', *New Technology, Work and Employment*, 18: 143–53.

Townley, B. (1998) 'Beyond Good and Evil: Depth and Division in the Management of Human Resources' in (eds) McKinlay, A. and Starkey, K., *Foucault, Management and Organization Theory*, London: Sage, Chapter 11, pp. 191–210.

Townley, B. (2008) *Reason's Neglect: Rationality and Organizing*, Oxford: Oxford University Press.

Trenholm, S. and Ferlie, E. (2012) 'Using Complexity Theory to Analyse the Organizational Response to the Resurgent TB Epidemic in London', *Social Science and Medicine*, in press.

Tsoukas, H. and Vladirimou, E. (2001) 'What is Organizational Knowledge?', *Journal of Management Studies*, 38(7): 973–93.

Turrini, A., Christofoli, C., Frosini, F., and Nasi, G. (2010) 'Networking Literature about the Determinants of Network Effectiveness', *Public Administration*, 88(2): 528–50.

Uhl-Bem, M. (2006) 'Relational Leadership Theory: Exploring the Social Processes of Leadership and Organizing', *Leadership Quarterly*, 17: 654–76.

Van Wijk, R., Jansen, J. P., and Lyles, M. A. (2008) 'Inter- and Intra-Organizational Knowledge Transfer: A Meta-analytic Review and Assessment of its Antecedents and Consequences', *Journal of Management Studies*, 45: 815–38.

Wainwright, S., Williams, C., Michael, M., Farsides, B., and Cribb, A. (2006) 'From Bench to Bedside? Biomedical Scientists' Expectations of Stem Cell Science as a Future Therapy for Diabetes', *Social Science and Medicine*, 63(8): 2052–64.

Wallace, M. and Tomlinson, M. (2001) 'Contextualizing Leadership Dynamics', *Leadership*, 6: 21–45.

Wanless, D. (2002) *Securing our Future Health*. London: HM Treasury.

Wanless, D. (2006) *Wanless Social Care Review: Securing Good Care for Older People—Taking a Long-Term View*, London: King's Fund Institute.

Waring, J. (2007) 'Adaptive Regulation or Governmentality—Patient Safety and the Changing Regulation of Medicine', *Sociology of Health and Illness*, 29(2): 163–79.

Waring, J. (2009) 'Constructing and Reconstructing Narratives of Patient Safety', *Social Science and Medicine*, 69(2): 163–79.

Waring, J. and Bishop, S. (2010) 'Lean Health Care: Rhetoric, Ritual and Resistance', *Social Science and Medicine*, 71(7): 1332–40.

Waring, J. and Currie, G. (2009) 'Managing Expert Knowledge: Organizational Challenges and Managerial Futures for the UK Medical Profession', *Organizational Studies*, 30(7): 755–78.

Webster, F. (2006) *Theories of the Information Society*, 3rd edition, London: Routledge.

Weick, K. and Roberts, K. (1993) 'Collective Mind in Organizations: Heedful Inter Relating on Flight Decks', *Administrative Science Quarterly*, 38: 357–81.

Weir, S. and Beetham, D. (1999) *Political Power and Democratic Control in Britain: The Democratic Audit of the UK*, London: Routledge.

Yin, R. (1994) *Case Study Research—Design and Methods*, Beverly Hills, CA: Sage.

Yin, R. (1999) 'Enhancing the Quality of Case Studies in Health Services Research', *Health Services Research*, 34(5): 1209–24.

Young, J., Forster, A., and Green, J. (2003) 'An Estimate of Post-acute Intermediate Care Need in an Elderly Care Department for Older People', *Health and Social Care in the Community*, 11(3): 229–31.

Zuboff, S. (1984) *In the Age of the Smart Machine: The Future of Work and Power*, New York: Basic Books.

Index

Index

Index